Moments in the Sun

Also by Claude Duval:

Lester: A Biography

Pat on the Back: The Story of Pat Eddery

Willie Carson: A Biography

Minter: The Autobiography of Alan Minter

The Real McCoy: My Life So Far

MOMENTS IN THE SUN

Tales from the Punter's Pal

Claude Duval

RACING POST

First published in Great Britain in 2017 by
Racing Post Books
27 Kingfisher Court, Hambridge Road, Newbury, Berkshire, RG14 5SJ

10 9 8 7 6 5 4 3 2 1

A catalogue record for this book is available from the British Library.

ISBN 978-1-910497-41-8

Designed by J Schwartz & Co

Printed and bound in the UK by CPI Group (UK) Ltd, Croydon, CR0 4YY

www.racingpost.com/shop

For Fiona, James and Jade, and grandson Dylan James

Contents

1

Doing National Service for Kelvin

'BUY ME A HORSE TO WIN the Grand National.' The words still haunt me, even though they were uttered way back in 1982.

I was at home casually doing my expenses, sometimes likened to *Tales of the Unexpected*, when my phone buzzed into life. It was *The Sun's* mercurial editor Kelvin MacKenzie, who can claim to have been the most successful red-top tabloid editor of all time, and whose volcanic outbursts were sometimes likened to Adolf Hitler on a quiet day.

He launched into his master plan. I was to buy a chaser, MacKenzie would organise a telephone competition for our lucky 12-million-plus *Sun* readers, one lucky winner would get to own the horse for the day of the world's greatest race, and it would run in *The Sun's* red-and-white-check silks. For our massive publicity stunt I was given a maximum budget of £15,000, which in those days meant we were not talking about a complete no-hoper.

I had become good friends with the genial Weyhill trainer Toby Balding, who had built up a fine reputation – he had trained Highland Wedding to win the 1969 Grand National. He also had a successful sideline of buying and selling horses. This distinguished wheeler-dealer was my obvious first port of call.

'You don't know how lucky you are,' Balding told me when I made contact. 'A horse called Blackwater Bridge arrived only today from Ireland. My former jockey Eddie Harty, who rode Highland Wedding in the National, has sold him on spec to me. He's proved already that he can jump round Liverpool – he was second in the Topham Trophy last year – and is now qualified for the National. He'd be just the job for you. *The Sun* can have him for ten grand. Eddie will want a bit of luck money in cash for his trouble – £250 – and so will the Irish horsebox driver.'

What did 'luck money' mean? I enquired, innocent as a lamb. In racing, Balding explained, it was always paid in cash to seal any deal. Subsequently the words were to appear so frequently on my expenses that *The Sun*'s top accountant contacted me for an explanation.

I rang a contact in Ireland, who said Blackwater Bridge would be an ideal horse for the National. Having managed to manoeuvre all this cash past the bean counters, I sanctioned the deal, and Toby Balding was happy to have a Grand National runner. 'My good friend Richard Calver' (a fellow Hampshire trainer) 'will have to look the horse over first,' he told me. 'He's an excellent vet, too. He originally bought Highland Wedding himself for £175, won six point-to-points on him, and then sold him on to me for five grand before he won the National. He'll want a bit of luck money.'

Calver rang me later. 'Blackwater Bridge is ten years old and has quite a few miles on the clock. But I've checked him over, and he's ideal for you and your exciting venture. Best of luck.'

Soon I was proudly visiting *The Sun*'s offices in Bouverie Street. From afar I could heard Kelvin MacKenzie's angry voice tearing into some poor reporter. When I revealed to him that we had purchased

Blackwater Bridge for £5,000 less than his limit he was clearly pleased. The readers' competition was going exceptionally well, with over 80,000 entries. The venture had already paid for itself.

Then came the first of many obstacles almost as daunting as Becher's Brook itself.

I showed MacKenzie pictures of Blackwater Bridge with Toby Balding, his new trainer. 'Never heard of him,' barked MacKenzie. 'There's only one man who'll train our horse Blackie, and that's the great Ginger McCain.' There was no point arguing.

Fortified by a few gin and tonics, I plucked up courage and rang Balding. He accepted the bad news with great dignity, almost laughing at the prospect of Blackwater Bridge being re-routed to Ginger McCain.

'Fantastic news! I'm f***ing chuffed,' said McCain on learning that out of the blue he had a Grand National-qualified runner joining him just weeks before the race. 'I'll send my horsebox driver down to Toby's tomorrow – he'll want a bit of luck money.' During this exciting period I was walking about with more wads of cash stuffed into my pockets than the Fleet Street print union boys who used to claim for false shifts as 'Mickey Mouse'.

MacKenzie's instincts were, as nearly always, spot-on. We were able to use pictures galore of Blackie in his box nuzzling up to the occupant of the box next door – the retired Red Rum, who'd won the third of his Grand Nationals in 1977. Three National wins, twice second, he jumped 150 Aintree fences without touching a twig, covering no less than 22 miles.

I booked into Liverpool's then-five-star Adelphi Hotel to make daily trips to Ginger McCain's famous yard in Southport, behind his second-hand car salesroom and a Chinese takeaway. It was a magic moment to see Blackie led out of that small cobbled yard each morning, along the wide avenues of posh Southport, and finally down onto the beach. It's well known that when Red Rum joined McCain in early 1972 he suffered from pedal osteitis in his off-forefoot, and it has always been claimed that the daily exercise in the sea cured the problem. Had he joined any other trainer but McCain I am certain he would not have become the great National treasure.

McCain was thrilled to have a National candidate again in his stables. 'The Grand National is the most important date in my calendar,' he told me – 'it's like a river flowing through my life. I was engaged to my wife Beryl in 1959 on the day Michael Scudamore won the National on Oxo. Two years later we were married on the day Bobby Beasley won on Nicolaus Silver, the grey – we went to the course from the reception!'

Now he was in full flow. 'I first went to Aintree in 1940 when I was nine, with an aunt from Crosby. I walked along the track beside the canal, which in those days was jammed with barges. It was wartime, and many of the spectators were in uniform. Bogskar was the winner – ironically, he was ridden by a serviceman on leave, Flight Sergeant Mervyn Jones. He was later killed in action in his Spitfire, doing photo-reconnaissance over the fjords of Norway.

'You can have Royal Ascot and the Cheltenham Festival. Aintree and the Grand National will always be the tops for me.'

Whenever people talk about the National, McCain's name will be high up there on the leaderboard: an ex-Liverpool taxi driver who ended up training a Grand National winner four times. If a Hollywood scriptwriter had penned a script about an Aintree legend it still wouldn't have matched the real-life Ginger McCain. He was as amusing as any of the long line of Liverpool comedians like Arthur Askey and Jimmy Tarbuck. He made great copy, and as I left the Adelphi Hotel on my daily missions to Southport I almost felt like an owner myself.

'I started off with horses when I was about fourteen,' Ginger reminisced. 'I used to drive harness horses and hackneys – I used to help out at shows, and I worked for Frank Speakman, the local Southport trainer.

'But after the war he moved to Cheshire, and I didn't fancy the move. So I bought an old taxi and built up my business from there. I used to drive Noel Le Mare, whose family were of Huguenot descent, to a dinner dance every Saturday night at the famous Prince of Wales Hotel in Southport. It cost three shillings each way, but he always gave me a pound tip.

'One night he casually asked me to buy him a horse to win the Grand National. I thought we were a couple of crazy dreamers. Red Rum was not the first horse I bought for him: that one had a heart complaint. The second one broke down. Then in 1972 I cocked it up and didn't enter his horse for the National.

'I was really devastated – I thought Mr Le Mare, who was then 85, would never have another chance to win the National. I was terrified to tell him the news, but he just said, "Pour yourself a drink, Ginger. Worse things happen at sea."

'Then I went to Doncaster sales in 1972 and got Red Rum for 6,000 guineas. He'd originally cost 400 guineas. He was ridden by 24 different jockeys – Lester Piggott rode him twice without success. In his first race as a two-year-old, in October 1967, he dead-heated in a Flat seller at Aintree.

'The very first morning I worked him on the beach at Southport, Red Rum was as lame as a cat. I was horrified, but after I cantered him through the surf all the lameness gradually disappeared. He never took another lame step until we were forced to retire him on the eve of the 1978 Grand National.'

From the massive response to our telephone competition we duly sorted out the lucky owner of Blackwater Bridge for the day. Our winner was a retired policeman from West Bromwich, who for some curious reason was very reluctant to be photographed with our now beloved Blackie. All the premium-rate phone calls more than paid for the purchase of the horse, the training fees – and, of course, all the luck money. As we watched the horse work out on Southport beach from McCain's car parked on the esplanade, we could all see Blackie's exuberance. 'He was a bit of a nutter,' Beryl McCain recalled years later. 'Some mornings our strongest lads couldn't pull him up, and we thought he'd end up in Blackpool.'

Meanwhile at the Adelphi the staff had found out I was connected with the Grand National. I was treated like royalty. Every night in the posh cocktail bar lovely Scouse girls would come up to me – I could never quite decide whether they were keen amateurs or professional ladies of the night. In true Fleet Street style I always made my excuses and departed.

It was always part of the agreement with McCain that Blackie would not run before the National. To have set up this magnificent publicity stunt and then suffer a late injury would be devastating. Twice a week I would get the cheerful call from MacKenzie: 'How's Blackie?' Each time I was able to give a positive update. Blackie had a lovely personality – he almost seemed to enjoy all the cameras clicking in his face. 'This is all going too well,' the editor said one day.

Then I had another call from him: 'We badly need some pictures of Blackie at Aintree next to Becher's Brook and the winning post.'

National horses are never allowed private gallops or photo calls at Aintree for pre-race publicity. Nevertheless, I contacted Aintree's clerk of the course, John Hughes, and relayed our unique request. I knew Hughes well, and had enjoyed many a glass with him during his spells at Chepstow and Lingfield.

'Out of the question!' he roared. 'No horse has ever set foot on the course before race day.'

Undaunted, I pressed our friendship to the limit. 'It would be worth a case of gin…'

'What time can you get him here tomorrow?' said Hughes. 'But our head groundsman will need some luck money for opening the Melling Road gates.'

The next day the famous iron gates were sneakily opened, and Blackie walked out onto the lush Aintree turf. He cantered down to Becher's, and was photographed having a private sneak preview of the world's most famous fence. I booked out of the Adelphi. My expenses that week included a receipt for a case of Gordon's gin… plus the mandatory £250 luck money.

Only one piece of the Grand National jigsaw remained – finding Blackie the best jockey available. Ginger McCain rang me one night – he was gaining in confidence by the day. 'Jonjo O'Neill doesn't have a ride at the moment.' He was the current champion jockey! 'I'm sure I can get him.'

There was one major problem, I pointed out. O'Neill had a ghosted weekly column in our main rival, the *Daily Mirror*.

'I'll fix it up with Jonjo,' said McCain. 'You reveal the ride exclusively in *The Sun*, and I'll say your paper has broken the news three days before the agreed time.'

In *The Sun*'s offices I was greeted by Kelvin MacKenzie in front of a crowded newsroom. He was thrilled by our *Mirror*-bashing back-page splash O'Neill exclusive. 'There's just one small thing,' I said casually. 'O'Neill wants the usual jockey's fee for the National for an outside ride – a monkey.'

'Are you telling me,' MacKenzie exploded, 'that he wants five hundred quid for what could be less than half a minute in the saddle? He could fall at the first fence!'

That was the going rate, I replied.

'Five hundred quid for 30 seconds' work! I'm in the wrong f***ing job!'

By now I was nearly at the end of my tether. 'You're not the only one who thinks that,' I whispered.

Fortunately, at that very moment MacKenzie's secretary rushed into the office. 'The chairman is on the line from New York and wants to speak to you urgently!'

In 47 years I suspect this was the nearest I came to getting the sack.

One evening Ginger McCain rang me out of the blue. 'Blackie is working so well he's far too buzzy,' he said. 'He'll have to have one more race before the National to calm him down. There's a race at Haydock over two miles early in March where I used to tune up Red Rum every year. He won't win it, but it'll be the ideal prep race.'

MacKenzie, I knew, would not be best pleased – but who were we, I told myself, to argue with a man who had trained a three-times Grand

National winner? Blackie had already been backed down to 50-1 for the National, and we had squeezed the publicity lemon as dry as we could.

So Friday, 5 March 1982 became D-Day for Blackwater Bridge at Haydock, and I set out to drive the long journey from Kent up to Lancashire. Jonjo O'Neill was not available, so the top northern jockey Ridley Lamb had been booked.

A new rug for Blackie had been organised – another £250 luck money – and as he emerged in the tree-lined paddock he looked an absolute picture. The new rug looked fantastic. On closer inspection, though, I spotted the word MURDER coming through from the inside. This, I realised, was the words RED RUM spelt backwards. It was his old rug.

I rang the office – there were no mobile phones in those days – to be told, 'You've got the back-page lead, a two-page spread on the racing pages, and something else as well for the front page.' No pressure then… Proudly, I took my place alongside McCain and the retired policeman as Blackie, a 20-1 shot, set off among the six-horse field.

On the first circuit he was showing prominently and jumping fluently. Then, after the eighth fence on the far side, I realised there were only five runners still on their feet. Blackie was missing.

'Follow me,' ordered McCain. We ducked under the running rails and ran straight across the track. The retired copper was tailed off in pursuit.

At the furthest point from the grandstands we arrived at a scene of absolute carnage. Blackie lay on the ground, motionless, the blood-stained Ridley Lamb concussed next to him. There was a huge V-shaped gap in the fence. That gallant warrior Blackie, it was clear, had not jumped it: he'd simply ploughed straight through. I imagined the twigs were still floating down right across Merseyside.

I recall looking up into McCain's face under his familiar flat cap. Notebook and pen in hand, I asked plaintively, 'Will Blackie still be able to run in the National?'

McCain said, 'He's f***ing dead, cock.'

My world had fallen apart.

In fact, Blackie was still alive, but very badly wounded, having suffered several fractures, and he was rushed to a Liverpool vets for an emergency operation. This was long before the days of At The Races and Racing UK, of course, and the Press Association merely reported that he had fallen.

'Ring me on Sunday,' said McCain.

I rang Terry Clark, *The Sun*'s racing editor, to break the bad news. 'They still want a spread on Blackie,' he said. I put a clean sheet of paper into my typewriter and began to type: 'A Nation Wept…'

On the Sunday Ginger McCain spelt out the seriousness of Blackie's condition. 'He's broken so many bones it's unreal,' he said. 'The vets are adamant: for his own sake he must be put down. I am so very sorry.'

I rang *The Sun*, to be told the editor urgently wanted to speak to me. He was at home. The telephone rang for ages, and I hoped I could just leave him a message back at the office. Then he answered. 'How's Blackie?'

Blackie, I explained, was not very well, not very well at all, and Ginger McCain wanted permission to have him put – I just couldn't finish the sentence.

'Put where?' said my boss.

Finally I blurted it out: he would have to be put down with a humane gun.

'Save a bullet for your f***ing self,' said MacKenzie.

2

In the Beginning…

MY FATHER, JOHN DUVAL, WAS DEFINITELY not a racing man. The only thing ever worth putting on a horse, he always claimed, was Lady Godiva.

From a Huguenot family, which explains our surname, before the war he was a tea-planter in India's Assam, where he met and married my mother Faith, a children's nurse, and afterwards he decided to buy a fruit farm in Kent. This would allow him his great passion of watching Kent County Cricket Club throughout the summer, before picking the apple crop in the autumn.

He was the most biased, one-eyed Kent cricket fan the game has ever known. His emotions swelled with unashamed pride even at the slightest mention of Kent's great players like Colin Blythe, Frank Woolley, Tich Freeman, Les Ames and Godfrey Evans. More recently his heroes were Colin Cowdrey – a fellow Old Tonbridge schoolboy –

Alan Knott and Derek Underwood.

He was especially proud that the famous 19th-century cricketer Edgar Willsher, a left-arm fast bowler who played 145 matches for Kent from 1850 to 1875 and took 1,329 first-class wickets, was born near our Osborne Farm in Rolvenden, Kent, in the adjoining Little Halden Farm. It was at the Oval in 1862 that Willsher was no-balled for six balls in succession by the umpire for having the temerity to introduce overarm deliveries with his hand above his shoulder. Previously all cricketers had bowled underarm. In protest, all Willsher's eight fellow professionals walked off the field. Later the MCC changed their rules, the umpire was replaced, and the game resumed. Willsher changed the whole history of bowling.

From 1947 to 1983 my father seldom missed a single day's play at Kent home matches, and was a permanent fixture, puffing away on his pipe, in the exclusive Band of Brothers tent, with a succession of black Labrador dogs waiting patiently at his feet. He kept up-to-date scorecards, and on the way home visited the same little hostelries in the Garden of England in the wild assumption that the early-evening locals wanted to know Kent's close-of-play score.

He was proudly in charge of the Band of Brothers flag for Maidstone, which fluttered over the unique little private pavilion at the Mote ground, the Tabernacle, and one day we had set off for the Mote when there was a three-car smash at Staplehurst and a rather stern policeman was stopping all cars. Undaunted, my father passed a long line of stationary vehicles, wound his window down, and said, 'I simply have to be at the Mote ground before the start of play. I have the Band of Brothers flag on the back seat.' The copper was so baffled that he let our Morris Traveller through. The famous flag was hoisted just as the first ball was being bowled.

While he adored watching Colin Cowdrey's classic innings, he took equal delight in lesser Kent players, and when Kevin Jarvis, arguably Kent's worst number 11 of alltime, with a career batting average in 180 innings of only 3.17, kicked a fluke four leg-byes to beat Yorkshire he rang me for the first time and only time in his life. He hated telephones.

He enjoyed the social life at Canterbury and at Kent's out-grounds at Dover, Folkestone, Maidstone, Gravesend, Tunbridge Wells and Blackheath. One evening at Canterbury, after a well-refreshed day, he was asked why he had lingered so long after the close of play. 'I'll have to wait until everybody has gone home,' he beamed: 'I've forgotten where I parked my car.'

For over 35 years my father was also president of Rolvenden Cricket Club, and was just as keen on watching his local side on the village green as his beloved Kent. I played in the second XI when I was only ten, and soon my father had arranged Easter coaching sessions on the magnificent old Sussex County Central Ground bang in the middle of Hastings (now disappeared under an ugly shopping precinct).

The coach was the Hastings groundsman Len Creese, a crusty old character, South African by birth, who had played as an all-rounder for Hampshire from 1928 to 1939, reached 1,000 runs in a season five times and taken over 400 wickets, and at Hastings was always followed around by three rather furious, snarling Alsatian dogs that used to terrify me. 'Get your foot to the ball, boy, and go right through with your shot,' Creese would bark from outside the nets.

After suffering the unbelievable tragedy at Hastings of running over his own grandson with the ground's heavy roller during a tea interval, Creese was moved by Sussex CCC to their main ground at Hove, where he was an excellent groundsman, took great pride in his work, and was famous for his beautiful hanging baskets. He had not been there long when Hampshire were the opponents and, after a flurry of wickets, complained about the pitch. Bert Lock, the head pitch inspector, he was informed, would be arriving the next day.

'If Lock so much as steps on one blade of grass,' declared an incandescent Creese, nearly biting his pipe in half, 'I will set my dogs on him.' He was especially irate that his very own county should complain about his wicket.

Creese later became an umpire, but loved a pint or two of Guinness at the lunch and tea intervals. Years later my good friend Fred Titmus told me a story of standing next to him at square leg when he was umpiring in a county game. 'He said, "I desperately need a piss – too late; I've started." I looked down and saw a great pool by his feet, but Len didn't bat an eyelid...'

Two other eager youngsters in our small exclusive group were Richard and Robin Burnett, grandsons of my father's idol, Frank Woolley, and one day a car pulled up on the Hastings outfield and out stepped Woolley himself: elegant, white-haired, bolt upright as a guardsman and wearing a Band of Brothers tie. My father nearly passed out with excitement – as a kid he had watched his hero at Kent's old Angel ground in Tonbridge (now sadly also gone, to make way for a Sainsbury's supermarket), and for over 50 years had regaled anybody wishing to listen with tales of the fine all-rounder's exploits.

Though my father hadn't the slightest interest in horses, he used to let the local hunt onto his land, and in return received free tickets for the point-to-point. He didn't go, of course, but from the age of ten I was taken by my mother, and it was at the Ashford Valley point-to-point at Charing that my love of racing was nurtured. The buzz and the excitement and the colours worn by the jockeys were a thrill that never left me.

When I left school I wrote to many local newspapers in Kent and Sussex, but to no avail. My father was bitterly disappointed that I had not the slightest hankering to take over our fruit farm from him. Eventually I had a reply from the *Hastings Observer* indicating that they had no vacancies for a trainee, but there was a position on a sister paper, the *Crawley and District Observer*.

Predictably, on the day of my job interview my father was watching Kent, and I had to get a bus from Rolvenden to Hastings, some 16 miles away. I recall being terribly nervous, but the editor, John White, could not have been nicer. About 20 minutes into the interview he suddenly said, 'Well, Duval, how do you like working for us?' This rather threw me, as I had not at that stage even been offered a job.

It transpired that the very likeable White was a recovering alcoholic, but did have the odd losing battle with the demon drink. Happily, however, I signed up my indentures and my father did agree – finally – to drive me to Crawley New Town, where the newspaper had kindly arranged my first digs. It was the start of 53 years in full-time journalism.

Crawley was a lively newspaper town with three evening papers – London's *News* and *Standard*, plus the *Brighton Evening Argus*, hitting the streets every afternoon, as well as the weekly *Crawley Observer* and our rival the *Crawley Advertiser*. So many local journalists, like Joe Moore, Norman Luck, Harvey Elliott, John Roberts and Ian Jarrett, went on to work for national newspapers in Fleet Street.

Weekly papers work round the all-important diary, and our chief reporter John Collins, Crawley's lineage king in selling articles to Fleet Street, duly marked 'CD' down for my first solo assignment. It was on my first Saturday, and the annual dinner dance of the local Three Bridges Cricket Club. It was the first of so many lucky breaks in my career.

I duly presented myself at the ballroom of the prestigious George Hotel in Crawley High Street, and was welcomed by Alan Perkins, the genial club chairman who, I discovered before long, was the manager of one of the betting shops owned by Crawley's main bookmaker, Bert Mitchell. The dinner over, Perkins and I adjourned to the bar and got on famously, and soon he was asking, 'Do you play cricket?' So from my very first job I joined Three Bridges Cricket Club, which was to prove an amazing shortcut to Fleet Street. I often wonder if I had joined any other local newspaper in the country, whether my career would have taken off in such a charmed fashion.

If you ever meet your boyhood heroes, it is claimed, you'll be disappointed. At the Oval, as a junior Surrey member, I used to marvel at Jim Laker's off-spin, and surely nobody will ever better his 19 wickets for 90 runs for England against Australia at Old Trafford in 1956. But in 1965 he played for Vic Lewis's XI against Three Bridges. I was only 20, and bowling my off-breaks, when the great man came to the crease. He pushed forward, left a big bat-and-pad gap, and was bowled first

News Chronicle

Telephone : FLEet Street 5000 (40 lines)   12-22 BOUVERIE STREET, LONDON, E.C.4.

22nd February, 1960.

Claude Duval,
Bethany School,
Goudhurst,
Kent.

Dear Claude,

        Thank you for your letter of February 16th.
I was very pleased to hear how enthusiastic you are
about sport and of your ambition to become a sports
journalist.

        Your friends who told you how difficult it is
to get on to the staff of a national paper straight
away were quite right.   At least three or four years'
experience should be gained on the staff of some good
suburban or provincial paper before an attempt is made
to come to London.   You see, the pressure of work is
so great on a newspaper like the News Chronicle that
there is no time to train beginners.

        I am sure that if you follow this advice you
will find it far more profitable than trying to take
a short cut to Fleet Street.

        With best wishes,

                    Yours sincerely,

                    W. J. HICKS
                    Sports Editor

Even as a 15-year-old schoolboy I was dreaming of a Fleet Street career.

ball. He was not best pleased. But he was a regular at Sandown in the winter, and we became great friends. A Yorkshireman by birth, he had a dry sense of humour, and used to introduce me as 'the man who takes three wickets every year for a Hundred Bridges.'

At the age of 21 I became sports editor of the *Crawley Observer*, and in the summer Three Bridges CC provided the main stories, which was easy for me as I was playing in their 1st XI. In the winter I followed the adventures of Crawley Town Football Club, who were soon to join the Southern League, and whose manager was the former Portsmouth goalkeeper Fred Cook, a really colourful character and a journalist's dream, to whom one weekly telephone call would provide masses of lively copy.

Alan Perkins's betting shop in Crawley's High Street, which got taken over from Bert Mitchell by William Hill, hosted a daily gathering of racing enthusiasts, and among the distinguished regulars listening to the old Blower system that relayed the results was the actor Peter Vaughan, who became famous as the sinister gangster Grouty opposite Ronnie Barker in *Porridge*, Irishman Bill Broderick, brother of the top northern jump jockey Paddy Broderick, and the Chelsea centre-half Marvin Hinton.

Another member of our magic circle was the local advertising businessman Dan Abbott, who owned horses with the Pulborough trainer Guy Harwood. As the first trainer to introduce open days in the spring for the press, Harwood, whose star horses included Dancing Brave, Warning and To-Agori-Mou, was years ahead of his time. I recall the very first one, when there were only six of us, plus stable jockey Greville Starkey, enjoying Dan Abbott's chosen fine wines and being entertained by his impersonation of a Jack Russell terrier. Over the years a full-scale media and TV turn-out saw the gathering grow to over a hundred. Harwood would stand proudly by his all-weather gallops and, as a youngster sped, would say, 'This colt has got Royal Ascot written all over him,' and Abbott would reply, 'I suppose my bugger has got Hamilton Park written all over him?'

After listening to the Blower we'd often adjourn to the Dragon Bar at the George Hotel, a lively spot. One day we were joined by the familiar face of the retired British heavyweight champion Don Cockell, who in 1955 had put up such a gallant but one-sided attempt to take the world title from Rocky Marciano. I plucked up the courage to ask Cockell about it. He was very reluctant to discuss the fight, but he did tell me, 'Rocky came into my dressing-room afterwards and said,

"You've got some guts. I don't think I ever hit anybody harder than you – or more often." Nowadays Cockell ran an ice-cream van.

I soon became aware of the Crawley Amateur Boxing Club, and in particular a fresh-faced young teenager called Alan Minter, who clearly had great potential. I watched him sparring in an old library in a drab back street near the main Queen's Square, and could not argue with his father Sid, a master plasterer and Les Dawson lookalike: 'The boy's a bleeding diamond.'

Alan never had as many fights inside the ring as the colourful Sid had in local boozers. On his birthday once he found a stranger sitting in his particular seat and, after 'a little slap' from Sid, the man called the police. An attractive WPC duly turned up. Convinced it was all a set-up and that the young woman was a stripagram, Sid bawled *'Get 'em off!'* and it took a lot of smooth talking for the incident to end without charges.

Subsequently I followed Alan Minter's career through all its highs and lows. In March 1980 he became World Middleweight Champion by outpointing Vito Antuofermo in Las Vegas, and the first British boxer in over 60 years to challenge successfully for a world title in the United States, and in June he successfully defended his title against Antuofermo at the Empire Pool, Wembley.

But the Empire Pool was where the Minter story ended cruelly, on the fateful night of 27 September 1980. For years he had been haunted by the knowledge that he would have to defend his title against America's awesome 'Marvellous' Marvin Hagler, but I lost count of the number of times he told me, after his fitness runs in nearby Tilgate Forest, 'I will never fight Hagler – that's not the way to beat him. I shall have to outbox him and be patient. If I get involved in a right old ding-dong, I shall get stuffed.'

In the meantime I was honoured to be chosen to work with Minter on his autobiography, and I had been so close to the entire Minter clan – his trainer Doug Bidwell was his father-in-law – that the words flowed easily. The book was serialised in *The Sun* in the run-up to the fight.

That same year I also wrote a book on Willie Carson, never my biggest admirer, and the two books were published within weeks of each other. With the proceeds I splashed out on a swimming pool at my home in Kent and, since one book did better than the other, I used to joke that 'Minter paid for the deep end, Carson for the shallow end'.

At a press conference a few days before the Hagler fight, however, I cringed as Minter said innocently, 'I am not going to lose my title to any black man.' All his camp realised the remark was a monumental mistake, but it was too late. The National Front saw their chance.

That night at Wembley was one of the unhappiest of my life – and certainly Alan's. With a sell-out crowd of 12,000 the atmosphere was electric, but his remarks had sparked a mass display of waving Union Jacks, with right-wingers singing patriotic songs. Minter stood to attention in his corner and sang the National Anthem heartily. Then the 'Stars and Stripes' rang out, and you could hardly hear the music for the sickening booing and cat-calls. It was a rather sinister and ugly spectacle.

When the bell rang Minter charged out of his corner like an angry bull. His avowed tactics went straight out of the window. Sitting ring-side I couldn't believe he had thrown away weeks of training and years of experience. Heads were soon clashing, and he was caught hopelessly off guard.

Minter was always prone to cut eyes, like his fellow southpaw Henry Cooper, and after just one round his face was covered in blood, or 'claret', as his camp always referred to it. No cuts man on earth could have staunched the flow. A bleeding diamond indeed. Round two was no better, and the referee halted the utterly one-sided contest in round three.

That's when Wembley exploded. Beer cans and plastic beer bottles galore came flying into the ring. I even suffered the indignity of being hit by a copy of Minter's book. The boxers were rushed away to their dressing-rooms by the police. Minter's career virtually ended that night. I could have cried when I saw him in his dressing-room after the fight. As doctors tried to ease the pain from his cuts and scars the matchmaker Mickey Duff was saying to him, 'Now you will find out who your friends are.' It seemed little compensation for his hiding.

Four days later my cricket match at Three Bridges was rained off, and I decided to drive back to Kent via West Hoathly, where Minter lived. He answered the door bell wearing the biggest pair of dark glasses I have ever seen. When I enquired how the old 'boat race' was, he asked his little boy to go and find us some ice for our drinks. I realised why when he lifted up his dark glasses: it looked as though he'd been slashed with a flick-knife.

Playing for Three Bridges, and later Hastings, plus several touring sides, enabled me to make countless genuine, lifelong friends. In my lengthy experience you don't meet many rogues in cricket flannels. One of our popular Sunday home-and-away games was with Walton-on-Thames, whose opening batsman was Steve Whiting, nephew of the legendary *Evening Standard* boxing writer George Whiting. We became good friends, and I introduced him to playing midweek games for Brighton Brunswick.

I knew he was chief sports sub-editor on *The Sun*, then a broadsheet and still owned by the Mirror Group, and a successor to the Labour-supporting *Daily Herald*, and one day he rang me at the *Crawley Observer* completely out of the blue. *The Sun* had just been bought by an Australian called Rupert Murdoch, he told me, and asked casually, 'Would you like to join as a sports sub-editor under me?'

I was astounded. 'But you don't know if I'm any good!'

'The sports editor is very keen to get a good *Sun* cricket team together,' he replied, 'and I've told him you're a useful off-spinner.'

Within a few days I was invited to do a casual subbing shift on the soon-to-be-closed old *Sun* and meet Frank Nicklin, whose great reputation was well known. When I arrived, Whiting said that Nicklin wanted to meet me 'in his office'. I was as nervous as a kitten, and even more so when it transpired that the office he referred to was across the road in Endell Street in the Cross Keys pub.

Many *Sun* journalists were being given big redundancy payments by the existing paper, and then signing up straight away for the new one, so the bar was a jolly place, and there I had my first sighting of a sports writer I had long admired, Hugh McIlvanney, then of the *Observer*. The colourful football writer Peter Batt was also much in evidence, and giving us the benefit of his Dean Martin-style singing repertoire.

'Off-spin, eh?' said Nicklin above the great noise, neatly balancing his pint in his left arm in the style I later discovered he'd perfected during his wartime days in the RAF mess bar. 'Steve says you're OK, so you're in' – and at 24 I became the youngest member of *The Sun* staff when Rupert Murdoch launched his new red-top tabloid on 17 November 1969. No mention at all had been made of journalistic ability.

3

The Controversial Captain

I'D JOINED *THE SUN* BACK IN 1969 as a sports sub-editor, but had quickly realised there was an opening for a racing writer. The sports editor, however, was soon getting pretty bored with my putting myself forward. One night, at one of his regular sessions in a Fleet Street pub, he said, 'Get an interview with someone in racing who's never been interviewed before, and the job's yours.'

Captain Ryan Price was one of the most talented and versatile trainers of all time. I'd followed his horses for years, captivated by the ex-commando with the battered trilby at a rakish angle. Many scribes said he looked more like a pirate. That he always led his horses right round the parade ring and out onto the racecourse himself only added to the mystique. He had been champion jumps trainer five times.

Just as I was later to find with Kelvin MacKenzie, Price was someone else who never minced his words. His colourful language could stun police dogs at a hundred yards. Told that Lord Belper had been involved in an unfortunate shooting accident on Yorkshire's grouse moors with the Newmarket trainer Bernard van Cutsem, Price remarked, 'Shit shot shit!' He had a quite remarkable facility with the f-word, and often even inserted it in the middle of other words. One of his favourite expressions was, 'Un-f***ing-believable.'

He had certainly never been interviewed properly before by any red-top racing journalist.

It was March 1970 when I approached the controversial Captain at the then leafy Lingfield Park and shyly introduced myself. I was from *The Sun* newspaper: would he, I wondered, grant me a one-to-one interview? I should have expected the explosive reply.

'Don't you think I've had enough of you bloody bastards already?' he yelled. Actually the two words he used were much stronger.

I stood my ground. A unique interview with such a private man, I explained, would give my career the dream lift-off.

The legendary hard man must have had a twinge of pity for me, because as he walked away to saddle a runner for the next race he barked in his harsh regimental voice, 'Be at my stables at 12.30 tomorrow – and don't be a bloody minute late!'

His stables, Soldiers Field, were at Findon in Sussex, and I was terrified at the prospect of going there. I recall passing by six times before I had the courage to finally drive in. It was 12.29. Unbelievably, next door was a hushed nunnery – a stark contrast to Price's harsh Anglo-Saxon phrases which I soon heard being bellowed from the main yard. ('He shouts a lot,' his brother Pendry would later explain in a TV interview, 'but that's because he is slightly deaf.')

But inside his new, French-styled home, sitting back in his reclining armchair, Ryan Price changed completely and opened his heart to an almost disbelieving novice hack. 'I'm not a human being when I'm racing,' he said. 'There's always some twat coming up to me asking a stupid question.'

I have often said that my very first racing interview was the best

I ever achieved. All the others, over the next 47 years, seemed like also-rans. Maybe I should have kept that quiet.

It was on the Sussex point-to-point circuit that Ryan Price had first come to people's attention. He had ridden over 200 winners in his teens. 'He was so determined,' his brother Pendry related, 'that he often actually got horses off the floor when they had fallen to go on to win races. Second was never good enough for him.'

Price started training in 1937 at Sutton Bank in Yorkshire, but when the war began he served as a commando and was involved in the D-Day landings. He loved to reveal how he often led his men with blasts from his hunting horn. I remember him reminiscing one day at Brighton. 'One day during the war I was in France' – he looked out to sea – 'and I thought, "You are a c***, Ryan. You will never see those white cliffs of Dover ever again."'

He had been training at Findon from 1951, and had opened his account when Broken Tackle won a selling hurdle at Plumpton. Times were hard: he and his wife Dorothy, whom he'd married after a whirlwind romance, spent the first seven years of their marriage living in a caravan.

Price showed an uncanny knack with hurdlers. In 1953 the black horse Clair Soleil from France won the Triumph Hurdle at Hurst Park, and later the Champion Hurdle and World Hurdle at the Cheltenham Festival. He won the Champion Hurdle twice more with Fare Time (1959) and Eborneezer (1961).

I started my interview, however, by pointing out to him that, while he was unquestionably a genius as a trainer, many had less kind things to say about his plots to land monster gambles.

He could not have been more direct. 'I know thousands of people in racing think I'm a rogue. I'm part of the racing scene. I'm always there to be knocked at. They reckon I've masterminded one successful betting coup after another. But it's all rubbish. I haven't had two bob on a horse in twenty years.'

In 1963 a new race was introduced: the Schweppes Handicap Hurdle, with a substantial prize in its first two years of £7,500. 'I was lucky enough to win four of the first five runnings of the Schweppes,' Price told me. 'I was the best advert they ever had.' But it was this race that also sparked the first great controversy of Price's career.

'The first race was at Aintree, with 42 runners,' he explained. 'Sadly, it was remembered for Stan Mellor being kicked like a football. There were too many runners round that tight circuit, and he suffered a fractured jaw.' But Price was victorious with his horse Rosyth. 'Rosyth was snapped up by a Kent farmer called Jack Sankey for only 430 guineas and sent to me. I discovered he had jarred up his shoulder, and he had several sessions swimming off Selsey Bill. He was an entire horse, and a spring horse. That was the only time of the year he flourished. You could see it in his coat.

'When the 1964 Schweppes was transferred to Newbury, the field was restricted to 24 runners. Rosyth repeated his Liverpool success, but I was immediately tapped on the shoulder by an official: "The stewards want to see you." I was asked to explain the horse's improvement since his previous race, when he'd finished sixth.

'At the inquiry in London I got the firm impression that the Jockey Club were out to get me. They didn't listen to a word I said. My licence was withdrawn until the end of the season. I was a disqualified person. Josh Gifford was banned from riding until 31 March.

'Josh and I were completely stunned. I drove all the way back to Findon and not one word was exchanged between us. Later Josh said he felt the two of us had been sent to the gallows. When we got home Dorothy was trying desperately to hold back her tears.

'The only crime in my book was that I had produced a horse to run to his very best on the big day. I got horses ready for special races, and the bookmakers didn't like it. My horses always ran on their merits. Nobody connected with me had a penny on him. In essence I was banned for being too successful.

'Thankfully, I found places for most of the horses. Only one owner said that he was taking his horses away because of Rosyth. It nearly killed me to see the horseboxes arriving every day to take over 70 horses away. It was a very difficult time – terrible – and I had no guarantee I would ever get my licence back again.'

John 'Jinks' James worked for Ryan Price as a jockey for five years during the jumping glory years at Findon. 'Ryan had a great list of jockeys,' he told me subsequently – 'Fred Winter, Josh Gifford, Paul Kelleway, Buck Jones, Jeremy Glover, Gordon Holmes, Taffy Salaman, John Jenkins and myself. If you worked at Findon you could get a job anywhere in racing. Everything *had* to be done properly.

'I remember somebody told me that the Captain had a golden rule through all his life of highs and lows,' – "I'd rather die than be seen to cry." When he was banned over Rosyth he was his usual barnstorming self, but he was very emotional and his voice nearly cracked up. "One day we will all be back!" he shouted. He made sure that everybody had a few quid in their pockets and arranged interviews for alternative jobs, but many of us decided to work for nothing until he got his licence back.'

Price was continuing with his story for me. 'Jack Sankey sent Rosyth to my old trainer pal Tom Masson at Lewes. The following year Rosyth ran three times unplaced before the Schweppes, and then carried 14 pounds more than he had for me in 1964. But he still finished a close second to Elan. That proved what I had said all along – Rosyth was a spring horse.'

Price resumed his successful run in the Schweppes in 1966, when Le Vermontois won by six lengths. But controversy seemed to follow him. 'I went to Gloucester to give a trial spin to a hunter called Sebastian. He was fantastic, and I decided to buy him and also take on a horse called Hill House at the same time. Sebastian gave me as much satisfaction in the saddle as any hunter I have ever ridden, and Hill House caused me more anxious moments than any horse I ever trained.

'He was not one of the easiest horses I ever had,' Price went on. 'Sometimes he refused to gallop, but if you got to the far end of the gallops and pointed him back to the stables he'd go like the wind. He always wanted to get home. We schooled him over fences and I can honestly say that he was the best potential novice chaser I ever had. If he had stayed with me I am convinced I would have trained him to win a Gold Cup.'

John James revealed to me that originally Price hadn't even planned to run Hill House in the 1967 Schweppes. But two months before the race the horse he'd earmarked, an ex-Noel Murless runner called Darfur, got loose on the Findon bypass, was hit by a car and had to be destroyed. Price ended up with two runners in it – Burlington II, who was owned the Jockey Club National Committee member Major Derek Wigan, and Hill House.

'The Major had warned the guv'nor,' James told me, 'that a Jockey Club member had told him that if Hill House won he would be warned off for life. People in the corridors of power were looking for him.'

Hill House stormed home by twelve lengths. 'I could tell the guv'nor was becoming more and more confident about Hill House,' its jockey, Josh Gifford, recalled years later. '"They will all piss off like scalded cats,"' he told me in the paddock. '"They will cut each other's throats. Just sit still, Joshua, and when you take it up at the second last hurdle, you'll come home alone." He got it spot-on. When I looked round on the run-in I couldn't see another horse.'

Price was reported again for the horse's improvement in running. 'I'll never forget the awful booing,' said Gifford. 'It was the bookies who started it all.'

'The crowd were going mad,' confirmed John James. 'I remember we got Hill House into our horsebox and the angry racegoers started to rock it. They were yelling, "Hang Him!"'

'It was horrible,' said Price. 'My wife Dorothy was worse affected, and she swore she would never set foot on a racecourse again. It was only when I trained a few jumpers to run in her colours that she relented.'

There was a further complication: Hill House failed a dope test. Six long and difficult months followed, the threat of another suspension hanging over Price, before it was proved that Hill House made his own cortisone, and Price was exonerated on both counts.

Hill House never ran again for Price. He was bought by the flamboyant bookie John Banks as an obvious publicity stunt. It backfired totally. Hill House ran another 22 times but never won. The last of his post-Price races came at Perth when he was tailed off last in a handicap hurdle. He went to Doncaster sales and Price, a hard man but sentimental at heart, paid 1,500 guineas to get him back to Findon. When he was unboxed in the yard both his secretary and his wife said, 'Don't you think we've had enough of that wretched horse?'

'As God is my maker,' Price declared to me in that interview, 'I have never stopped a single horse in my life. I'm especially proud that I made both Fred Winter and Josh Gifford champion jumps jockeys four times. You don't do that if you're stopping horses all the time. Ask Fred and Josh, plus Paul Kelleway, and anybody who has ever ridden for me.

'But people at the races are so fickle. Like in other sports they love a champion, but the moment he fails to please they turn on him. When I run two horses in the same race they always think I'm up to something and cheating.

I remember one day at Sandown when Fred Winter rode four winners. But he had a crashing fall in the last race when he was riding the favourite. I rushed down to the fence to see that he wasn't too badly hurt, and sections of the crowd were booing. One punter shouted, "Up to your old tricks again, Ryan?"'

Price performed wonders over jumps – Champion Hurdles, a Gold Cup and a Grand National. But he confided to me that Persian Lancer's win in the 1966 Cesarewitch, at the then record age of eight, gave him most satisfaction, 'and surpassed all my other training achievements.

'He was trained as a three-year-old by Sir Gordon Richards. He finished third in the 1961 Cesarewitch after making most of the running. Then he broke down and was given by his owner, Stavros Niarchos, to his racing manager Lord Belper. He came to me, but was the most difficult horse I ever had to train. Every time I had him ready to run something went wrong. Once he was turned out in a field in

Gloucestershire but got loose, and ended up under a bus. They had to jack up the bus to get Persian Lancer free.

'I got two unplaced runs out of him as a five-year-old, but then he was fired and spent another two years on the sidelines. I risked him over hurdles, but he was always a tricky ride and had to be held up to the very last moments.

'Five barren years after his first Cesarewitch bid I eventually got him fit enough to run again in that Newmarket marathon. Doug Smith had ridden him in the Cesarewitch all those years before and was on him again. He timed his run to perfection and won by three-quarters of a length. I didn't have a penny on him, but he was backed from 33-1 to 100-7 and plenty of my owners and friends cashed in.

'I loved Persian Lancer. He had a great character, and I'm so proud that, after five losing years and numerous injuries, I got him back to win a long-distance race like the Cesarewitch. He was my second Cesarewitch win, as Utrillo had won in 1963, ridden by Joe Sime at 100-8. The third win came with Major Rose, ridden by Lester Piggott, in 1968.'

The owner Charles St George had horses in training with the very aces of the profession – Noel Murless, Henry Cecil, Barry Hills and Vincent O'Brien. But his only Classic winners were Ginevra (1972 Oaks) and Bruni (1975 St Leger) – both trained by Ryan Price. But they had a fiery relationship, Price always referring to him as 'Cab', after his initials.

Price had rung St George days after he had purchased Ginevra. 'Are you sure they've sent me the right filly? She's only a 13.2 hands pony…'

Two weeks later he'd rung again. 'She's grown two inches. I'll keep this one. She's a charming ballerina and I love her.'

Three days before the 1972 Oaks, Ginevra escaped from her paddock and jumped to freedom. She was found an hour later by the Findon dual carriageway. 'You never knew which direction she was going in,' Price mused. 'I walked hundreds of miles trying to find the bitch.'

But he had trained the bay filly to perfection. On the big day, Price at his flamboyant best in his huge sunglasses, top hat at a typically jaunty angle, she came from last to first and, superbly handled by Tony Murray, won by a length and a half.

The winner's enclosure was memorable. Price stormed in, shouting to St George and his co-owner Peter Richards, 'What did I tell you? You buggers didn't believe me!'

'My orders from the guv'nor were simple,' Murray recalled: 'Be last at Tattenham Corner, and you'll win the Oaks. She was a very frail filly, and the Captain's training was a miracle. He spent hours working with her. I have never seen a training feat to match this.'

For the 1975 Derby, Charles St George wanted his great pal Lester Piggott to replace Murray on Bruni. 'I never wanted to run Bruni in the Derby,' Price said, 'and Tony Murray knew the horse better than anybody. The Derby was a disaster. Piggott was carried wide on the 16-1 outsider, and they finished fourteenth behind Grundy. Worse still, Bruni finished with very sore shins and was off the course for three months. Tony Murray was put back on him in the St Leger and duly trotted up by ten lengths. He had the satisfaction of looking round and seeing Lester Piggott finishing a faraway second on King Pellinore.'

Looking down on Price as he opened up his heart to me were striking framed photographs of his finest triumphs. He chuckled: 'These horses have to have won over £10,000 before they can join my select band of pictures.'

Then Price took me up onto his windswept gallops. He yelled at a group of faraway horses. Immediately we were joined by Hill House, Persian Lancer, Charlie Worcester, What A Myth and Kilmore. 'These horses are my favourites,' he said, patting them emotionally, one by one. 'They all ran their hearts out for me and gave me everything. Without them I would have gone skint. They never let me down. I loved horses with determination and guts – bags of guts. In life bloody cowards get nowhere, and it's the same with horses.' Years later, in 1981, I spotted Price at Plumpton, standing in his usual position inside the track. 'Bloody sad day, m'boy,' he told me – he was fighting back the tears. 'We had to put down Kilmore this morning,

17 Mar 70   THE SUN, T...

Sun Racing

It's exclusive! Ryan Price talks to Sun Sport

I WILL LET THE PUBLIC JUDGE ME

By CLAUDE DUVAL

THOUSANDS of punters think trainer Ryan Price is a National Hunt wizard .. but others are less kind about his money-spinning achievements.

Genius or not the racing public have only two weeks to make a final decision. After the Grand National on April 4, Ryan hands over his string of jumpers to his rider and friend Josh Gifford.

Relaxing in the luxury of his new French-styled home in the Sussex village of Findon, Ryan came straight to the point.

"I know thousands think I am a rogue. I'm part of the English scene. I'm there to be to be knocked at. They reckon I've planned one coup after another.

'Rubbish'

"But it's a lot of rubbish. I sleep easy at nights. It's only the unjudicated who curse me. I often wonder whether I will be remembered as the trainer of some great horses, or for the controversy which has surrounded me.

"My wife Dorothy, whom I met on a Sunday and married on the Tuesday, won't go racing any more—and I can't blame her. After the Hill House affair, she begged me to get rid of the animal.

"Dorothy loves racing and owns horses. But I cannot get her near a track now. The insults and abuse we had to put up with was just too much. Some of her friends would turn away.

"I can remember the days when I couldn't afford a matchbox let alone a haversack.

"When I started training had along the way my wife and I lived in a caravan and she drove the horsebox when I finally got one. If I was a gambler, I wouldn't be in my position now.

Personality

"I've seen all the big punters in my time. Brick and income and a few thousand quid in the bank are more important to me.

"And yet I admire one of today's big punters ... bookie John Banks. Racing could do with 10 more like him. He's got personality and is prepared to lay £10,000 in one hand.

"I train the way I want to. Even big owners like Nat Cohen have come to realise that."

There is one horse Price would dearly love to train again—Hill House, the jumper who was said to have made its own dope.

"I'd give his new owner a guarantee that I would win with him.

"He was the easiest horse I have ever trained. And he was the best novice chaser I ever schooled. If he had stayed with me he would have won a Gold Cup. The big thing was that he couldn't be hit.

"One day he refused to work on the gallops. He was given a sharp reminder and reared off through a wood. I'd have no trouble getting him to win again—over hurdles or fences.

Brilliant

"Little credit is given to Josh Gifford for the brilliant way he won the Schweppes on him. It was the old, old story. They all went off like mad.

"After a mile and a half they had all cut their throats and Josh only had to wait and then canter past the lot. I should know all about that race. I've won it four times."

Price chuckles happily at the pictures on the walls of his home. They have to win over £16,000 prizes—money to join his select band of pictures.

"I knew that I am smug and self-satisfied, but don't forget that I and my family had to put up with a lot when I was banned over Rosyth.

"But I'm a bloody professional. I'm a master of my art .. and nobody can take that away. You won't find me knocking English racing—it's the straightest and fairest in the world.

"People are so fickle. They just love to think that there is something going on when I have made them see horse in a race. It's like other sports, they love a champion but the moment he fails to please, they turn on him.

Favourite

"One day at Sandown, I spotlighted the novelty of our game and the moods we have to live with. Fred Winter rode four cracking winners and it the last race was made a firm favourite.

"He looked all over a winner and then fell at the last. I rushed down to see whether he was OK and we were greeted by booing from the bookmakers."

The ex-commandos may have had some of his greatest triumphs with the ring of ugly racecourse booing in his ears. But he still has other wonderful memories.

"Like when Kilmore won the National and the best horse I ever trained, Clair Soleil, won the Champion Hurdle. They were great times and I've been lucky to have had two grand champions riding for me—Fred Winter and Josh Gifford.

"What other trainer can boast that? And when I start on the Flatweiwisweekly this year I'll have another genuine riding a lot of races for me—Lester Piggott."

And the other trainers?

"I've always admired Geoffrey Champneys from Lambourn. We would have my horses if I wanted to be an owner with another trainer."

With the wind blowing coldly off the sea, Ryan surveyed the spacious gallops on the top of his beloved Sussex Downs.

"It's up here away from it all that I love.

"It won't worry me if I never saw another racetrack in my life. I live for hunting but I've still got ambition ... to win the Derby. I reckon I've not 20 years to do it in.

Challenge

"The Flat will be a new challenge to me and perhaps I can follow Vincent O'Brien, who was a brilliant jump trainer before concentrating on the Flat."

Besides hunting, 58-year-old Ryan's other loves are boxing—he's at the ringside for all the top fights—and Aston Villa.

"Yes, I've always supported the Villa, although I have never seen a professional game. If I had a million quid I'd love to restore that club.

"I know that I have been successful, but in this game I've had to take some terrible knocks. I guess I will just have to let people judge what kind of man I am."

■ **TOMORROW:** Josh Gifford, who takes over from controversial trainer Ryan Price, is featured in The Sun.

Ryan Price ends his days as National Hunt trainer after the Grand National on April 4.

My exclusive interview with Ryan Price which clinched my job as *The Sun* racing correspondent.

---

at the age of 31. He was virtually blind. It was the kindest thing to do.'

'It's up here on the gallops that I'm at my happiest,' he told me that day of my very first interview. 'I love getting away from it all. It would not worry me if I never saw another racecourse in my life. I used to live for hunting, but now only have one big ambition – to win the Derby. That would be the crowning glory of my career.'

Sadly, the Epsom Classic always eluded the Captain.

I learned a lot about Ryan Price from that memorable first interview. For example, despite never having seen a professional football match in his life, he claimed for some unknown reason to have always been an Aston Villa fan. When it was time to leave I was still chuckling about his claim that 'I haven't had two bob on a horse in twenty years'.

'You don't bloody well believe me, do you?' he shouted. 'You're laughing at me!'

He went on to tell me one last story. 'Many years ago I borrowed £2,000. I put the lot on a horse of mine at Wincanton, which won at 7-2. I was at Doncaster, and after I heard that result, I had the lot on a Flat horse of mine, which was then pipped in a photo-finish. Then I discovered that the Wincanton horse had been disqualified, and placed second. I learned my lesson. It's a great myth that I was always after the bookies.

'I know I've been successful in racing,' he reflected, 'but I can remember the days when I could hardly afford a matchbox, let alone a horsebox. In the early days I had to gamble to survive, but that's not the case now. And nobody should forget that my family and I have been forced to put up with a lot. I have had to take some terrible knocks. I often wonder whether I'll be remembered for the big races I've won, or the great controversy that has surrounded me.

'I know I'm smug and self-satisfied, but I always sleep easily at night, and it's only the uninitiated who curse me. The Jockey Club could take away my licence, my horses, my staff and my livelihood – they could never take away from me one thing: I'm the f***ing master of my art. In the end,' he concluded, 'I guess I will have to let the public judge what kind of man I have been.'

The Sun used that exclusive interview under the headline, I WILL LET THE PUBLIC JUDGE ME.

I got the job as its racing correspondent, and went on to cover the rest of Ryan Price's career, and hear a lot of other people's stories about him.

Sally Masson was his secretary, and to my complete surprise revealed another side of the Captain. 'I used to take Ryan's children for a day out at the Brighton ice-skating rink,' she told me. 'One day the guv'nor said he would join us. He put on the skates and was brilliant. He'd been brought up in a Sussex village called Wisborough Green, and spent a lot of his youth skating on the local ponds when they were frozen over in the winter. He even claimed that at one time he'd skated for Brighton Tigers' (the local ice hockey team). Many cynics would claim that the ex-commando spent most of his life skating on thin ice.

John James had lots of touching stories about Price, including one about his stint of jury service at Lewes Crown Court. 'He'd tried desperately to get out of it, as it was during the busiest time of the season. He told me about it standing at the top of the gallops wearing that headscarf that made him look like a gypsy.'

The case had been about a man who'd discovered his wife was having an affair. He'd watched his house one day, seen the chap go in, waited ten minutes, and then burst in and caught them at it, and blasted the man with his gun. 'I would have done the same,' James remembered Price telling him, 'but all the other jury members wanted to get a rope round this man's neck. But after my begging I managed to get him off with diminished responsibility. I've always been too bloody soft-hearted.'

Then again, there was James's story of the French Champion Hurdle. 'One day the guv'nor asked me if I spoke French. I told him no. He said, "You've got three weeks to learn." I duly went over with Burlington II to run in a trial, and then unplaced in the French Champion Hurdle. The horse went back, but I was left over there for five months. Ryan forgot all about me. Eventually, when I got back, I asked for a holiday. "You've had five months!" he exploded. "How much longer do you want?"'

'He had one hell of a bark,' James conceded, 'but he never bit. Sir Mark Prescott has the reputation of being a hard taskmaster, but he told me, "I was a pussycat compared to Ryan Price."'

At Plumpton in 1982 Price greeted me with a typically robust, 'Three score years and f***ing ten, my boy, as it says in the Bible!' But then his health declined, and four years later, on Saturday, 16 August 1986, he passed away in Brighton Hospital. It was his 74th birthday.

A rare visitor during his final days, while he had been in the King Edward VII Hospital in Midhurst, was Tim Neligan, his one-time secretary at Findon, who went on to be United Racecourses' managing director at Epsom and Sandown.

Nurses explained to Neligan that the Captain was very weak. He found Price in a darkened room, sitting up in bed with a faraway look. The great lion's roar had been silenced.

'I could not get a word out of the Captain,' Neligan recalled, 'which was a first. Finally, to make conversation, I told him that Dancing Brave had been considered an unlucky Derby runner-up earlier in June. I said that in time the winner, Shahrastani, might turn out to be a better horse. It was then that I could see Ryan's lips move slightly. I bent down to hear him properly. He just whispered, "You always were a c***!"'

Ryan Price's funeral took place later in August, in the 12th-century church overlooking Findon village. His wife Dorothy said that the one thing she could not do was follow his coffin into the church, so it was carried in before a vast congregation arrived. It bore one floral tribute from Dorothy, in his racing colours of yellow and purple.

The church was packed, with standing room only at the back. People had travelled from America, Ireland and the length and breadth of England to be there. The congregation was a brilliant cross-section of racing's great and good. I sat next to the owner Charles St George and Jack Doyle. As Peter Bromley made the address, memories came flooding back. These were Peter's final words:

Ryan was a marvellous judge of character, demanding and receiving intense loyalty. His whole life was conducted at breakneck speed, and he had an enormous love of life.

I fear the real knowledge has died with him, because so much of it was pure instinct. He was a very complicated character. He was the hardest taskmaster imaginable. He would bellow at everybody, but underneath all the hardness he was very generous. With horses, he was simply a genius.

With great gusto we sang the very apt farewell hymn of 'Onward Christian Soldiers'. As we filed out, the church's ancient organ was belting out the Frank Sinatra classic, 'My Way'. That really summed up Ryan Price's lifestyle.

Afterwards, to fulfil Price's last request to throw a 'Pearly Gates party' for all his friends, champagne flowed at Soldiers Field. I was a non-runner at the party as Goodwood races were on in the afternoon. But one thought occurred to me. I rang the Jockey Club's press officer, and asked whether the Club had been officially represented at the funeral of one of racing's biggest personalities.

She rang me back. 'Members may have been present,' she admitted rather sheepishly, 'but nobody was there to officially represent us.' And that prompted my final Price scoop in *The Sun*: 'Even to the grave the Jockey Club snubbed the great dual-purpose trainer…'

4

The Horse That Could Do Anything

ALL SPORTS WRITERS YEARN TO SEE their stories splashed across newspapers' front pages. But one headline still haunts me, from *The Sun*'s front page on 1 September 1972: WONDER HORSE BREAKS HIS LEG.

Sports and racing journalism have greatly changed over the years. The advent of modern internet and Twitter communications means that the old-fashioned exclusive stories have virtually disappeared. Nowadays news of a horse's possible injury before a big race can usually be gauged accurately from dramatic moves on the internet betting exchanges. On the other hand, it's even been known for some unscrupulous people to lay horses at generous odds on the betting exchanges knowing perfectly well that they were actually already dead.

Mill Reef's tragic accident on the Kingsclere gallops was not an exclusive story for me, but I was hours ahead of the news, and *The Sun* was able to give it a big splash and a two-page feature inside. I often wonder what racing story would make the front pages of national newspapers these days.

In 1971 Mill Reef, whom I always likened to a little battleship, had won the Derby, the Eclipse, the King George VI by a runaway six lengths, and the Arc de Triomphe. His form in 1972 was just as brilliant: he had sauntered to victory in the Prix Ganay and the Coronation Cup, and he was a short-priced ante-post favourite for a repeat win in the Longchamp autumn thriller. As Chris Poole told his *Evening Standard* readers, 'It will take an Act of Parliament to stop him winning a second Arc.' I totally agreed.

Then, in a routine dawn gallop, disaster struck, and Mill Reef fractured his near foreleg. He broke a part off his cannon bone, shattered the inner sesamoid and damaged his main pastern. Lesser horses would have been humanely put down on the spot. But such was the money-spinning potential of Mill Reef as a likely super stallion that vets fought hard, and successfully, to save his life.

Shortly after dawn on the fated day I had an exclusive tip-off that Mill Reef had suffered this life-threatening accident. Making calls to trainers when disaster has struck is never an easy task. But in his autobiography, *Making the Running – A Racing Life,* Ian Balding kindly acknowledged that I was first on the trail:

> *I had no sooner put the telephone down to convey the news to Mill Reef's owner Paul Mellon in America's Virginia when Claude Duval, a young racing reporter for* The Sun *whom I knew quite well, rang and asked if the rumour about Mill Reef was true. I found it unbelievable that the news had leaked out already, having purposely delayed informing the Press Association until I had managed to contact Paul Mellon.*
>
> *Apparently I was remarkably polite to Claude, but inwardly I was seething that somebody close to us all must have contacted him.*

I.A. Balding, a fine all-round sportsman, is a true gentleman, and over 40 years later he has never once quizzed me as to who at Kingsclere spilled the beans. On the day itself he could have given me a right earful, but he answered all my questions as though he was giving me his big-race runners for the weekend. It's at times like these, when disaster strikes, that you discover the real quality and depth of someone's character.

Most papers had Mill Reef's accident on the front pages, with the story turning inside, and most of them carried the same headline: WILL MILL REEF EVER RACE AGAIN? Balding later revealed that he received one massive bill from a vet for 'Saving Mill Reef's life'. He queried the sum, but Paul Mellon, the quiet, courteous Virginian, said simply, 'Pay him.'

When Mill Reef made his two-year-old debut at Salisbury, my friend Chris Poole was a sub-editor on the *Daily Telegraph's* racing desk. In the same race was a horse called Fireside Chat, owned by Charles Engelhard of Nijinsky fame, who had previously destroyed his rivals on his debut at Newmarket. Lester Piggott was riding him, and the colt was heavily odds-on at 2-9. Poole was surprised, however, when he received Peter Scott's 'Hotspur' copy and saw that he had napped the unknown debutant Mill Reef, and presumed Scott had failed to notice that Fireside Chat was in the same race. He rang Scott only to be firmly put in his place: 'Oh, thank you so much, Chris,' said a rather irate Scott. 'Just please leave my copy and selections as I phoned over.'

Geoff Lewis had never sat on Mill Reef before, but stormed home unextended by four lengths at 8-1. Somebody had marked Scott's card. Lewis jumped off and, with his usual delightful little stammer, told Balding, 'This is for sure the best horse you have had, and I suspect the best horse you will ever have.'

Mill Reef went on to win the Coventry at Royal Ascot by eight lengths on fast ground, and York's Gimcrack Stakes, where the ground was so heavy that Balding approached Paul Mellon over lunch and expressed his desire not to let the horse run. Geoff Lewis was also much against putting Mill Reef on testing ground, on which he had previously been beaten by a head by My Swallow at Maisons-Laffitte. Mellon heard them out, but then said, 'I have never seen Mill Reef run before, and I have a feeling that everything will be all right.' The little star duly ploughed through the mud to win by a staggering ten lengths.

Mill Reef went on to win the Dewhurst, his first race further than six furlongs. Yet again he surged away from his rivals, and won impressively by four lengths. 'On firm ground in the Coventry,' Balding told me years later, 'and heavy ground at York for the Gimcrack, I am sure he was the best two-year-old I have ever seen.'

There was now tremendous betting interest in the 1971 2,000 Guineas. The official handicapper rated Mill Reef one pound better than the Dick Hern-trained Brigadier Gerard, who had won the Middle Park at Newmarket. Besides Mill Reef and Brigadier Gerard there was the unbeaten My Swallow, who was rated a pound above Mill Reef after winning the Prix Robert Papin.

I was firmly in the Mill Reef winter supporters' club, mainly because Ian Balding was so accessible about his Kingsclere superstar. Dick Hern was one of the old school, making it quite clear to me at the races and on the telephone that giving information to the distinguished *The Sun* newspaper was not his first priority in life.

Mill Reef duly reappeared in the Greenham, and won easily by four lengths. Now everything was set for the Gunfight at OK Newmarket – a three-way shoot-out between My Swallow, Mill Reef and Brigadier Gerard. It was a sad day for the Mill Reef fan club when he was beaten by the Brigadier by three lengths, with My Swallow back in third. My pockets were jammed with ante-post betting vouchers for Mill Reef to win the Guineas and the Derby double, and hefty singles on each race. It was a long drive home to Kent.

I still maintain that Mill Reef (6-4 favourite) and My Swallow (2-1) cut each other's throats up at the front, and Joe Mercer was able to sail home by three lengths on Brigadier Gerard (100-30), a great miler. 'I can recall being disappointed after the 2,000 Guineas more than at any time in my training,' says Balding.

Next up was the Derby, and in a pre-Epsom gallop at Kingsclere on a very foggy morning Balding's heart sank. The trainer could hear the horses galloping along before he could actually see them. 'As they came out of the thick mist I thought that it was a lead horse Aldie in front, and no sign of Mill Reef. Then I realised that I had got the horses confused, and it was Mill Reef striding eight lengths clear.'

I shall be able to picture Mill Reef's two-lengths Derby win to the grave. The little colt stormed ahead and was never going to be beaten, although there were not the same commanding winning distances of his outstanding two-year-old triumphs. Geoff Lewis, who won the Oaks on Altesse Royale and the Coronation Cup on Lupe at Epsom's big June meeting, rode Mill Reef to perfection. Linden Tree was second and Irish Ball, who later won the Irish Derby, third.

'Ask I.A Balding how he arrived at Epsom,' whispered one kindly fellow hack to me by the winner's enclosure. I thought he was kidding – but I did ask the question.

'The police in their wisdom have redirected all the traffic away from the Downs,' replied Balding. 'When we were two miles from the course all the traffic ground to a halt. After ten minutes of no movement I jumped out of the car and told my wife Emma to drive. Running with my top hat on and tails took 20 minutes, and I was nearly exhausted when I arrived at the track.' Balding probably raced further than Mill Reef that epic day.

Next up was the all-age Eclipse at Sandown, and Mill Reef beat the classy French four-year-old Caro by four lengths. It was the same winning margin when he won the King George VI and Queen Elizabeth Stakes at Ascot from the four-year-old Ortis.

Covering my first Arc de Triomphe was a nervy affair. For 23 years the vast Longchamp straight had proved a graveyard for many British hopes. Park Top, Sir Ivor and Nijinsky had all arrived in Paris with such high hopes, only to see their challenges beaten.

But Mill Reef won by three lengths, in a then-record time of two minutes, 28.3 seconds. I recall little Geoff Lewis jumping off Mill Reef, and his first words after the Arc: 'Can anybody give me a tipped ciga-rette?' He went on to tell me that Mill Reef had always been in the first six and had never galloped out better in his life – 'in the end I had a job to pull him up.' I was guilty of journalistic licence when I wrote in *The Sun*, 'The French flags fly at half-mast above the fabulous Longchamp stands tonight – lowered by the greatest horse in living memory.'

Freddy Head, the jockey on the runner-up, Pistol Packer, claimed, 'If I had been better drawn I would have run Mill Reef very close.' I beg to differ. Mill Reef was all class. He seemed to float across the ground, which made his Gimcrack win as a two-year-old on near bottomless ground at York all the more remarkable. 'I simply pushed Pistol Packer out of the way,' said Geoff Lewis.

In 1972 everybody was excited about the prospect of the unbeaten Brigadier Gerard clashing head-on with Mill Reef in the Eclipse, in a replay of the previous year's 2,000 Guineas. For the duel of the season

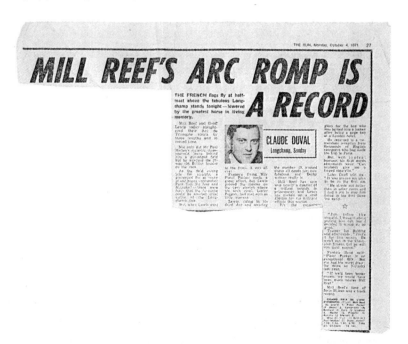

A lucky early assignment ... my report on Mill Reef's 1971 Arc de Triomphe romp.

the bookies were quoting both colts at virtually the same ante-post odds. I still chuckle at the story of the Queen's racing manager, the late Lord Porchester, who by virtue of his position knew the Dick Hern and Ian Balding camps only too well, approaching Ladbrokes' much-respected rails bookmaker Dickie Gaskell a few days before the Eclipse to place a sizeable bet on Brigadier Gerard.

'I suppose that means that Mill Reef is not working as well as Brigadier Gerard?' said Gaskell's clerk that day, Derrick Smith.

Gaskell, a wise old sage with an amusing eye twitch, looked down at him. 'No,' he replied. 'It means Mill Reef is a non-runner.' Days later Mill Reef was scratched from the Eclipse, and the Brigadier won a thriller by a length from Gold Rod.

Brigadier Gerard went on to win 18 of his 19 races. His only defeat came in the Benson and Hedges Gold Cup at York, where he started 3-1-on favourite but could not match the Vincent O'Brien-trained Roberto, who was virtually friendless at 12-1, but went on to a shock victory. 'He was a sick horse when he was beaten at York,' insists his jockey Joe Mercer. 'At the time most of Dick Hern's horses were suffering from the virus. When I put my foot on the pedal in the straight there was nothing there and Roberto had gone. Still, Brigadier Gerard had given twelve pounds to the Derby winner and still finished second when he was a sick horse.'

At the start of his four-year-old career Mill Reef went back to Long-champ for the Prix Ganay and won by ten lengths. Then he was struck down by a virus. When he reappeared in the Coronation Cup at Epsom he was not seen at his best, as he beat Homeric by only a neck. But the form did not turn out to be too bad, as Homeric won two races in France, and was an unlucky third in the Arc de Triomphe behind San San.

But on the last day of August 1972, Mill Reef's career was suddenly over. He had won nearly £300,000 in prize money, which at that time was a record for a horse trained in England. He was saved for a stud career, and he did breed Lord Halifax's 1978 Epsom Derby winner

Shirley Heights. 'He was the easiest horse to ride I ever experienced,' says Geoff Lewis. 'He was so small, but had a powerful neck. You had to give him a bit of rein, and he could do anything.'

5

In the Press Room

MY FIRST EXPERIENCE IN 1970 OF Newmarket's hallowed haunt, for the Craven meeting, was slightly embarrassing. As my friends know, I am a stickler for punctuality – like the Test umpire Dickie Bird I always get there hours before the scheduled start. When I arrived at the Rowley Mile course, therefore, the press room was completely deserted, and with its rows of tables and empty chairs looked more like a school classroom. I placed my bag down in one of the empty places.

Within minutes, in walked the well-known figure of ITV's trilby-raising racing presenter, John Rickman. My mother considered the charming, immaculately dressed Rickman to be the perfect English gentleman. He did once raise a few eyebrows, however, when he raised his hat and said, 'Welcome to Redcar… Sorry, I meant Newcastle.'

Rickman approached this callow newcomer and, in a perfectly friendly fashion, said, 'Do you mind moving, young man? I have been sitting in this spot for 37 years…'

Since the early seventies the press rooms have changed beyond all recognition. In those days it was almost back to William Caxton, with newspapers produced with ancient hot-metal setting. All the articles that came in from the press room were dictated via the various telephones to copytakers.

With three London evening newspapers alone covering racing in the 1960s deadlines were vital, competition was intense, and all the *Evening News*, *Standard* and *Star* reporters had a second man to re-dictate the articles at breakneck speed into the newspaper offices. Many of the evening paper reporters became speedy ad-libbers – my special friend Chris Poole of the *Evening Standard* could ad-lib 600 words on the outcome of a Derby before the winning colt had even made its way back to the racecourse stables. So the press room was a noisy place, far removed from the current set-up with earnest young men staring into their laptops.

It was also something of an upmarket social club, with larger-than-life characters galore. I recall one early day at Newbury when the *Daily Mail*'s Tim Fitzgeorge-Parker took me aside and put a fatherly arm round me. 'You see the *Daily Mirror*'s Dick Radcliffe over there?' he said. 'He's the biggest shit in racing. Have nothing to do with him.'

'That's odd,' I told him. 'That's exactly what he's just told me about you.'

Nowadays the atmosphere has changed greatly, and the press room has more in common with a public library, with hardly a murmur of conversation – and precious little laughter.

Most racecourses even provided free drinks. I spotted one well-known figure filling up his hip flask from a bottle of whisky before hiding it in his inside pocket. Doncaster was one course where the free booze really flowed, and the press room became noisier and noisier as the afternoon wore on. On one occasion a northern press colleague became terribly drunk and, after the respected Sir Noel Murless had won a major race and we all gathered round for the eagerly awaited quotes, realised he was about to fall over. He grabbed hold of Murless's overcoat lapels and dragged him to the ground. It was an unsightly spectacle, but to his eternal credit Murless shook off the incident with a sheepish smile.

When I started out as a racing correspondent, top trainers like Murless and Bernard van Cutsem could not have been kinder to a mere novice. When I asked van Cutsem once if Lester Piggott had confirmed a likely ride in a Classic he replied, in his lordly manner, 'There's been no word yet from Mount Sinai.'

In July 2000 I was invited by Julian Muscat, the then editor of *Pacemaker* magazine, to write an article about how the press rooms at racecourses had changed in the thirty years since I'd first ventured into these inner sanctums, and pick my top six daily racing journalists. The ones I chose were all so very different, but all had memorable careers, and I could count on them as true and loyal friends. Here they are.

SIR PETER O'SULLEVAN

In my formative years Sir Peter reigned supreme. With his powerful, former German submarine binoculars, and his honey-toned, quick-fire coverage behind the microphone for the BBC, he became the greatest racing commentator of all time, no question.

Sport has been graced by some great broadcasters and commentators – John Arlott, Brian Johnston, Richie Benaud, Henry Longhurst and Bill McLaren – but these legends of sound never had to pick out 40 runners in a split-second travelling at 35mph in the hurly-burly of a Grand National field, with all the frantic blur of colours. 'If Peter had been on the rails at Balaclava,' Hugh McIlvanney famously wrote, 'he would have kept up with the pace of the Charge of the Light Brigade and would have listed all the fallers before they hit the ground.' He was peerless.

As the *Daily Express*'s racing newshound he was also virtually unbeatable. He had started with the Press Association in 1944 before joining the then almighty *Express* in 1950, and held his post for 36 years. The combination of a razor-sharp brain and superb contacts, especially in France, made him a very formidable foe. The former champion Flat trainer Peter Walwyn, a great character in his own right, dubbed him 'Peter the Fisherman', after the Biblical disciple, because, he said, 'Peter was always angling for something.'

But Sir Peter O'Sullevan was ultra-secretive over his stories. In over 30 years I never heard him telephone over a single word of copy. Driving away from small racecourses I would spot his company Jaguar parked near some remote public phone box – always a worrying sight, as you knew he probably had some fine exclusive up his sleeve. He was never part of the press corps: he was the cat who walked by himself. He sometimes ended his copy with the best story of the day – in his last throwaway paragraph casually informing his readers that Lester Piggott would be riding so-and-so in the Derby.

But for all his brilliance Sir Peter was incredibly modest. 'I had terrible acne,' he recalled of his youth, 'and this made me very nervous about entering a room full of people I had not met before. I was always very shy.' One day I travelled with him by train to Haydock, via Warrington. As usual, we were fortified by a glass or two of claret as he produced his crib-sheet and coloured in all the silks the runners were to be carrying that afternoon. When we reached the course it was announced that number 28 in the first race of 30 was a non-runner. 'Bugger,' grinned the silver-haired maestro. 'It was the only one I knew the colours of.' He found himself commentating on his own two best horses, the ace sprinter Be Friendly and little Attivo, when they won major races, but from his unbiased description you would never have known.

He had grown up near Reigate in Surrey – 'I used to hand my bets to the local butcher in his sawdust-filled shop,' he recalled, 'and in front of all his customers he would say, "This order will be taken care of, young man." In 1925 I sneaked round Epsom's Tattenham Corner on my pony Fairy. In 1928 I had sixpence each way on the 100-1 Grand

National winner Tipperary Tim. I listened to the race on the radio, and I was hooked on racing from that day onwards.

'My first visit to the Cheltenham Festival came in 1935, when Golden Miller won the Gold Cup. I drove there in my beloved old Morris Coupe, but coming down Cleeve Hill the brakes suddenly failed. Luckily, a five-bar gate to a nearby field was open, and I sailed in.'

He was devoted to his dear wife Pat, who in her later years suffered from Alzheimer's. 'I came home from the races one evening,' Peter once told me ruefully, though alive to the humour of it, 'and she said, "Scobie Breasley rang up earlier."' Breasley had been dead ten years. 'I said, "I hope he didn't reverse the charges."'

He loved his glasses of chilled Brouilly. On one press trip to Chantilly it was three in the morning when some of Fleet Street's finest drinkers stumbled off to bed, leaving the great man as a solitary figure in the bar. The next day, all suffering from terrible hangovers, we congratulated him. He just smiled. 'It was nice to have an early night for once...'

But while O'Sullevan was the epitome of courtesy and quiet civility, he could also swear like a trooper. One year I was picking up my hire car at Charles de Gaulle Airport en route to Longchamp, and O'Sullevan was at the next car hire desk. Usually he had a limousine to take him to the races in style. But this year the *Daily Express* bean-counters had downgraded him to a much smaller vehicle. When he got back, I heard, he stormed into the *Express* offices in Fleet Street and, in front of a huge audience, called the sports editor a very rude word.

'You can't call me that!' protested the man.

'OK,' replied O'Sullevan. 'Like everybody else on the newspaper I'll just think it.'

In 1996 he commentated on the first four of Frankie Dettori's 25,059-1 Magnificent Seven at Ascot, but it was his faithful sidekick John Hanmer who did the rest, and someone suggested that 'the Voice' hadn't wanted to do the last three as he'd taken a glass or two in the BBC's private box. But 20 years later, when Ladbrokes sportingly hosted a dinner to celebrate Dettori's unique achievement, Hanmer revealed that 'Peter and I once shared two bottles of champagne before a Grand National. It certainly did not bother him at all.'

Even in his final days, at the age of 97, he instructed a visitor to bring some screw-topped bottles of red wine to his hospital bedside: 'I don't want the nurses to hear any corks popping.'

When he died, in July 2015, I could hardly believe that the veteran 'Voice of Racing' was finally silent. His ashes were scattered in a hotel garden at Gosnay, near Bethune en route to Paris from Calais, where his wife Pat's ashes had previously been scattered.

'It must be nice to be famous,' I said to Peter once.

He smiled. 'I'd rather be famous for being nice.'

JOHN OAKSEY

If Sir Peter O'Sullevan was the greatest news gatherer, Lord John Oaksey, previously John Lawrence, was the most outstanding writer. In his heyday he doubled up as a Corinthian amateur jump jockey and the *Telegraph*'s racing correspondent, under the by-line 'Marlborough'. From 1959, and for nearly 30 years, he was also 'Audax' of the *Horse and Hound*. His brilliant essays, and books on horses like his favourites Red Rum and little Mill Reef, made their exploits simply jump out of the pages. Wonderful phrases flowed from his pen; he was never boring. Nobody before or since has ever quite captured the excitement of jumping.

In 1946 his father, Lord Justice Lawrence, had presided over the International Military Tribunal at Nuremberg. At New College Oxford, John rode in several point-to-points, winning his first race at the Pegasus meeting in 1951. From 1955 he rode for 20 years as a fearless amateur jockey, having started on the *Daily Telegraph* two years earlier. Peter Walwyn once described his riding style as 'a fine example of the Old English lavatory seat.'

In 1963, on Carrickbeg, his 11th big race ride, he looked as though he was going to achieve his life's ambition of winning the

Grand National. But near the winning post, in the last few agonising strides, he was overtaken by Pat Buckley on the 66-1 Ayala, trained by Lester Piggott's father Keith. Having met this heartbreaking defeat with his trademark roar of laughter, John changed out of his silks and returned to the press room to write 1,500 wonderfully descriptive words.

'Round the elbow in the lead and into the straight,' he wrote. 'The final dregs of stamina were draining fast for horse and man alike. A hundred yards to go, and in the shadow of the winning post, and then Ayala's head appeared like a Nemesis at my knee…' Brough Scott had it spot-on: 'It was the greatest single piece of first-person sports narrative ever written in the English language.'

From his 'Audax' articles in *Horse and Hound* I grew up to appreciate John Lawrence's great gift of getting right to the heart of racing. His admiration of Arkle knew no bounds: 'Until some flaw is revealed in Arkle's armoury,' he told his readers, 'I for one will continue to believe that, in him, we are lucky to have seen the perfect, complete chaser.' After Arkle was given an injection to end his life on 31 May 1970, John was at his brilliant best. 'Now he has gone,' he wrote,

and we must search for others to warm our blood on winter after-noons, to fill the stands and to set the crowds on fire. No doubt we will find them – but they will be pale shadows of the real thing. For those who saw Arkle will never forget the sight, and until we see another like him, will never believe that two such miracles can happen in a lifetime. Arkle was always brave in defeat, magnificent in victory, and gentle in repose.

I once played cricket for Oaksey's XI against his local village. I remember Mick Jagger playing for our side, and I've never forgotten the rather strange aroma in our dressing-room. His lordship had been telling me for years that the village had a butcher who would belt me to all parts of Wiltshire. Luckily for me he was run out.

Oaksey's after-dinner speeches were fabulous. 'Two retired cavalry officers were in their gentlemen's club in London's St James's…' began one of his favourite jokes. 'One asked, "Whatever happened to Carruthers?"

'The other one replied, "Didn't you know? He's retired and living out in Malaya with a chimpanzee."

'"Not a male chimpanzee?"

'"Oh, Lord, no. There's nothing queer about Carruthers."' John was later to name his horse Carruthers, which he'd bred himself, and back him at 1,000-1 one day to win a Gold Cup. In fact, in 2011 Carruthers became the fairytale winner of the Hennessy, and that day at Newbury battle-scarred punters were seen to wipe away the tears.

He made a brief appearance in the film version of Dick Francis's thriller *Dead Cert*, to utter the single line, 'Sorry, guv'nor, the urine sample isn't good.' He didn't pretend to be an outstanding tipster. Once in the 1990s, when one of his tips had been short-headed at Warwick, he exclaimed angrily, live on Channel 4, 'Bugger! Damn it!' 'Dear Bastard,' one viewer wrote in, 'I am writing to tell you that you could not tip more rubbish on Channel 4 if you drove a forklift truck.'

In April 1975 I visited him in hospital in Folkestone after a bone-crunching fall at the local track. His face and mouth were completely wired up. His TV rival Julian Wilson had sent him a huge box of chewing gum. John promised me there and then that if he ever decided to retire he would let me know. Some months later, on a Friday afternoon at Ascot, he took me aside. 'That's it, Claude,' he said. 'I am retiring. I promised you the story.'

The Sun's sports editor Frank Nicklin was a great fan of this amateur jockey with the cavalier attitude, and the following Saturday his retirement was duly splashed all over the back page. Unfortunately, John was then racing correspondent of the *Sunday Telegraph*, and had planned his own exclusive for the following day. On the Friday night, puzzled *Telegraph* racing staff saw the first edition of *The Sun* and contacted John in his Wiltshire village with the news. 'F***ing hell!' was his response.

I felt terrible. John accepted my word that I'd honestly thought he was going to reveal his retirement that Saturday as well. But he held no bitterness, and indeed thereafter always greeted me with a cheerful 'Hello, Scoop!' John McCririck always called him 'the Noble Lord'. I always said that if racing writers could be handicapped for life's Grand National, John would have carried top weight of 12st. – and won every time. He was a Group 1 nice guy.

'Nothing has given me more pride in racing,' he said, 'than the creation of the Injured Jockeys Fund,' and Oaksey House at Lambourn, opened by the Fund, is a testament to his life and endless charitable works. When he died in September 2012, at the age of 83, I wrote an obituary in *The Sun*; the headline was SWEET LORD.

JIM STANFORD

Amongst my Super Six for *Pacemaker*, jolly Jim Stanford was the only non-public schoolboy. He'd started on local and evening papers in his native Yorkshire town of Leeds, and progressed to being an ace news gatherer on the *Daily Sketch* and then 'Captain Heath' for the *Daily Mail*. He had far more than his share of exclusive stories. It was he, for example, who broke the story that Michael Dickinson had left Manton and the owner Robert Sangster, which, predictably, was strenuously denied at the time. 'The office will be getting you out of bed tomorrow,' he often chided Chris Poole: 'I've got a belter of an exclusive.' Most times we looked at the *Mail* and there was nothing of note from 'Captain Heath'. He always had the same reply: 'Too good a story. Couldn't get it past the lawyers.'

I once wrote rather harshly that Stanford proved that not all the Beefeaters are in the Tower of London. He had a rare appreciation of Beefeater gin. At one posh press drinks reception I heard a rather effeminate flunkey enquire, 'Ice and lemon, Mr Stanford?'

'Only if there's f***ing room!' he retorted.

Life with our red-faced colleague was never dull. Some of his exploits, indeed, have been carved in racing history by those of us to whom it fell to witness them at close range. Most notorious is the time when, unprecedentedly in their august history, the Jockey Club were persuaded by a new PR, Tony Fairbairn, that the top pressmen of the day should be invited by the senior steward Lord Howard de Walden to a black-tie dinner. So, for the first time ever, a select handful of us were admitted to the hallowed inner sanctum of the fabulous Jockey Club rooms in Newmarket's High Street.

I remember walking down this long corridor, adorned by the most marvellous racing paintings, worth millions. 'Are they all here yet?' said Lord Howard.

'We're waiting for Jim Stanford,' said Fairbairn.

At that precise moment, and clearly already the worse for wear, Jolly Jim staggered into view.

Sadly, Stanford had enjoyed more than a few after-race drinks at the course with his friend the trainer Bill Marshall. He flopped down in his seat opposite me, and fell sound asleep before we'd even said Grace. The smoked salmon came, and then several more courses, all placed in front of him by the waiters, and then taken away untouched as he sat slumped motionless.

When the after-dinner port was being passed round he finally opened his eyes. He took a swig, and I feared the worst. He was sick.

I'd just managed to say, 'Thanks for bringing that up, Jim,' when Lord Howard de Walden rather saved the show.

'Let's all go and see the cups Jim Joel has donated to the Jockey Club,' he said – and we were quickly ushered away from the scene...

Most men would have hidden away for a few days, but not our Stanford. He was at the races the next day, and rather regarded himself as something of a hero.

When the Maktoums took over Newmarket's Dalham Hall they threw a party for Her Majesty's press corps. Pink champagne flowed, but one waiter had a special bottle of Beefeater gin for the ever-thirsty

Stanford. Well refreshed, he finally went to leave and walked off down a long corridor. Horror of horrors, we realised he had not spotted a plain glass door. He walked straight into it.

'With all their f***ing money,' he spluttered, nose streaming with blood, looking like he'd been clobbered by one of 'enry Cooper's 'ammers, 'you'd have thought they could have afforded a handle on the door...'

Then there was the time at Charles de Gaulle Airport for the Arc de Triomphe when a once again well-refreshed Stanford stumbled up the steps to the plane and at the top decided to turn and give Paris a presidential wave. Sadly, he then fell down the entire flight and was stretchered away with several broken bones and a huge bill from a Paris clinic.

For the York Festival he always stayed at the Dean Court Hotel, a hundred yards from York Minster. One evening, in front of a shocked gathering of American tourists, in a slurred voice, he asked the manager loudly, 'What time in the morning is f***ing Quasimodo going to start ringing those bloody bells?'

Another day he arrived at Doncaster to casually announce that 'I've driven up with the mother-in-law in the boot.' It transpired he was referring to his mother-in-law's ashes, which he was to scatter at a particular spot in Leeds, where they all hailed from. Next day he arrived even more red-faced than usual: 'Disaster. A sudden gust of wind came up and they flew all over the place...'

Although not graced with good looks, Stanford assumed that women, and especially racecourse barmaids, were all yearning after his body. Knowing the attractive girl behind the press bar at Doncaster was a miner's wife, he would always ask, 'Is your husband on nights?' Romeo Stanford really was one of life's great triers.

RICHARD BAERLEIN

'Now is the time to bet like men,' Richard Baerlein notoriously commanded all his readers in 1981, like Henry V on the eve of Harfleur.

After ten years on the *Evening Standard* from 1947, he joined the *Observer* in 1963, and then worked for the *Guardian* until his retirement in 1994. A proud Old Etonian and ex-fighter pilot with a fearless style of writing, it is correct to assume that he did not share the *Guardian*'s left-wing inclination.

In the golden age of racing just after the war he was a master punter, with excellent inside information from particular trainers and jockeys, and often concentrated on his long list of ante-post betting vouchers at the expense of the daily grind from the racetracks, and landed sizeable bets. In this respect his friendship with the legendary professional punter Alec Bird proved extremely profitable. I recall one day at York when the pair were welcoming an obvious coup into the winner's enclosure, and Sir Peter O'Sullevan coldly asked them, 'Have you ever backed a loser?'

The outspoken Baerlein's 1981 pronouncement came after he had just seen Sir Michael Stoute's Shergar, owned by the Aga Khan, win the Derby Trial at Sandown by ten lengths with great ease. The race was then sponsored by the *Guardian*. Money piled in on Shergar at 8-1 for the Chester Vase, and he duly won by ten lengths again. He then turned the Derby into a procession for the 19-year-old Walter Swinburn, to win as 10-11 favourite by a record ten lengths. John Matthias was on the runner-up Glint Of Gold: 'I really thought I was about to achieve my life's ambition and win the Derby. I looked round and there were no challengers. Only then did I spot Shergar so far ahead on the horizon.'

The glee on Baerlein's face after this truly remarkable romp will live in my memory for ever. He loved landing these coups. He was so impressed by the colt's stunning win that when he moved to Felpham on the Sussex coast he named his new house 'Shergar'.

Baerlein loved the good life. A glass of champagne was never far from his lips. But his love of food ran even deeper. He loved crab claws as a starter. When the great sports writer Hugh McIlvanney came down from Scotland to join the *Observer*, he was overawed by Baerlein who, he later recalled, 'thought nothing of ad-libbing a thousand-word feature to copytakers while sitting up in bed eating a pheasant.'

As well as being giant bookies, in the 1970s William Hill used to host a pre-Flat-season party for a few pressmen at Bentley's fish restaurant just off Regent Street. I can picture Baerlein, with a white napkin tucked into his collar, devouring one oyster after another. 'We mustn't leave any,' he beamed to Chris Poole, a fellow big eater. When he had polished off 12 dozen (yes, all 144) of Bentley's finest oysters, Baerlein announced loudly, 'That must be a record at one sitting.'

'No, sir,' replied the manager: 'the England cricketer Percy Chapman once ate 21 dozen… all in one evening when he was playing in a Test match at Lord's.' For once Baerlein looked deflated.

The night of the Great Storm, which swept through the south of England destroying thousands of trees, I was staying at the Old Bridge Hotel in Huntingdon. Racing at Newmarket the next day was abandoned, and I visited the track to see the devastation. All the Rowley Mile hospitality tents and running rails were scattered across the course.

Baerlein emerged in the press room with a look of horror on his face. I couldn't even get a phone call through to my home in Kent, but I asked him if his house 'Shergar' had survived the tornado. The great man was in tears. 'The house is OK, but a tree has fallen on one of my outbuildings and crushed six big freezers. I've lost wild ducks, lobsters and crabs galore!'

PETER SCOTT

'Bravo, Geoff! Bravo, Geoff!' I shall never forget those words yelled in my ringing ears high in the Longchamp grandstand as Geoff Lewis entered the straight in the 1971 Arc de Triomphe on Mill Reef, the pocket battleship trained at Kingsclere by Ian Balding. He went on to beat Pistol Packer by a comfortable three lengths.

The man standing next to me in a state of unbridled euphoria was Peter Scott, the *Telegraph*'s much-respected racing correspondent. Always immaculate with his trilby hat and a rolled umbrella, the bespectacled, pipe-smoking Scott looked far more like the scholarly headmaster of a rather run-down prep school. He was very old-school-tie material.

He once told me about the day his train back to King's Cross made an unscheduled stop at Peterborough, where earlier that afternoon West Ham had been playing the Posh in an FA Cup tie, and was invaded by hundreds of tattooed, Julian Dicks lookalikes. They had used language the cultured Scott had never heard before.

In the 1970s there was a German racing journalist, a regular visitor to England, who raised a few eyebrows in the Ascot press room when he claimed, 'Adolf Hitler was not all bad – he loved horses.' Scott and I travelled up to York one morning with him, in a packed first-class compartment, and he greatly embarrassed us when, in a loud voice, he asked, 'Are all the brothels close to the railway station?'

Scott worked with the Press Association from 1950 to 1956, before joining the *Daily Telegraph* and working under the nom de plume of 'Hotspur' until he retired in 1991 and handed over to Jim 'Croc' McGrath. He was a very friendly colleague, and helped me immensely when I started. He had an odd trait of greeting virtually everyone with a cheerful 'Hello, fairly honest sportsman'. If he ever said, 'Oh, how interesting. Do you really think so?' that meant he thought you were talking absolute rubbish. A fellow Kent cricket supporter from his youth in the Garden of Kent, he often hailed me to ask, 'Is Arthur Fagg out yet?' This rather baffled anyone within earshot, as the Kent opening batsman had retired in 1957, years before Scott and I had even met.

A huge admirer of Major Dick Hern, Peter didn't suffer fools at all. I greatly respected his very firm opinions. He loved Classic Flat races, and was a mine of information on breeding. His knowledge was immense. I heard one self-opinionated young journalist singing the praises of the current champion racehorse. 'Ribot would have trashed him by 20 lengths with his two back legs tied together,' said Scott.

When two-year-olds scrambled home in small autumn races Scott would always approach Ladbrokes' PRO Stanley Longstaff and enquire with a grin, '6 to 4 for the Triple Crown, Stan?'

But he had no time for jump racing. This opinion, of course, was entirely at odds with his *Telegraph* colleague John Oaksey. They were workmates, but could never be described as press room chums. I used to travel back on the Euston train from Aintree with Scott. He always ordered his favourite Medoc wine and was a generous companion. As the train rattled over Runcorn Bridge and we watched the twinkling lights of Liverpool receding, every year he would announce, 'Thank God that bloody dog race is over for another year.'

He was not a great fan of American racing, either, with its drug-riddled horses, most of them running on Bute and Lasix. 'Fairly honest,' he told me, 'I have no desire to attend the Breeders' Cup. It's a junkie's jamboree and the dopey Derby.'

MICHAEL SEELY

The first time I saw this lovable Old Etonian, in the Doncaster press room, he was rather tired and emotional. The Press Association's northern racing correspondent, however, was in a far worse state, an empty bottle of Gordon's on the bar indicating the state of play. But Seely gathered himself together, and proceeded to write 1,500 words in a longhand scrawl, before dictating his article to a copytaker. The next day I bought *The Times*, and was amazed to read such a brilliant description of the afternoon's racing.

Michael Seely was sadly flawed, but you could only admire him for the way he resolved to win his lifelong battle with alcoholism. He slipped back a few times, but generally held the demons of the bottle at bay. And he could paint a vivid picture of a race with a style and flair that put lesser writers to shame. Great horses and the major races always brought a twinkle to his eye. Many of his racing essays were masterpieces, notably the one on his great friend, Gordon Richards, the Penrith jumps trainer, which was read out at Michael's memorial service at St Bride's. When in full flight penning his colourful *Times* articles, he had a rather alarming habit of taking out his false teeth and stuffing them in his pocket.

His personal life may have been disorganised, and he was far removed from the average Fleet Street racing hack, but his nose for a good story was as keen as anybody's. Even though Seely was working for *The Times*, I greatly admired the way he chased after headlines with all the energy of a tabloid writer. He spent hours on the telephone getting exclusive stories from his long list of special contacts – on Sunday mornings he would make up to 50 calls in the hunt for an exclusive angle. He developed close friendships with the trainers Major Dick Hern and Sir Michael Stoute.

One Sunday he rang his great pal Stoute: 'You'll never guess what the devious Wop [the outstanding Newmarket trainer Luca Cumani] is up to now.' Unfortunately he had rung the wrong number and was actually speaking to Cumani.

A true gentleman with a great sense of humour, fortunately Cumani saw the funny side. 'No. What *is* that devious Wop up to now?'

When my son James Charles was christened (after the great off-spinner J.C. Laker), Seely got to hear about the party I had organised for it. 'It sounds the kind of thing my wife and I would love to attend,' Seeley told me – the most obvious hint for an invitation I had ever heard. I couldn't turn him down.

'Are they all here?' the vicar (Canon Philip Duval – a second cousin) asked me as we stood gathered outside Rolvenden's church of St Mary's. I replied that we were just waiting for the Seelys, when a battered old green car came chugging round the corner like something out of a circus, with sets of windsurfing gear loosely strapped to the roof.

'That's *The Times*' racing correspondent,' I said. To this day I suspect the good Canon never believed me.

6

The Scarlet Pimpernel and the Major

DURING MY EARLY GROUNDING AT THE southern tracks Plumpton, Lingfield and Folkestone I soon realised that Albert Davison, the Caterham-based trainer, was one of the shrewdest trainer-gamblers on the circuit. He was the unrivalled betting king of the selling race, but ran his whole operation in a cloak of secrecy. He disliked the press intensely, and would only talk to the *Evening Standard*'s Christopher Poole and myself, presumably because we were regulars at his local tracks.

One day after racing at Plumpton, the flat-capped Davison beckoned me into a corner of the Frank Muggeridge owners and trainers' bar. 'I've got just the horse you and your fat friend should buy,' he said. 'We'll run him in somebody else's name, and you won't have to pay any training fees for two years. But on the appointed day, when I give you the green light, I want a £5,000 bet on the horse to win for me.'

I admit I was rather tempted by the intrigue of such a venture. But Poole was having none of it. 'We'll lose our press badges – and our jobs – if we're ever found out,' he said. 'Anyway, I'm not sure I can find £2,500 out of mid-air.'

I had to give Davison the thumbs-down, but I always wondered what horse had been selected for our proposed betting coup, and what the outcome would have been. Within two years Davison duly won a seller at Folkestone and pointed out the horse to me with a grin: 'See what you missed.'

Before the compulsory overnight declaration of jockeys, Davison very rarely revealed who his riders would be until the last possible moment. I recall another Folkestone race when one of the Caterham wizard's horses was due to be ridden by an unknown apprentice claiming seven pounds. Minutes before the race there came an announcement over the tannoy: 'Number eight will now be ridden by L. Piggott.' The horse duly won, and had been backed from 33-1 to 4-1 favourite. Most betting shop punters were blissfully unaware of Piggott's only ride at the meeting. But no rules had been broken.

Davison's great ploy was to be very patient and secretive, and then back two horses on the same race card in each-way doubles. If both horses were placed at 10-1 or better he made a healthy profit. If they both won, he had landed a typically crafty betting coup.

One of his biggest came at Leicester on 18 December 1978, when Great Things won at 33-1. Richard Rowe, now a trainer in Sussex, was the jockey. 'I was still a conditional jockey,' 'Rosie' told me, 'but Albert booked me for Great Things, and another Josh Gifford conditional rider, Christy Kinane, rode his second runner, Minigold.

'There was no sign of Albert or his two horses in the paddock, and Christy and I stood there like two lemons. When the bell went to mount, two horses appeared, but still no sign of the trainer. It was only when I was going out onto the course that Albert appeared out of the crowd, grabbed my leg, and told me, "Don't bother coming back if you get beaten."

'I jumped the last with three horses in front of me, but I recalled Albert's words and forced Great Things up to win by half a length. Minigold was eighth.'

'I went into the ring and made a big point of letting everybody know that I fancied Minigold,' said Davison years later. Six days earlier Great Things had finished unplaced. Punters couldn't have been inspired by his previous form figures, which read 00/0-PP0. 'I won over £250,000,' Davison confided, 'which was worth many millions in later years. But many of the bets were in Ireland, and the bookies welshed on me and I never got the full amount.'

Davison landed many gambles, amounting today to well over a million pounds. But he was most reluctant to reveal any details, and would only say, 'Sure, there have been a lot of lovely weddings... but there have been far more funerals.'

'I rode for Albert for many years, but I can't honestly ever remember riding a trier,' revealed one ex-jump jockey, who would rather not be named. 'It drove me crackers when I saw that one of his horses I had stopped for years had finally won, and I was still blissfully in the dark.'

Taffy Madden was one of Davison's few trusty cohorts. 'Albert was a brilliant trainer,' he said, 'especially with horses which had previously had leg problems. He had the patience of a saint, and was quite happy to keep a horse quiet for over two years, waiting for the big day when the money was down. He played all his cards very close to his chest, and few of his staff ever saw the last gallop before the attempted coup. He'd always make an excuse and say that his cows had broken out and his lads had to go and search for them.'

When the jockey David Mould reached 50, Davison arranged a black-tie Saturday night dinner in his honour, and Christopher Poole and I made the cut for this exclusive gathering. I got directions from Davison for the most secretive stables in racing, and spent many minutes driving up and down the Caterham bypass before I spotted a few cars vanishing through a gap in a hedge.

When I arrived at Davison's substantial property, there was the selling-race king in all his glory. The old flat cap was hanging up in the hallway, and for the first time in over 25 years I realised that he was completely bald. It was a great night, and it seemed that virtually all Epsom's trainers were present.

In 1992 Davison gave me a rare exclusive interview in *The Sun*. 'I'm on the way out,' he reflected. 'I'm part of a dying breed. Nowadays the little man has no chance. Tracks like Plumpton and Fontwell are trying to attract world-beaters and cutting back on their number of sellers. I say that we want *more* sellers, not fewer. Sellers generate real betting turnover and must be good for the Levy. Trainers like me have to have a couple of touches a year to survive. It's the only way we can pay the wages. I don't want to end up skint or scratching about just to survive.

'I've got selling platers jumping out of their skins, but there are too few opportunities. It was an old unwritten rule that small-time trainers never bid against each other at the selling auctions. Now all and sundry, mostly riff-raff, are bidding me up.

'In my heyday trainers like Peter Cazalet, Fulke Walwyn and Fred Rimell would never have dreamed of coming to a small track to have runners in lowly sellers. But it comes to something when Martin Pipe, with all his hundred-plus horses, runs horses in sellers. I have a great admiration for Pipe, but these sellers were designed for lowly horses, many recovering from leg injuries. I saw David Loder won a seller at Lingfield recently – and he has all the might of Sheikh Mohammed behind him.'

In 1998 Davison was warned off for six years after Will I Fly won at 13-2 at Leicester, and then failed a dope test for the banned substance Procaine. There were claims that the horse was not trained by Anne Jermy in Wiltshire, but by the shrewd Davison in the Surrey hills. Typically, Davison managed to escape any press attention after the lengthy Jockey Club hearing by sneaking away via a fire escape.

After serving his ban, he made a comeback in 2004. 'I spent most of my time in exile flitting between Ireland and Tenerife,' he told me subsequently. 'Maybe one day I'll write a book that will cause a few red faces at the Jockey Club.' Having been stung so many times in the past, bookies now rarely let his runners go unnoticed in the betting ring.

Years later, it became apparent why Davison's kingdom was tucked away so secretively. Millions of tons of building waste and industrial rubbish had been dumped on his illegal landfill sites, with lorry drivers handing over £50 in readies. When a council helicopter spotted mountains of dumped rubbish he was in severe trouble, but he had cleverly sold off parts of his land. I never drive on the M25 without a glance across at the Caterham hills, which could tell a few fascinating stories of the coups planned by Davison.

Davison died in 2011, leaving his two wives to bitter legal financial wrangles. 'Some of his riding instructions to me when I was riding as an amateur were hilarious,' his bubbly daughter Zoe told me. She now trains a small string of horses enterprisingly at Ashurst Wood, near East Grinstead, so the surname still appears on race cards. But now bookies are not quite living in the utter terror they did when the infamous Albert Davison was plotting his secret exploits. 'Dad was like the Scarlet Pimpernel,' says Zoe. 'They sought him here and there, and they sought him everywhere!'

It was also at Folkestone where I recall the notorious Davison coming up against the equally redoubtable clerk of the course there, Major David Cameron. After another selling winner, Davison was required by the rules to unwrap the bandages of all the horse's four feet before the auction. 'He'll fall over if I take them off,' he pleaded with the Major. 'He's a cripple, really – shouldn't have run.' Davison got his way, and predictably there was no bid for the horse and it returned to Davison's stables.

David Cameron was a typical ex-army officer who became a racing official – the sport was full of them, in varying roles. He always wore a battered old trilby perched at a zany angle, the military tie, and puffed away on the inevitable cigarette. He was immensely proud of little Folkestone, tried to run it with military precision, and didn't want it to go on the scrap heap like nearby Wye. The *Evening Standard* once conducted a survey of catering at southern racecourses. It read, 'Brighton – marvellous value.' But for Folkestone it said, 'Simply awful – bring your own sandwiches.'

The Major rang me. 'Brighton and Folkestone have exactly the same caterers,' he raged, 'so this is simply rubbish! Anyway, your mate Poole doesn't exactly look like he's f***ing starving!'

Cameron always invited selected journalists to share a glass of wine with the officiating stewards after racing. It was a bold move and, since he was splendid company, a great PR exercise, although my wife Fiona once asked me, 'Why does it take you longer to get back from Folkestone than Doncaster, when we live only twenty miles away?'

I witnessed more than one Major alert in Cameron's company.

One afternoon while we were enjoying a glass, his mobile phone suddenly sprang into life. 'That's all I need,' he exploded, before departing in a cloud of cigarette smoke. 'Some bloody kid has fallen in the goldfish pool.'

On another sweltering afternoon at Folkestone, Cameron was taking the auction. The winning connections were obviously keen to retain their horse, and were enraged when rival bids were being accepted. In the ding-dong battle the price went up dramatically and soon attracted a large audience. But the Major kept taking bids from a scruffy-looking, red-faced racegoer with his shirt hanging out, who appeared to be clinging onto the rail for dear life.

Eventually, after the bidding was knocked down to him for over 10,000 guineas, the mystery man turned away. He let go of the rail as a prop and proceeded to fall flat on his face. It transpired he was drunk out of his mind and had spent the morning drinking cider on Folkestone beach. Chaos reigned, and the whole auction had to be cancelled.

Major Cameron fought like a lion to keep Folkestone alive. At one stage some Americans wanted to buy the track and turn it into a ghastly leisure park. Later, plans were drawn up to run the Channel rail link straight through the middle. My last meeting with the Major was a typically jolly occasion. But he had some serious reflections. 'All the letters I get are complaints,' he said, 'even though we now have marvellous new facilities. That's the trouble with life now. Nobody ever writes to say thank you. Some morons actually wrote to me asking Folkestone to ban all jeans and T-shirts like Royal Ascot. I ask you! Perhaps we should have accepted all the millions for the site and all lived happily ever after.'

'In my father's day, racing was fun and full of great characters,' says David's son Fergus, who has been in charge at Wolverhampton's sandy expanses since 2001, and has not had to endure the same skirmishes with officialdom his popular father suffered. But, admits Fergus, 'Now it is more of a blame culture.'

But even the Major's enthusiasm would surely have been vanquished by the multi-millionaire property tycoons the Reuben brothers when they got their hands on his friendly Kent track. The die was cast. In 1990 Major Cameron was struck down with a fatal heart attack when mounting the starter's rostrum at Fontwell. 'There was a tremendous hailstorm just before the start of the race,' the jockey Ray Goldstein told me, 'and when we all eventually got to the start the Major said, "Why aren't all you bloody little blighters soaked like me?" He had just adjusted my girths and gone up to start the race when he keeled over.'

Now that Folkestone is lying idle he must be spinning in his grave in the nearby Stanford churchyard.

7

The Grand Old Man of Yorkshire Racing

LIKE RYAN PRICE, PETER EASTERBY WAS a dual-purpose trainer, and I appreciated the singular talents of his rival. 'Ryan was a lovable old rogue,' he laughs: 'there was one time he and the trainer Denys Smith bought four horses from him at the sales. 'They all had to go back. There was something wrong with all of them.'

The only trainer who has won over a thousand races both on the Flat and over jumps, the flat-capped Peter the Great became a training legend at his base at Great Habton near Malton. Most journalists never had much joy with the busy Easterby – 'Mek it quick!' he would say. Now in his late eighties and assistant to his son Tim, he still has a razor-sharp memory, and when we met up to walk down his memory lane his eyes sparkled. His nags-to-riches story is real fairytale.

'I first got my licence in 1950,' he said. 'You had to have seven horses. I only had three, but I included an old broodmare and some hunters to qualify. I also borrowed two from my uncle Walter, who was a trainer. I had to wait three years before my first winner. The horses weren't any good. They were all useless. Finally Double Rose won at Market Rasen on 7 March 1953. It was worth £102 to the winner and my training fees were five guineas a week. I had to wait another two years before King's Coup was my first Flat winner at Thirsk on 15 April 1955 at 25-1. In 1959 he also won the Rose of York Handicap at the Ebor meeting.

'In 1951 I had cycled the five miles from my father's home at Great Habton to Malton, where I got a lift to the Newmarket sales in a horsebox. I bought three yearlings for a total of 380 guineas. By the time I got home I had sold all of them. That got me started.' Mick once told the Tote's Roger Easterby (no relation) that he had traced their family history, and that in the early 19th century the Easterbys were horse thieves. 'Nothing has changed much, then,' was Peter's straight-faced response.

It has been claimed that, if Castle Howard did not get in the way, the Easterby brothers, Peter and Mick, own most of the lush acres in North Yorkshire. But 'our success has all been self-made,' Peter points out. 'No silver spoons at the start. There was a limit to what we could spend. I've done well with a lot of horses who were bought cheap. The reason I never bought expensive horses was quite simple. I couldn't afford them! Anyway, no expensive horse ever did me any good. The main thing was to get them sold.

'They were tough times with little money. But you didn't know any differently and just got on with it. After the Beeching cuts I even built some horseboxes out of railway sleepers. There were many times when it was touch-and-go to survive in racing. But it's when you're in trouble and nearly skint that you think quickest. I soon learned that the more money you started out with, the less chance you had of making a success, because you weren't hungry.

'Goldhill was my first big winner on the Flat,' he went on. 'He was a very good horse, but nobody bid for him, and that's how I got him. He won at Ascot as a two-year-old, and then won later at Royal Ascot.

'Saucy Kit was my first runner at the Cheltenham Festival, and in 1967 he won the Champion Hurdle after a brilliant ride from Roy Edwards. He was one of the very few ungelded horses ever to win the Champion Hurdle, and only the third ever to be trained in the north of England. His secret was his jumping – he was a brilliant leaper.

'I spotted him at the sales ring and saw that he was a good sort of 'orse. When I got him I realised that he'd been heavily bandaged. There were rings round his joints, and I feared he was not 100%. Then the chap told me that all his horses were bandaged like that and there was nothing wrong with him. I could have kissed him!

'He pulled like mad at home, and it was almost impossible to settle him. That got some head-scratching, but in the end I settled him by using him to round up cattle. It was unusual, but it worked. I didn't have proper gallops in those days, and Doncaster refused to let me work him on the racecourse. But I used strips of land inside the track. I worked him on his own, but I could tell he was in grand form, and had a few quid on him at 33-1. He won by four lengths at 100-6.'

Although he had a galaxy of stars to pick from, Easterby made no secret of the fact that his favourite horse was probably Night Nurse, who won the Champion Hurdle in 1976 and 1977. People still talk about his epic battle with Monksfield in the Templegate Hurdle at Aintree in 1977. 'Night Nurse won 37 of his 85 races,' Easterby told me, 'but his problem was he was so miserable in his box and would kick and bite you.

'He cost me 1,100 guineas. The problem was, I could not sell him – I couldn't give him away. I thought I'd end up being landed with him. Eventually, the eighth person I showed him to agreed to buy him. He wore very thick glasses and couldn't really see a thing. One day I casually told him that Night Nurse shaped like a jumper. But his girlfriend was soon on the telephone and said that Night Nurse would only jump a hurdle or chase fence over her dead body.

'So I sold him to Reg Spencer, and a week later he won for him at Market Rasen. I met Night Nurse's ex-owner and his girlfriend at the

Nottingham races and asked them to join me for a drink. The girlfriend snarled, "I'd rather drink poison!"

'He went on to become a top-class chaser. In 1981 Night Nurse and Little Owl, my second runner, jumped upsides together at the last fence in the Gold Cup. I thought to myself, surely both the buggers can't fall! If Night Nurse had won, he would have been the first horse to pull off the Champion Hurdle-Gold Cup double. Dawn Run did it five years later. I was thrilled for Little Owl, but Night Nurse was running out of time – he was already ten. He was a great horse, and because of him we all had a great time.'

Wise old Easterby will always be remembered for Sea Pigeon's heroic efforts over hurdles and on the Flat. Sea Pigeon was a son of the Derby winner Sea Bird II, hailed by many as one of the greatest Arc de Triomphe heroes after romping home at Longchamp in 1965. 'Sea Pigeon was the cleverest horse I ever trained – he had the brains of two horses. He was one of the most popular horses ever trained in Yorkshire. He had finished seventh in the 1973 Derby for Jeremy Tree, and had previously been trained by Gordon Richards – he and the owner, Pat Muldoon, fell out over something.

'Everybody remembers his win in the 1979 Ebor – it was a great York meeting, as I'd won the Gimcrack earlier with Sonnen Gold. I was the first trainer to win both races in the same year, and both horses were owned by Pat Muldoon.

'But then in 1980 and 1981 Sea Pigeon won the Champion Hurdle for us.' In the 1979 Ebor, Sea Pigeon fought out a thrilling photo-finish with Donegal Prince. 'My heart nearly stopped,' said Easterby. 'I reckon I've had numerous heart scares ever since. Jonjo O'Neill rode him, and dropped his hands near the line when he thought he had won. Actually, Jonjo had ridden him with a broken foot. He was passed by the doctor after he showed him the wrong foot.

'It took ages for the verdict to be announced. We only heard the word "Sea" because there was such a roar of approval – we never heard the word "Pigeon". It was the biggest roar I have ever heard on a racecourse. The winning distance was officially a short head.'

The story of Alverton was one that combined glory and great unhappiness. In 1979 he won the Cheltenham Gold Cup by a runaway 25 lengths, and afterwards Easterby was keen for him to follow up in the Grand National. 'He would have been an absolute certainty with only 10st 13lb, and he would have been the first to achieve the double since Golden Miller in 1934.

'He was only cantering when he had a crashing fall at Becher's on the second circuit, and broke his neck. I'm sure he must have had a heart attack. It was a tragic day. And every National day after Alverton was killed for the next three years, I arrived at Aintree and there was a telegram waiting for me in the weighing-room. It was from a gypsy who wanted to put a curse on me.'

Easterby's last runner as a trainer was a winner. On 24 January 1996, Balhernoch won the novice hurdle at Sedgefield by a neck from the 8-11 favourite Welsh Mill. Since he handed over the reins at Great Habton to his son Tim, the Easterbys' romantic dynasty has galloped on. Tim trained Bollin Eric to win the 2002 St Leger, and had joined his father on the Cheltenham Festival scoreboard when Barton won the Sun Alliance Hurdle in 1999.

Easterby grinned. 'Everybody should enjoy the job they are doing. It's the key to any success.' The biggest mystery is why he is universally known as Peter. He was christened Miles Henry. 'Where Peter came from,' he says, 'nobody knows…'

8

Epsom Heroes

BACK IN THE 1970S I INTERVIEWED many of the old-time Derby-winning jockeys. It was an insight into a fascinating, now vanished age.

Tommy Weston had won ten British Classics, including the 1933 Derby and St Leger on the immortal Hyperion. I had an audience with him in his flat in Newmarket's tree-lined Avenue, near to Lester Piggott's one-time home 'Florizel' – but only after I'd put a ten-pound note through his letter box.

The door was opened by a frail little man. I immediately noticed his tiny hands: they looked more like the claws of a mole. Hyperion – the 'Little Horse' bred by the 17th Earl of Derby he rode to glory – had been just as diminutive. 'He was so small at the start of his life,' Weston told me, 'that they had to create a special manger for him. At first he was so small that they considered putting him down. When he went into training he was 14 hands two inches, and only 15 hands and one and a half inches at his tallest.

'I certainly didn't rate him when he was given his first gallops. I told everybody that he was either dead lazy or completely useless. Luckily, we found out that he had huge ability. Every time I gave him a few reminders he literally took off.'

Hyperion was always greeted with a tremendous reception when he won his big races. In 1935 he was retired to stud, and sired 118 stakes winners from 527 foals. There is a striking statue of him in the court-yard of the Jockey Club's headquarters in Newmarket High Street.

Tommy, the son of a wagon driver for the Lancashire and Yorkshire Railway, was extremely popular with racegoers himself during his career. In retirement he lived modestly, and it was often a sad sight to see him hanging around the entrances to Newmarket's two racecourses hoping to cadge a free ticket from one of his old acquaintances. He was always greeted with affection – and I suspect a few readies – whenever Lord Derby arrived.

Harry Wragg, who won three Derbys on Felstead (1928), Blenheim (1930) and Watling Street (1942), I found to be a charming person. He later trained Psidium to win the 1961 Derby. His shock win at 66-1 was considered a big fluke, and he returned to Epsom's winner's enclosure to be greeted with near silence.

In his riding days Wragg was always known as the Head Waiter, as he so often used waiting tactics and only pounced in the last few strides. Later he was one of the first trainers to adopt timing tactics on the gallops. He was very helpful to a young scribe, and his genial spirit carried over into his son Geoff, who acted as his assistant for nearly 30 years before he took out his own training licence and won the 1984 Derby with the Lester Piggott-ridden Teenoso.

I often stayed in the same Millstream Hotel in Bosham as Geoff for Glorious Goodwood, and after dinner he would regale us with stories about 'the old man' and his riding days. One tale still makes me laugh. 'One day at the old Birmingham racecourse the twelve jockeys were down at the start, and Gordon Richards asked, "Who is off?" It transpired there was not a single trier in the race. One jockey must have been slammed by his connections when he beat an entire field of non-triers!'

Eph Smith, the older brother of Doug Smith, won the 1939 2,000 Guineas and Derby on Blue Peter. The horse was especially impressive at Epsom where, as 7-2 favourite, he romped home by four lengths. 'Only one person is stopping Blue Peter from winning the St Leger and the Triple Crown,' Smith told the horse's owner, Lord Rosebery, and trainer Jack (later Sir Jack) Jarvis after the race: 'Adolf Hitler.'

He was dead right. War was declared on 3 September, and the St Leger meeting at Doncaster was abandoned.

The passing years were not kind to Eph Smith. When I visited him on a hot summer's day his wife pointed to the figure reclining in a garden chair. 'I'm afraid he's not very well,' she said. Sure enough, there was a half-empty bottle of brandy on a nearby table. A year later, his body was found in a shallow brook near Newmarket, and a verdict of death by misadventure was returned at the inquest.

But of all the Derby-winning riders I interviewed, the one I found most fascinating was Fred Templeman. Born in 1890, and in 1971 the oldest living Epsom hero, he had won the first post-war Derby in 1919 on the 33-1 Grand Parade, a foal who had been bought by Lord Glanely for 470 guineas. He was also the first black-coloured colt to win the Derby since Smolensko in 1813. Later Templeman had gone into training, and won the 2,000 Guineas in 1930 with Diolite, and again with Lambert Simnel in 1941, as well as the 1933 Oaks with Chatelaine.

Templeman was a delightful little character. Like Weston, he had remarkably small hands. His sight wasn't good – wearing large dark glasses he told me he had had three operations on his eyes in the past two months – and needed a stick to get about the house, but when I arrived at his white-painted mansion high in the hills above Lambourn he gave me a firm handshake. He had clearly been clever with his investments, and had no financial worries.

'I was only four foot four inches when I rode my first winner,' Templeman told me, 'at the old Gatwick racecourse in 1905. I had to get special permission to ride, as the horse carried 9st 5lb in a handicap. The penalty weighed more than I did! But I could always control massive horses. It was all in the hands. It's the ability to control a horse with the lightest touch which is the secret.

'I was second in my first Derby in 1910, on a horse called Greenback, who was beaten by a neck. They didn't have photo-finishes in those days, of course, but the paintings are correct, and Lemberg was the winner. I also rode in the 1913 Derby, which was famous for the Suffragette outrage. But I was up with the leaders, and didn't hear about the incident until I was having a wash afterwards. I lost by a head on Kwang-Su in 1916, and it was only in the last ten yards that I was headed.

'But I was lucky with Grand Parade in 1919. Two weeks before the Derby he worked very badly, and the trainer Frank Darling's first stable jockey Arthur Smith switched to Dominion. Grand Parade had not had a previous run that season, and he drifted out to 33-1. But we won by half a length. I remember I got £3 for riding in the Derby, and the happy owner gave me £5. Imagine one of Vincent O'Brien's owners giving Lester Piggott a fiver for winning the Derby!

'In those days jockeys like myself used to hang around the weighing-room entrance, touching our caps to wealthy owners and almost begging to get big race rides – nowadays the jockeys are the kings, and the owners fight to get them for the main events. Oh, how times have changed!

'I rode against all the greats of my era,' Fred went on, 'like "Brownie" Carslake, the Aussie, Jack Brennan, Tommy Weston and Joseph Childs. But the great Steve Donoghue was the best, although Danny Maher, who rode a lot in America, was by far the best judge of pace.

'It's odd that I should end up living comfortably here,' he reflected, 'just a furlong or two from where Steve ended his days – penniless. He was a fool to himself with money. He was too kind, and gave much of it away. I saw him shortly before he passed away and the sight was pitiful – he didn't have a shilling. He had frittered away a quarter of a million pounds he had made from racing. That would be worth a king's ransom today…

'There must be something about Lambourn. Long after Steve Donoghue died, a young lad used to ride in all the local shows. He really cleaned up, and his name was Lester Piggott. When I trained I put him up often as an apprentice. His allowance was an absolute steal. He could outride jockeys with hundreds of winners behind them. I always found him a very sensible little boy.'

My *Sun* feature on Fred Templeman appeared just days before the 1971 Derby. As we parted, and I experienced that ancient firm handshake again, he said, 'I can't see anything to touch Mill Reef at Epsom. He's the only one with real class. I'd have a really hefty bet if I were you.'

I took his advice. It was with great sadness two years later that I learned Fred Templeman had passed away. But like the mighty Mill Reef, his Derby-winning exploits will never be forgotten.

9

The Greatest Comeback Since Lazarus

THERE HAVE SELDOM BEEN MORE EMOTIONAL days at Prestbury Park. I well recall the Cheltenham crowd going mad in 1974 when Captain Christy crashed through the last fence and outgunned Ron Barry on The Dikler to win the Festival showpiece, the Gold Cup, by five lengths. Jubilant racegoers from the Emerald Isle heartily sang 'Danny Boy' and 'When Irish Eyes are Smiling'.

It was one of the greatest sporting comebacks of all time, because the crack Irish jump jockey who had masterfully steered the winning horse to victory had conquered alcoholism to do so, and win his second Gold Cup. 'In the hefty archives of horse racing's unlikely comebacks,' someone wrote, 'from National Velvet to Aldaniti, the story of Bobby Beasley was perhaps the most heart-warming of them all.' The *Racing Post*'s Steve Dennis summed it up best: 'They called it the greatest comeback since Lazarus, but let's not forget that Lazarus had everything done for him. Bobby Beasley got himself into the worst kind of a mess and then got himself out of it. Lazarus had nothing on Beasley.' Thanks to Beasley thousands of hangovers were soon in the making, but he had miraculously beaten the bottle.

Years later, with the top racing photographer Ed Byrne, I tracked Bobby Beasley down to the cosy Hare and Hounds Inn at Peasmarsh, on the outskirts of Rye in East Sussex. Working as a publican would not be considered the ideal career for a reformed alcoholic, but that's where I interviewed him, by then retired from racing, for two of the most poignant hours of my life. Slightly stooped and balding, he might have lost his boyish good looks, but his vivid blue eyes still twinkled when he recalled a roller-coaster career that had taken him from the very depths of despair to be cheered home at Cheltenham like a saintly hero.

'I come down every morning,' he told me, 'and touch all the optics of spirits – the little bastards. Once they ruled – and almost destroyed – my life. Not now. Booze was once my god, but now I am the master. Running a pub may seem an odd challenge, but I can honestly stand here, serve drinks all day, and know that I have beaten it.'

Beasley was the last line of the well-known racing family from County Kildare in Ireland. It was quite a dynasty, although Bobby was actually born in 1935 in London's Cromwell Road, and went with his parents to Ireland when he was only one. His father Harry had been a leading jockey on the Flat, winning the 2,000 Guineas in 1929 on Mr Jinks. He later became a successful trainer, but was more intent on steering Bobby in the direction of a career away from horses. Amazingly, Bobby never sat on a horse until he was 14. But he soon loved riding his father's horses, and at 16 rode his first winner as an amateur on the Flat – Touareg at Leopardstown in May 1952. His first win as a professional came on Brenair II at Naas in 1955.

But the Beasley family were steeped in jumping's record books. His grandfather Thomas Beasley rode in twelve Grand Nationals and won three times – Empress (1880), Woodbrook (1881) and Frigate (1889). Another relative, Harry Beasley, trained and rode the 1891 Grand

National winner Come Away. 'Age is all in the mind,' Bobby reflected that day in Peasmarsh: 'even now, at 69, I might try and ride in a few charity races. But I will have to go some way to match Harry Beasley. He holds the record for riding in a Flat race at the Curragh when he was 85 years old. Health and safety officers would have something to say about that these days.

'But I suppose disaster was always lurking there – some people even claim you can be born a would-be alcoholic. I never touched a single drink until I was 23 and won the Galway Hurdle on Knight Errand in 1960. Afterwards the other jockeys encouraged me to have a celebration glass of champagne, and said, "You've been a boy long enough: now is the time to become a man." That was it. I was hooked by the evils of the demon drink, and in the end it completely wrecked my first marriage and career.'

In between puffing on his cigarettes (it was legal in pubs then) and serving his customers, Beasley went on: 'When I started drinking I knew it would be my downfall. It's like a spiralling circle downwards – you have no control. People like me never really change. It's like having a nuclear bomb inside us. Just *one* drink and we activate the warhead.

'I used to celebrate riding winners by drinking champagne in London until dawn. Then I'd sweat it off at the Turkish Baths in Jermyn Street. Then I'd dash off the next day to some faraway track and ride a treble.'

Beasley had been champion amateur jockey in Ireland in 1953; three times he became champion jumps jockey, in 1958, 1959 and 1960. For a spell he trained horses from Lewes and Marlborough. 'When I trained at Lewes I was desperately trying to give up the booze, but high on the gallops I could smell the beer from the local Harvey's brewery. That didn't help. I never thought that one day I'd earn a living selling beers like Harvey's but never touching a drop myself.

'Even my best friends would not send me horses because they knew all about my drink problems.

'I suppose my very lowest point was in 1970, when I was sitting all on my own in tiny digs in Leamington Spa, drinking bottles of vodka non-stop, and watching Soloning winning the Arkle Chase. The previous day Bula had won the Gloucester Hurdle at the Cheltenham Festival. They were both my rides for Fred Winter, but I had lost the stable job, lost the will to live almost.' Paul Kelleway partnered them both to victory. Bobby's weight had ballooned to over 15 stone.

'That was the turning point. People say you have to be virtually in the gutter before you realise you have to beat the booze. Friends in the Midlands and AA meetings came to my rescue – thank God. I spent a lot of time with Alcoholics Anonymous, and that got me back on the right path. But I did not want to go to AA meetings for the rest of my life. I did not want to use them as a crutch. I decided when I was at my very lowest to rehabilitate myself with a normal life. I was desperate to prove that alcoholism is a disease, and not a weakness of character. Nobody ever sets out to become an alcoholic.

'I finally sorted myself out, and one day in Ireland I was standing outside a weighing-room when Pat Taaffe, who by then was a successful trainer, offered me the chance to ride some of his horses. Everybody remembers him for his career with Arkle, but he was a truly great rider – he won so many races out in the country that people don't know about. Don't forget he had a terrible fall once, and was unconscious for six weeks.

'Pat Taaffe was a wonderful man, and so, at 35 years old, he gave me a second bite at the cherry. I stood in for the injured Francis Shortt at Leopardstown, and won on Norwegian Flag.

'I knew that Captain Christy was headstrong and had caused many problems when being schooled – I was told that three work riders had ended up in hospital in one day after he'd turned sour. But I became used to working with him. I won on him the first time I rode him at Naas. I was also with him when he made his novice chasing debut. I always maintained he was a better horse over hurdles than fences – he won the Irish Sweeps Hurdle in 1972 and the Scottish Champion Hurdle in 1973. If I had used different tactics in the 1973 Champion Hurdle I'm sure I would have won and not been third behind Comedy Of Errors.

That would have meant he would have beaten Dawn Run to be the first horse to achieve the Champion Hurdle-Gold Cup double.

'In his best-ever season he starting by winning a novice chase at Powerstown Park by a distance as the 2-1-on favourite. Then he coasted home by 20 lengths at Punchestown in December. He didn't win his next four races, but came back to winning form by another 20 lengths at Punchestown in February.

'That's when Pat Taaffe and I openly talked about taking him to the Cheltenham Festival for the Gold Cup, even though he was still a novice. When he won the MZ Mower Chase at Thurles in late February it was definitely decided to go for it.'

Fred Winter's Pendil was the red-hot 13-8-on favourite, and minutes before the off Captain Christy was backed from 8-1 to 7-1. Everything in the race changed at the tricky third last fence (its position has since been changed), when a 100-1 outsider fell, and Richard Pitman on Pendil – arguably the best horse never to win a Gold Cup – had no chance and was cruelly brought down. 'I was absolutely cantering at the time,' Pitman would insist for years to come.

At the second last, Captain Christy and Bobby Beasley ranged upsides the giant-sized The Dikler and Ron Barry. At the last obstacle Captain Christy reverted to his frightening days on the schooling grounds and made the most horrendous blunder. But Beasley staged a miracle recovery and powered away up the gruelling Cheltenham hill.

That's when all hell broke loose round the old Cheltenham winner's enclosure. It had been 15 years since Beasley had last won the Gold Cup on Roddy Owen. So much had happened in the intervening years for the stylish jockey – good and bad. 'That day,' he told me later, 'I regained all my dignity, which I thought that I had lost for ever. I was so proud to have beaten the drink problem.

'Looking back, I think I was too old to have ridden Captain Christy that day at Cheltenham. After that he fell in the Irish Grand National, before I won on him in the Power Gold Cup at Fairyhouse in April. I never rode in public again. Captain Christy and I were two old rogues on the comeback trail together,' Bobby reflected. 'We were pure theatre. I was the reformed alcoholic, too old at 39 to be riding at the highest level, on a completely wild horse, who used to bury his work riders in his younger days.'

It was closing time for lunchtime drinkers in the Hare and Hounds but, having bolted the doors, Beasley just carried on reminiscing. 'The happiest days I had in racing,' he confided, 'were the early ones with Paddy Sleator, the Irish trainer. I always thought he was the shrewdest man I ever rode for. But he didn't like humans very much. On a return visit to Ireland once I went to see the old boy. He was sitting in the same seat I'd last seen him in 30 years before. He looked at me and said, "You look bloody bad." He didn't realise it was the best I'd looked for years.'

In the 1950s many of Sleator's horses were housed in England near Warwick with the trainer Arthur Thomas, and the combination was greatly feared by the bookmakers. From 1955 onwards he was the leading trainer for seven consecutive years. He won the Galway Plate nine times. In 1960 Bobby won the Champion Hurdle by two lengths on Sleator's Another Flash, the 11-4 favourite, and the trainer had five more Cheltenham Festival winners. 'He was a truly great trainer – a genius with horses: he'd school a horse for a year before ever thinking about running in a race. People would never believe half the stories about him.

'It was probably a mistake when I came to England later to ride for Fred Rimell. I always got on well with him. But his wife Mercy was one of my most severe critics, and after one of her rows with Paddy Sleator I went back to Ireland. But that only increased my drinking problems.

'My hero was Bryan Marshall. I still think he is the greatest jockey I ever saw, or rode against. He was a heavy man, but he was the complete jockey and rider. He won the Grand National on Early Mist in 1953 and Royal Tan in 1954.

'Richard Dunwoody reminded me of him, and there's no bigger compliment I can pay. The secret with the best jockeys is in their hands. They could jump on an ass and it would run for them.' Beasley was less complimentary about some of his contemporaries, saying of one top Irish jockey that he was 'the model of piety, but he was one of the toughest riders I ever raced against. He'd cut up Jesus Christ on a bike if he got half the chance!

'Roddy Owen was probably my favourite horse of them all – and that's including Captain Christy and my Grand National winner Nicolaus Silver. Roddy Owen was not a natural, and his first schooling sessions were a nightmare. He had a mind of his own, and a very exaggerated action. For the first five times I schooled him over hurdles, he dropped me every time. But the penny dropped in the end, and I shall always remember in 1958 when Roddy Owen carried 12st 7lb to victory against Mr What, who was carrying 10st 7lb. We pulled away to win by ten lengths, but three weeks later Mr What won the Grand National.

'I well recall the 1959 Cheltenham Festival. It never stopped raining in England that year, and in February 38 meetings were lost to flooded courses. It seemed to suit the Irish, and they won six of the sixteen races. Roddy Owen powered through the mud up the hill, and we beat a rather unlucky Linwell by five lengths. Many thought that Pas Seul and Bill Rees would have won but for coming crashing down at the last fence.

'Arkle, Mill House and Fort Leney were the best I saw. It all came so easily to them. Arkle seemed to know that he had a divine right to win his races. I still reckon his trainer Tom Dreaper was the nicest man ever to set foot on a racecourse. He was totally loyal to his jockeys. After that, Desert Orchid was my absolute favourite. But, unlike Arkle, he did it by sheer toughness and bravery.'

Bobby Beasley retired after twelve years as landlord of the Hare and Hounds and moved just over the border to Sandhurst in Kent, where he used to pick grapes every year for a local vineyard. He even took up umpiring for his local Newenden cricket club on the Kent-Sussex border. 'I always feared that one day it would be the men in white coats taking me away,' he told me with a grin in one of our last conversations. 'Now I've ended up wearing one.'

One evening he invited me round to see a new video he had been sent by the BBC: grainy old black and white footage of the 1961 Grand National with Peter O'Sullevan's peerless commentary. An excellent host, Beasley was always happy to pour welcoming drinks for others. At one point I glanced across at him and he was grinning. 'Here we come,' he announced, as Nicolaus Silver emerged from the pack – being a grey he was easy to spot. Indeed, he was probably the best-looking horse ever to run in the National, as well as a natural athlete with a fluid action – he could have been a showjumper. He was almost foot-perfect all the way round, and the punters who'd backed him down from 40-1 to 28-1 had few scares as he beat the previous year's winner Merryman II by five lengths. The whopping 25lb he'd received at the weights was clearly decisive.

'I first saw Nicolaus Silver run at Naas before he even came to England,' Bobby told me. 'I didn't dream that one day he'd win a Grand National, as at that stage I didn't think his jumping was nearly sound enough. But it transpired that he really hated soft or heavy going.

'Tim Brookshaw and I were employed as Fred Rimell's two main jockeys, but neither of us was particularly keen to ride Nicolaus Silver in the National, although he did win his prep race, the Kim Muir at the Cheltenham Festival.

'But Fred Rimell trained four Grand National winners' (the last was Rag Trade in 1976) 'and he always told me that the one horse who filled him with the most pre-race confidence was my winner.'

Nevertheless, drama surrounded the grey's win. At that time massive doping plots were the talk of racing, and several big-race favourites appeared to have been nobbled. 'Fred Rimell decided to swap Nicolaus Silver from his usual box for another grey in his yard, High Spot. Nothing could ever be proved, but one morning High Spot appeared listless. He was in such a poor state of health that he never raced again.'

To his very end Bobby Beasley mounted a one-man crusade against the evils of drink. On Friday, 2 January 2008 some of jump racing's old familiar faces, including ex-champion jockey Josh Gifford, gathered at St Nicholas Church in Sandhurst for his funeral. Hymns like 'He who would valiant be' and 'Lord of all hopefulness, lord of all joy' seemed entirely appropriate. The Kent trainer Linda Jewell gave a very touching appreciation of a remarkable man, who in his later years had helped at her Sutton Valence stables, never without a quiet quip or a merry yarn. 'I never saw Bobby drink,' she said, 'and he had packed up for nearly 30 years when I met him. He had tremendous willpower. But he was never without a cigarette. One day we were walking on the schooling ground and he was really puffed out. He said, "It's these bloody fags." He threw the remaining packet away, and never, ever smoked again.

'I was thrilled to train his part-owned horse Contented, aptly-named, to win a Goodwood apprentices' race in August 2007. We have a special bench for him at our stables, and some of his ashes were sprinkled under it, the rest being scattered on the Curragh. We will all miss him so much.'

But it was Linda's daughter Karen who rather stole the show with an emotional poetry reading:

The day my final race is run,
And win or lose the sinking sun
Tells me it's time to leave the track
And gracefully hang up my tack,
I'll thank the Lord the life I've led
Was always near the thoroughbred.

And in the fields of life
Let shirkers stand aside.
Make way for those who want to work,
And those who dare to ride.
The only one who's worth a place
And risk a fall with fate,
Is he who steels his gallant heart,
And rides his fences straight.

10

What a Waste

BUT WHAT HAPPENS IF, UNLIKE BOBBY Beasley, you can't conquer your demons and find a fulfilling existence after racing? I think of two other jockeys I knew – two of the finest there have ever been.

Pat Eddery was one of the greatest-ever Flat jockeys: 11 times champion – the first time at just 19 – and winner of 14 British Classics, including three Derbys. He closed his 36-season riding career with 4,632 winners. Only Sir Gordon Richards, on 4,870, ever rode more. In the jockeys' hall of fame Eddery is bang up there in a golden era with Lester Piggott, Willie Carson and Steve Cauthen. But he was arguably *the* most naturally gifted horseman of them all.

In the saddle the modest Eddery was a king. He rode his first winner – Alvaro at Epsom in 1979 – at the 72nd attempt. But it was on Epsom's unique twists and turns that he won his three Derbys, on

Grundy (1975), Golden Fleece (1982) and Quest For Fame (1990). 'Pat was pure magic,' Grundy's trainer Peter Walwyn told me. 'He never lost a race for me he should have won. I never gave him any orders. He would not have obeyed them anyway.' Other trainers would say the same thing: Eddery was the last jockey you ever gave any instructions to: he was such a natural you didn't want to clutter up his mind.

'I'll always recall him winning the 1985 Breeders' Cup Turf on Pebbles,' said the Newmarket trainer Clive Brittain – the first English-trained horse to win at the meeting. 'Pebbles was drawn 14, but Pat just said, "It's a race. She's the best horse and will win." Pat was at the top of the tree for so long – he made so few mistakes, just like Ryan Moore today.'

His darkest hour in the saddle came in the 1984 Derby, when he rode the red-hot 11-8-on favourite El Gran Senor, trained by Vincent O'Brien, on whom he had previously won the 2,000 Guineas. He hit the front, but was pipped by a shorthead by 14-1 Secreto. To the end of his life Eddery was still beating himself up about it. 'There's not a day goes by when I don't think about that Derby,' he told me. 'Of course I should have won. It was my worst bad day. I messed it up and I went to the front too soon. He should have pissed it. It was a massive cock-up, and I was suicidal that night when I got home. Often you have to take defeat on the chin, but not that day. There's only one Derby chance for a horse, and I messed it up big-time.'

But his last-to-first win on Dancing Brave in the 1986 Arc de Triomphe was a fantastic, ice-cool ride. For that win alone he will always be a Longchamp legend for the 10,000 'Brits' who roared him home. He won four Arcs in all. 'Guy Harwood asked me in the paddock how I was going to ride him,' Eddery recalled years later with his impish grin. 'I said I would come as late as possible. Guy went mad! If he had had a gun on him, he would have shot me!'

Eddery's 1997 St Leger win on the grey Silver Patriarch was another memorable moment, as it gave him his 4,000th career success. For once the gods wrote the perfect script.

Sadly, when he retired from riding in 2003 at the height of his powers, his life seemed to take a downhill spiral. 'The tragedy with Pat was that he never really readjusted after he retired,' said Willie Carson. 'That's when all the problems started.' Eddery admitted he never hit the heights as a trainer. 'Training is tough. It's far harder than I ever thought when I was a jockey. I don't have a massive number of horses, and it's very difficult to compete.'

In 2010 his brother Paul sued him for wrongful dismissal, but lost the case. Carolyn, his wife for 25 years and mother of their three children, left him and later divorced him. He then enjoyed a relationship with Emma Owen, 24 years his junior, who played a major role in Eddery's training career in recent times.

In 2015, Eddery, not averse to a glass or two of brandy, and struggling with ill health, was a noticeable non-runner when Ascot invited him to be part of their 40th-anniversary celebration of the epic 1975 King George VI when he rode Grundy to beat Bustino. In that year's Flat season, out of 62 runners, he saddled only one winner.

The last time I spotted him at the races, wearing dark glasses on a dull day, I barely recognised him, he looked so frail. He died not long after, at just 63. But if you simply mouthed the word 'Pat' anywhere in the racing world, everybody knew who you meant.

FIFTY-FIVE WAS, TRAGICALLY, AN EVEN YOUNGER age to die for Walter Swinburn. Sadly, as with Pat Eddery, his life was affected by alcohol.

The son of the former Irish champion jockey Wally Swinburn, who rode three Irish Classic winners – Pidget and Prince's Polly (Irish 1,000 Guineas in 1972 and 1982) and Blue Wind (Irish Oaks 1981) – Walter was a boy-wonder nicknamed 'the Choirboy' because of his angelic looks. He joined two of Britain's best apprentice academy schools with trainers Reg Hollinshead and Frenchie Nicholson.

At only 19 he won the 1981 Epsom Derby on Shergar by ten

lengths, with Peter Bromley famously shouting, 'You need a telescope to see the rest!'

Swinburn was modest about his own contribution. 'Anybody could have won on Shergar,' he told me. 'You never realised how fast you were galloping until you saw all the other horses disappear.

'All I can recall from the Derby were the crowd shouting. "Go on, Lester!" They could not believe that any other jockey was winning the race so easily. When we went round Tattenham Corner I had to pinch myself as I was travelling so easily. I gave Shergar one slap and he took off. I always regretted afterwards that I whipped him – I would have won without carrying a whip. There was a big party that night, but I didn't drink in those days, and I celebrated by having a ham sandwich and going to bed early. To me it was all a fairytale, riding the winner in my teens and in a record time.'

Swinburn was banned when it came to the Irish Derby, and Piggott replaced him to win, but he was back on board Shergar when he won the King George VI at Ascot. Shergar won six of his eight races, and ironically both of his defeats were at Doncaster: as a two-year-old he had been second in the Racing Post Trophy, and in his farewell race he started 9-4-on but trailed in fourth in the St Leger. Two years later the horse was famously kidnapped by the IRA, who demanded a ransom from the Aga Khan. But he had syndicated him for £10 million to 40 shareholders. Shergar was thought to have been destroyed, and his disappearance remains one of racing's biggest unsolved mysteries.

'The trouble with Shergar,' reflected Swinburn, 'was that even at that early age I knew I would never ride a better horse. He was a steering job. It gave me even greater satisfaction when Lammtarra won the 1995 Derby. But Zilzal, who won five of his six races, was argu-ably the best horse I ever rode, including winning the 1989 Breeders' Cup Mile.'

Like Lester Piggott he was tall for a Flat jockey, and at Sandown in April 2000 Swinburn retired. 'It's the weight,' he confirmed.

'He had weight problems as a jockey which were far worse than

Left: Cricket has always played an important part in my life. Bowling off-spin for Three Bridges in the Sussex League actually helped me get my job on *The Sun*, when Rupert Murdoch started the red-top tabloid in November 1969.

Above: Danoli was one of the greatest Irish fairy tale winners at the Cheltenham Festival when he won the 1994 Sun Alliance Novices' Hurdle. This picture was taken at Tom Foley's County Carlow stables just days before his terrific triumph.

Left: Thanks a lot… England and Surrey cricket legend Jim Laker is not best pleased when I bowled him first ball with one of my off-spinners in a charity cricket match at Three Bridges in 1965.

I loved going on cricket club tours to Australia and made countless friends. Keith Miller loved horse racing but this photograph shows an after-match barbecue in Adelaide with Barry Jarman, one of the nicest Australian Test cricketers.

I ghosted Tony McCoy's column in *The Sun* for over ten years. Here we are pictured at Stratford on the last day of the season when he was first crowned champion jumps jockey in 1996. I hope his fierce competitiveness and modesty shone through our articles.

Happy and contented in retirement, this is a rare photograph of Peter Easterby, the only man ever to trainer over 1,000 winners on both the Flat and over jumps, with a photo of his debut Cheltenham Festival runner, the 1967 Champion Hurdle-winner Saucy Kit.

Bobby Beasley behind the bar of his pub in Sussex – the reformed alcoholic who rode Captain Christy to a quite remarkable win in the 1974 Cheltenham Gold Cup. 'We were two old rogues together,' Beasley beamed.

Ginger McCain and I at Aintree on the day before Amberleigh House became his fourth Grand National winner in 2004. We became involved in the well-known Grand National story of Blackwater Bridge, who was due to run in *The Sun*'s colours.

Above: Joining in the special happy celebrations with John Gosden and his wife Rachel Hood, when he won his second Flat trainers' title in 2015.

Right: A number 11 in between two England and Kent opening batsmen – Rob Key (left) and the late Peter Richardson. They came to Lingfield when a race was run to celebrate my 40 years on *The Sun*.

Rupert Murdoch, the world's leading media mogul, was a rare visitor to the Cheltenham Festival in 2010 when his daughter Elizabeth rode the Andy Stewart-owned Watergate in a charity race.

Rupert Murdoch
Chairman and Chief Executive Officer

10201 West Pico Boulevard
Los Angeles, CA 90035
310 369 1226

December 8, 2014

Mr. Claude Duval
The Racing Reporter
c/o The Sun
London

Dear Claude,

I simply couldn't allow this momentous milestone to pass without personally thanking and congratulating you for your 45 years of service and dedication to The Sun and News Corp.

Your racing expertise and capacity to bring readers on a journey from their workplaces or home to the stands of racing tracks the length and breadth of Britain continues to be the envy of Fleet Street and remains unparalleled in its field.

Who'd have thought after that first triumphant night of The Sun in November 1969 that just the two of us remain now. 'Horse Dope Sensation' was a great splash to launch our paper and paved the way for thousands more great Sun headlines. Fittingly, you are fondly known in your circle "as big a national treasure as The Sun itself".

I'm sorry I can't be with you today Claude but hope you enjoy celebrating with colleagues and friends.

Best wishes,

Rupert Murdoch

'Just the two of us remain now…' *The Sun*'s owner Rupert Murdoch was kind enough to write me a personal letter from Hollywood when we celebrated 45 years on the newspaper.

Frankie Dettori and I celebrate him winning the 2004 champion jockeys' title. *The Sun* presented a cup as at that time there was no prize for the achievement. Nobody has done more to promote racing that the popular little Italian.

Lingfield has always been one of my favourite racecourses and Kate Hills, then working for Arena Leisure, organised a series of races to celebrate various milestones in my career. Here I am greeting a happy winner.

A happy group celebrate my 60th birthday at a London dinner. Left to right: Alan Lee, Colin Mackenzie, Jim 'Croc' McGrath, Geoff Lester, George Irvine, Chris Poole, Trevor Clements, Rob Hartnett, Jim McGrath, Adrian Pratt, CD, Jimmy Blackshaw, Alan Byrne, Wally Pyrah, George Ennor, Cloudesley Marsham, Mike Dillon, Jeremy Cassel, Andy Stewart and Cornelius Lysaght. Mascot: John Maxse.

Above: Martin Pipe comes to my birthday parties and always creates an individual card. He remains one of the most intriguing people I have met in my 47 years in racing. He smashed records galore from a humble, non-training background.

Right: My last working day at Ascot in October 2016 with the peerless Tony McCoy. We have so many memories together going back to his first rides in England before he rode 4,358 winners and was champion jockey for 20 consecutive seasons. He is the Real McCoy.

Barry Dennis, the king of the betting ring, let me work on his pitch at Plumpton in October 1998. 'Here come the mugs,' the Romford Foghorn bellowed as the London train, full of punters, pulled in. He was not quite so happy when a string of favourites trotted up.

To Claude.
Happy Retirement
Nico de Boinville

Might Bite on his way to winning the RSA Chase at the 2017 Cheltenham Festival. He is part-owned by Simon Philip, my good friend and Kent County Cricket Club Chairman. Jockey Nico de Boinville was kind enough to send me a photograph of them both for my retirement.

anybody imagined,' said John Francome, later a broadcasting colleague when Swinburn joined Channel 4 as a racing pundit.

'Riding has been all my life,' admitted Swinburn ominously to me when he gave up, 'and it will almost be the end of my world when I retire.'

When Walter passed away I had pangs of guilt about the nickname 'Bunter' I'd given him, as he was frequently putting up overweight. A good cricketer, who'd been coached at his public school in Ireland, Swinburn had both Sir Colin Cowdrey and Garry Sobers caught off his bowling in charity matches – Sobers on the boundary in Barbados. Sir Michael Stoute, who was also playing said the catch was taken so deep it was nearly on another island. It was when Swinburn was playing for a Newmarket XI against Lambourn, with my pal Chris Poole acting as an umpire, that I got my comeuppance.

'Right arm over, Bunter?' said Poole when he came on to bowl.

'What did you say?' asked an astonished Swinburn, and when Poole told him I'd given him that nickname, retorted, 'Well, f*** him!' I was subsequently forgiven, and when he won a big handicap with a masterful riding display he spotted me and grinned. 'Not bad for a Bunter...'

Swinburn made a successful switch to training, married the Tring trainer Peter Harris's daughter Alison, and they had two daughters, Claudia and Milly. He seemed to enjoy training, but then in 2011 he quit. It was well documented that he had dark days. A troubled soul, he often turned to the bottle to try and lessen his troubles. 'He always seemed a very sensitive person,' reflected John Francome. He was fined £500 for assaulting a Newmarket restaurant owner and damaging a glass door. He moved into a London flat with a male partner.

It was a sad day, then, on 29 December 2016, when a funeral was held at Newmarket for Swinburn after a fatal accident at his flat. 'Walter was happiest on a horse,' said his great friend Michael Haggas, the brother of trainer William Haggas. 'He never found anything to replace the buzz when he retired. We all knew that he had plenty of demons. But he fought all his many problems with great dignity and courage. He had a certain swagger, but all that confidence was left behind in the weighing-room. His closest friends all knew how humble and shy he really was.'

I leave the last words with Sir Michael Stoute, his greatest ally. 'There were times when he drove me mad,' he says. But he had so much talent and a brilliant temperament that I always forgave him. He definitely had a vulnerability, but that often comes when you have as much talent as he had.

'Even on the big racing days he was totally unfazed. When I went round to pick him up on the morning of Shergar's Derby he was still in bed. Then he fell fast asleep in my car all the way to Epsom.'

11

'He Could Teach Birds to Sing'

IF I EVER WANTED LESSONS ON the background to Irish jump racing, the cocktail bar in Upper Dublin's massive Burlington Hotel in Leeson Street was the ideal venue. Before and after racing at nearby Leopardstown the Irish racing fraternity assembled, and tales of monster gambles and unbelievable characters abounded. It was in the 'Burlo', as Dubliners loved to call it, in the 1970s that I first encountered Mick O'Toole, one of the most colourful figures Irish racing has ever known. Not only was he one of the shrewdest dual-purpose trainers, he was also a fierce gambler prepared to back his judgement with colossal sums of money.

Born in the Liberties area in Dublin's heartland, he trained over 800 winners, including eight at the Cheltenham Festival, and it should have been nine if his 1980 Champion Chase hero Chinrullah had not been disqualified for contaminated foodstuffs.

But still so vivid in my mind are the tears unashamedly trickling down his chubby face as he walked into the winner's enclosure at the Cheltenham Festival with his usual swagger. This was 13 March 1975, and he had trained his first Festival winner with Davy Lad in the Sun Alliance Novices' Hurdle. Seeing O'Toole completely overcome with emotion, you would have thought he was following the funeral cortege of one of his closest relatives. Instead, it was one of the happiest moments of his life.

Remarkably, Davy Lad had not set foot on a racecourse since the previous November, but, despite his non-appearance, punters had piled into him all winter and he had started a heavily supported 5-2 favourite. Trained to perfection by ex-butcher and greyhound trainer 'the Tooler', and ridden to perfection by an ice-cool Dessie Hughes, Davy Lad trounced his nineteen rivals by an easy three lengths. Race-goers were rain-lashed but happy. At the very shrine of steeplechasing, Irish priests and punters alike had pulled off a monster gamble on Davy Lad.

A year later, marvellous Micko proved that Davy Lad's win was no fluke when his Parkhill won the Sun Alliance Novices' Hurdle from twenty rivals at 4-1, and in 1977 Davy Lad returned to the Cheltenham Festival to win its biggest prize, the Gold Cup, at 14-1. During the winter O'Toole had struck a bet of £500 each way at 50-1, and Davy Lad duly won on St Patrick's Day. Davy Lad was owned by Anne-Marie McGowan, and was the first horse ever to run in her colours. Talk about beginner's luck.

After Davy Lad's first Festival win I travelled to Ireland for an exclusive interview with O'Toole, who had so often been the court jester in the boisterous bar at the Burlington. 'Go to the Curragh, turn left, and then ask for the Maddenstown stables,' was the simple advice from a local. 'Ask the sheep,' he added – 'everybody knows Micko.'

Sure enough, as soon I left the Curragh the country road was blocked by a flock of sheep. But after negotiating that hazard, the first sighting of Maddenstown was the huge, blue-painted horse barns and the new covered gallop. This was the place O'Toole had turned into a winners' factory.

As I studied O'Toole, a jovial character with a high-pitched voice, yelling orders across his yard, it was hard to take in just how much he had achieved in such a short time. He is as well known in his native Ireland as the prince of punters as the actor Peter O'Toole (no relation!). Relaxing in his spacious bungalow after introducing me to his splendid wife Una, O'Toole smiled. 'When I bought Maddenstown for £45,000 I didn't have the price of a round of drinks. I was virtually skint, and my gambles simply had to come off, or nobody in racing would have ever heard of me again. But I built up a string of over 100 horses, and increased the boxes from 40 – and all paid for with bookies' money.'

Any conversation with O'Toole is always interrupted by one of his trademark bursts of laughter. Of course, not all his attempted gambling coups have come off, but many times he has left the bookies crying into their empty satchels. As he warmed to his life story I was concerned that my notebook would not be big enough. When the legendary Irish bloodstock agent Jack Doyle joined our little party I was scared there would be a real paper shortage.

Doyle was an ex-Irish rugby international, champion sprinter, and representative boxer who'd turned bloodstock agent. It was said of him that he'd sell sand to the Arabs and the next day they'd come back for more. 'He told me once his secret was to spot yearlings at the sales with big ears and a clear eye,' said one of Micko's top owners, Barney Eastwood, who was involved in the demolition business in Belfast – not a bad job at that time, as most of his job seemed to be already done for him. 'If only it was that easy.'

So how did O'Toole's fairytale start?

'It was a plot,' Doyle assured me. 'You couldn't call it anything else. I got Micko's first horse when he got his licence in 1966. I came over to Epsom and bought a three-year-old filly for 800 guineas called Lintola from Syd Dale, who had been Captain Ryan Price's assistant for many years. If you didn't learn something at Findon you deserved to be shot.

'She had won the Acorn Stakes at Epsom as a two-year-old and had looked a speedy sort. In those days the ownership and training rules were very different. I watched Lintola working for Micko and I could sense that he was getting excited. I favoured taking her back to Epsom, but Micko had sorted out a five-furlong race at the then Edinburgh racecourse. An O'Toole runner at a Scottish track would have set off the bookies' alarm bells, so she ran in the name of Syd Dale. It was a hush-hush operation, and everything was a deadly secret.

'Micko couldn't afford an aeroplane horse transporter in those days, so she went on the ferry to Scotland. We reserved a special space for her. But Lintola could have been a circus performer, and walked calmly up the tiny gangplank. She was as quiet as a sheep, but one slip and Micko's first gambling coup could have really ended up in the drink. Micko was always absolutely certain that she would provide him with his first winner.'

'The way she had been working at home made me sure that she would win,' added O'Toole, 'although I virtually only had selling platers to work her against. I was so sure of myself that I even went round Dublin borrowing money to back her.

'The famous day came on 18 April 1966, and the North Berwick Handicap. The good lightweight Johnny Murtagh – no, not that one – was booked to ride the filly and sworn to secrecy. I had my army of backers to place bets on her in London. So as not to arouse suspicion they were told not to place their bets until minutes before the off, and take the official SP. Then my lady luck turned sour on me.

'When the runners got down to the start, Lintola's price was 100-8. But one of the runners had to have his girth completely readjusted. Then just as they approached the gate another horse broke a girth. The start was delayed for several more minutes, and when they finally got under way Lintola's starting price was 6-1. Some of our money in London had obviously been relayed to the track, and the SP was shortened to avoid bookies' losses.

'Watching the race I was always sure she was going to win. She was always cantering, but the winning distance from Lionel Brown on Stranded was judged to be a neck.

'I had landed a dream betting shop coup. But I hadn't! But for the delays I reckon she would have started around 10-1, and I would have cleared over £100,000 – a fortune in those days.'

Readers may be surprised to learn that O'Toole's first ambition was to be a jockey. He actually rode for his two uncles, Willie and Michael Byrne, who were very much involved in racing, in bumper races, but had five or six point-to-point winners. But then he decided that his future professional career was to be a butcher.

For six years he had a flourishing butcher's business in Santry, two miles from Dublin Airport. 'Micko was a bloody good butcher – very, very popular,' Jack Doyle recalled. 'Customers used to drive from miles around to hear his non-stop banter. He looked a picture in his white apron!'

But Micko was always restless, and for three years he switched his attentions to being a greyhound trainer. In 1965 he sent over Marjowe win the English Oaks at Harringay. It was not to be his last Classic win on English soil, and he enjoyed his fearless forays with the bookies.

'I think Micko was pretty skint when he started with his greyhound kennels in Dublin,' says Cecil Hobson, who at the time was working closely with the much-respected Dickie Gaskell on the rails for Ladbrokes. 'But he was always plotting some coup or other in Belfast. We soon learned to fear his name on the race cards.'

O'Toole was soon getting restless again. This time he switched his career to become a horse trainer. 'I started at some stables at Castleknock,' he went on, 'which were close to the old Phoenix Park racecourse in Dublin. I started with three racehorses and 25 grey-hounds! Lintola was my first-ever success at Edinburgh, but my first winner in Ireland was Gail Time, who was ridden by one of our most promising jockeys at the time, Tony Murray, who would later have a great career in England.

'When things got going I paid off all Maddenstown's loans, and actually turned down over half a million punts for it. Some people may wince at some of the bigger bets I have had. But having over £10,000 on a horse has never worried me. It's only money, for Christ's sake. I get far more pleased after winning a big race through clever training than landing a big gamble. In the early 1970s I had a smashing mare called Shore Drive. She won eight races on the trot in one year. It was a licence to print money when she was running.'

Jack Doyle described O'Toole as 'an animal man – he could teach birds to sing a particular song. He is happier when he is with animals, and seems to have a special rapport with them.'

I recalled the time I'd found myself flashing down some Irish country lanes on the way to Punchestown races with O'Toole in his cherry-coloured BMW, when he'd told me of his absolute pet hate: 'I don't have too many dislikes, but I loathe people tapping me for readies at the racecourses. I don't know why, but I detest it.'

Now Jack Doyle butted in. 'It's odd, because Micko would take the clothes off his back if he had a friend in need. He hates being tapped for readies because in the past, when he was financially up against it, he asked friends for help and was turned down. He never forgot it.'

'I love a gamble,' said O'Toole, 'but whatever the result I would never sulk. I'd rather be dead than be seen as a bad loser. There's always tomorrow, and the worst mistake punters can ever make is to chase their losses. It's fatal.'

Una had overheard our conversation. 'When Mick walks through the front door after a day at the races I never know whether he has won or lost,' she said. 'I defy anybody to tell by the look on his face. We are forbidden to moan. Later he might tell me quietly, "I lost my tonsils today," but he is never upset for long.'

'Even the night before one of his major gambles he sleeps like a baby,' confirmed Doyle.

'Unlike most people in racing I don't have any superstitions,' O'Toole reflected. 'It's all rubbish. Whatever will be, will be.'

By now he was in full flow, and opening yet another bottle of champagne. 'Have a large brandy with it to take the harm away,' he giggled.

'Chinrullah's disqualification was a big blow,' he said (when traces of theobromine and caffeine were found in his sample), 'but the Jockey Club were very fair, and accepted I was an innocent party. We were refunded the prize money as the horse-feed people took full responsibility.

'Balios winning the 1972 Ascot Stakes at the Royal meeting by 25 lengths was a great thrill. Like my first winner Lintola, he only cost 800 guineas. He was once trained by Sir Noel Murless. We had 25-1 that day, and I remember the triple Champion Hurdle hero Persian War finishing tailed off last.'

O'Toole also won the 1975 Norfolk Stakes with Faliraki (backed from 6-1 to 13-8), and towards the end of his glittering career his attentions were clearly centred more on the Flat. His best horse was Robert Sangster's Dickens Hill, who was second to the outstanding Troy in both the 1979 Epsom and Irish Derbys. But he did win the Irish 2,000 Guineas and the Coral-Eclipse that year.

'It's not been all weddings and piss-ups,' O'Toole stressed. 'I've had quite a few funerals. Happily, I once had £3,000 at 16-1 with Sean Graham' (the Belfast bookmaker) 'on Do Me A Favour in a bumper race at Navan. He won, thank God.'

'Financially he has kicked me in the balls so many times,' confirmed Graham. 'But he never gloats. I've had my moments with him, of course. It's never been one-way traffic. Every credit bet is on the nod of the head. Funnily enough, I'd trust him with my life. He's not a knocker, unlike a lot of Irish so-called high-rollers I could name. Sometimes I can hardly speak after he has had it off. But, win or lose, O'Toole is always smiling. He is never in bad form.'

O'Toole's greatest coup came on 27 December 1980, when he invited Ladbrokes' Mike Dillon to breakfast at Maddenstown on the morning of the fiercely competitive Sweeps Hurdle. Over the meal O'Toole backed his horse Carrig Willy at various odds from 40-1 downwards. By the time breakfast was over, O'Toole had £64,000 in betting vouchers burning a hole in his pocket. Carrig Willy duly got home by a head at 33-1.

Even now O'Toole laughs. 'There are some lessons that people have to learn the hard way. Mike had been a close friend for many years, but that morning he learned an expensive lesson – bacon and eggs don't come cheap on the Curragh!' In Dillon's defence, it must be pointed out that Carrig Willy had been well beaten in his four previous races. It was a great payday for the O'Toole family. Mick picked up £64,000 in bets, while Carrig Willy was owned by his wife Una and the race was worth £21,642.

One of the highlights of the Irish Derby at the nearby Curragh was the exclusive pre-Classic annual party at the O'Toole household. Wexford spring lamb had been specially kept for the occasion, and exquisite wines flowed. Micko and Una's hospitality was truly fabulous, and you usually left with a parting gift of a delicious side of smoked salmon – Micko always seemed to have more smoked salmon available than Dublin Airport's duty-free shopping halls.

In retirement O'Toole was given a surprise special award for his contribution to Irish racing, and he remains a welcome figure at Royal Ascot and York's big May and August meetings, so proud that both his children have adopted successful roles in racing – son Ciaran as a jockeys' agent, and daughter Mags as a bloodstock agent, buying many horses for the Gigginstown House stud, owned by Ryanair's controversial boss Michael O'Leary.

Mick O'Toole has lived life to the full, and I am a self-confessed fan. Memories could scarcely be richer. The best question I ever put to this ex-butcher, greyhound trainer and master trainer-gambler was: what's your greatest secret? He beamed the old Micko grin and, laughing loudly, walked away with a typical swagger. 'Always travel first class.'

12

Marvellous Martin

I RECALL STANDING NEXT TO MY friend Chris Poole in the press room at Cheltenham in 1981. A grey horse called Baron Blakeney had just won the Triumph Hurdle at 66-1. The trainer was one MC Pipe. Chris and I looked at one another and said, 'Who the hell is this?'

It was the moment Martin Pipe announced his presence on the big race scene. In his first six years as a trainer he had saddled just 31 winners; in the next six he had 219.

Martin Charles Pipe is the most intriguing racing personality I have ever met. Small in stature, as true training legends go he is a giant. Bare statistics show that he produced 4,180 winners (3,927 over jumps and 253 on the Flat) spanning 32 years, scored eight double centuries, and was champion jumps trainer fifteen times in seventeen seasons. Only David Nicholson broke his monopoly. His career total beat Arthur Stephenson's 2,644 winners by miles.

He had 34 Cheltenham Festival winners, won two Group races on the Flat, and six races at Royal Ascot. In the 1999–2000 season he trained a record 243 winners.

The intriguing thing about Pipe is that he did not have the usual background for trainers. Most are relations of trainers, ex-jockeys, or people who have worked in stables to gain a vital apprenticeship. Pipe was none of these.

His father Dave Pipe was well known on the West Country racing circuit as an on-course bookmaker.

Martin was educated at King's College, Taunton, where he showed potential at cricket and was coached by the colourful Australian Bill Alley, who had enjoyed great success as an all-rounder for Somerset and went on to become a famous Test umpire. Pipe became the youngest-ever boy in the 1st XI. He left school to work in some of his father's 45 betting shops, and when Pipe senior sold them to William Hill for many millions, found himself out of work.

Dave Pipe started the Pipe fairytale when he bought a pig farm down a quiet Somerset lane on the outskirts of Wellington, and Martin started training a few point-to-pointers for him. 'I didn't have a clue when I started,' he said. 'I used to read books to try and pick up knowledge. When I started I definitely felt I was a complete outsider. I never worked in any other trainer's yard for a single day.'

As a jockey Martin shattered his ankle in 1972 at Taunton at the last hurdle on a horse called Lorac (his wife Carol's name spelt backwards), and when he won a solitary point-to-point on Weather Permitting at the lowly Tiverton Stag Open race at Bishopsleigh in Devon in May 1975, he jumped off and retired on the spot. 'I was a pretend jockey,' he says, 'and I was determined not to become a pretend trainer.'

His first winner as a trainer came at Taunton with Hit Parade in a selling hurdle. 'One certainty in racing,' his father had predicted as he drove off to the race, 'is that you will never train a winner.' He was way off the mark by exactly 4,180. Pipe and his jockey Len Lungo had arrived very early at a deserted Taunton and craftily loosened from the rails the second section of each of the eight hurdles, in the knowledge that this was only the second race on the card and Hit Parade would attempt to make all the running. Hit Parade was backed down from 2-1 to 13-8 favourite, flicked over the loosened hurdles, made all and won by seven lengths. Prize money for the winner was £272. 'You learn very quickly,' reflects Pipe, 'when you're doing it through your own pocket.'

One year I was staying at Southport's Prince of Wales Hotel for a Grand National meeting when Martin Pipe and his entourage entered the dining room only to be told that the restaurant had taken its last orders and was now closed.

Shortly afterwards, Pipe and his faithful sidekick Chester Barnes returned with bags full of takeaway Chinese meals. Using the hotel's plates and cutlery they tucked into a minor feast. The other diners looked on in amazement. 'Never tell Martin that he can't do something,' I recall Dave Pipe telling me: 'He's guaranteed to do it.'

'My dad never gave me much credit,' Martin says, 'but maybe he did that to make me more determined…'

At his Pond House training base at Nicholashayne, Pipe recalls, 'We built a fabulous gallop on the top of the Blackdown Hills of a mile and a half round, and they used to gallop up there flat out. But I never trained a winner. That's when we created our all-weather gallop, five and a half furlongs uphill, and started interval training. They would canter up the hill and then canter back downhill. If you climb up stairs you are using certain muscles. Then if you go down stairs you are using completely different muscles. Basically, everybody thought I had revolutionised the game, but it was all down to common sense. You never see fat athletes winning big races. I was always good at doing jigsaw puzzles. Training is just like putting all the pieces together.'

Captain Tim Forster was a famously pessimistic trainer of the old school, but when he left Letcombe Bassett after many years and moved to Ludlow, he adopted Pipe's methods, with interval training on an uphill all-weather gallop. 'I realise now,' he admitted, 'that for over 20 years my horses have been on holiday. Now they're fitter than they've ever been.'

Pipe landed his first monster gamble in January 1980, when his home-bred filly Carrie Ann won a selling hurdle at Haydock by two and a half lengths, with Rod Millman, now a successful Devon trainer, as the jockey. On course she had drifted from 14-1 to 20-1, but Pipe and Chester Barnes, who was dressed in a wolfskin coat, both looking like a pair of rascals on the evidence of photographs from the day, managed to get on at odds as long as 33-1, and won nearly £60,000. But at the selling auction Carrie Ann did not raise a single bid.

My first dealings with Pipe were sometimes tricky. He would enter six or seven horses for the big Saturday races, and then never answer my questions about which of them would run: 'We don't know the state of the going or their fitness.' I had the same conversation dozens of times. Getting information over the phone was just as difficult – I christened his long-time secretary Gail Harrison 'Geoffrey Boycott', because it was impossible to get anything past her. Her loyalty to 'Mr Pipe' knows no bounds.

Then the bookies would reveal – on Fridays, surprise, surprise! – that one of Pipe's horses had been backed, and when his horses were declared just that one same horse was in the field. It was his secret operation to hoodwink the bookies. To add to the intrigue, his jockeys in the major races were never announced until the last possible moment. Names like Peter Scudamore or Tony McCoy were only revealed after the declaration. When he had a winner, Pipe, rolled up *Sporting Life* always in his hand, was usually courteous with the press – but he seldom gave anything away. 'He did it nicely, didn't he?' was his standard post-race comment.

Pipe loved the guessing game. He even sponsored a race at Taunton and called it the Martin Pipe Am I That Difficult? Hurdle. He once took me aside and said, 'People in racing are so suspicious. They can't believe you are so successful unless you're doing something wrong.'

In May 1991 Pipe's inner circle came under immense pressure when, on ITV's *The Cook Report*, Roger Cook questioned his training methods and alleged a high turnover and excessive mortality rate among his horses. Pipe was openly accused of blood doping. Jenny Pitman and Ginger McCain appeared on the programme, McCain, who loved controversy, to pronounce that 'I don't want a horse once Martin Pipe has had it'. One rival trainer called him 'Dracula'. I know Pipe suffered months of anguish before the programme was finally screened. 'You can't believe the strain the guv'nor and his wife Carol were under,' said Chester Barnes. 'Some people are very jealous of Martin.'

'Two days after the programme I went to Exeter races,' Pipe recalled. 'I was full of aggression but very depressed. I even thought of committing suicide. One of the first people I bumped into was the Exeter steward Peter Brown. I was prepared for an argument, but he said, "I want to send you a horse to train for me." That really got me back to life. I was at a very low ebb, and he gave me a lifeline.'

I found it extraordinary that *The Cook Report*, which won 11 television awards, should include the champion trainer in a series of exposés which included programmes on the IRA, the National Front, and all sorts of unpleasant villains and spivs. Under the headline CARRY ON MARTIN! I reviewed the programme in *The Sun*. 'If this was trial by television,' I concluded, 'Pipe is still a winner.' Cook's hatchet job failed totally.

A month after the programme the Pipes entertained their close friends, and members of the press who had supported him, to a lunch party at Pond House. After a long drive from Kent to Somerset with my wife, I was delighted to see Barrie Cope's racecourse fish catering van in the driveway. As the wine flowed there was genuine relief that the *Cook Report* nightmare was over. I didn't spot Mrs P. or McCain tucking into the oysters and lobsters. 'It cost my family over £30,000 to defend ourselves,' said Pipe. 'Imagine what would have happened to an innocent individual who could not afford to fight?'

The doping issue reappeared many years later, when in February 2002 Jockey Club officials mounted dawn raids on the stables of Pipe, Venetia Williams, Paul Nicholls and Len Lungo. Altogether 408 of their horses were tested for the illegal drug EPO. All the tests proved negative. The Jockey Club confirmed they were freezing some of the samples in case

My angry response to the TV's 1991 Cook Report.

in future years the testing procedure became more sophisticated. 'They can keep the samples of my horses until kingdom come,' fumed an angry Pipe. 'Don't you think somebody would have talked if I had been using an illegal drug?'

Despite all his great successes, one big race always eluded Pipe. Between 1988 and 2006 he had 31 runners in the Gold Cup, the Cheltenham Festival's glittering showpiece, but his best runs came from Rushing Wild (second in 1993 at 11-1), Beau Ranger (his first runner, third in 1988 at 33-1) and Miinnehoma (third in 1995 at 11-1).

In 1992, however, his outstanding chaser Carvill's Hill was the red-hot even-money favourite. Since joining Pipe in June 1991 from the Irish trainer Jim Dreaper, Carvill's Hill had put up a fantastic weight-carrying performance under 11st 12lb to surge home in the Welsh Grand National by 20 lengths, beating the subsequent Grand National hero Party Politics into second. Then he had a glorious Irish homecoming at Leopardstown in front of 17,000 appreciative race-goers, when he flew home by 15 lengths. 'It wasn't even a race,' observed wise old Barney Curley. Pipe was given an especially warm reception by the Irish crowd, considering that one of the most popular horses in the Emerald Isle had left Jim Dreaper.

I travelled down to Somerset to see Carvill's Hill in his last piece of full work before his date with destiny. There was no hiding Pipe's pre-race confidence. 'I can't see any danger in the Gold Cup,' he announced.

There was always the odd fear, however, about Carvill's Hill's jumping technique. In the 1989 Gold Cup, while trained by Jim Dreaper, he had fallen at the seventh fence behind the dream winner Desert Orchid. After the Leopardstown win, Peter Scudamore had revealed, 'He hit the third fence very hard.'

'Carvill's Hill has a fantastic engine,' said Jim Dreaper, 'but there are flaws in his chassis and suspension. So every time he approaches his fences he knows it will hurt.'

In that controversial Gold Cup, Jenny Pitman was running two horses: the 15-2 Toby Tobias, and Golden Freeze at 150-1. Carvill's Hill was evens favourite. Mrs P.'s last words to Michael Bowlby, the jockey on Golden Freeze, were, 'Don't forget what I told you.'

From the start Bowlby's tactics were blatantly obvious. He galloped off alongside Carvill's Hill, in a cat-and-mouse ploy to expose any flaws in Carvill's Hill's jumping. If the Pitman plan was to upset Carvill's Hill's sky-high wonder-horse reputation it worked to perfection. At the first, Peter Scudamore tried to maintain his place at the head of the field, but Carvill's Hill clobbered the fence. Bowlby actually took a pull on Golden Freeze when he went ahead of Carvill's Hill. Then Carvill's Hill hit the ninth, and then the twelfth. For those of us unashamed Pipe supporters, the sight of Carvill's Hill so obviously facing a shock defeat was distinctly unpleasant.

Eventually Golden Freeze was pulled up seven fences out. Carvill's Hill led to the fifteenth fence, but was then soon headed. He faded back into fifth place, and after the last fence was virtually pulled up. Toby Tobias finished fourth, but broke down and left the course in a horse ambulance. 'The heart had been taken out of Carvill's Hill after he jumped the last fence,' Scudamore said sadly. 'I sensed that he'd had enough.'

'I'm truly shattered,' Pipe told me. 'This is the most disappointing day of my life.'

I must stress that the stewards quizzed Pipe and Scudamore about the favourite's total flop. 'Scu' could not have put it more plainly: 'I simply could not ride a race.' But these local worthies completely failed to inquire into the tactics of Golden Freeze: Mrs P., it must be reported, was never asked to explain her tactics. In my opinion, however, and for thousands of others, Golden Freeze did not adhere to the strict rules of racing: that all horses must run on their merits to obtain the best position in a race. 'Carvill's Hill goes into turf history,' I reported in *The Sun*, 'as the heavyweight champion who was knocked out by unfair tactics.'

Many people – the usual anti-Pipe jealousy army – claimed that to be a true champion in any sport you must battle against unsuitable tactics. 'If Carvill's Hill was in the army,' David Elsworth – never a fully paid-up member of the Martin Pipe Fan Club – told me that day in his usual controversial manner, 'you would have to say that he lacked moral fibre.'

As for Mrs P., 'Golden Freeze's owner backed him at 200-1 to finish in the first four,' she said on the day. 'I have done nothing wrong.'

Martin Pipe refused to be drawn, but one of his staff said sadly, 'If that wasn't intimidatory tactics I don't know what is. I thought this was supposed to be a sport.'

Years later, in his book – written, ironically, with Richard Pitman – Pipe recalled:

> *Carvill's Hill virtually walked across the finishing line. I was speechless, drained, and hurting for the large number of people who would share my sorrow for the horse himself. The next day we discovered that the main flexon had broken down. He also had severe cuts to the outside of his fetlock joints.*
>
> *Many people remain convinced that he was exposed as a wimp or that he was not as good as we believed. I only make one observation: How much fuss would Jenny Pitman have made if the roles had been reversed?*

The row rumbled on. 'The matter is over,' Mrs P. went on to say.

'There will be no Jockey Club inquiry. I'm not backing down. I've been in the game 20 years and it's not all about shaking hands. Do you expect Ian Botham to bowl underarm to the Australians?'

Now BBC TV's Julian Wilson entered the fray. 'The tactics were unsporting,' he told me. 'It was a very sad day for racing. Jenny's subsequent various interviews were full of crass hypocrisy. She shot herself in the foot, reloaded, and shot herself again. At first she said, "I didn't do it," and then later said, "OK, I did it – but why I shouldn't I?" If the Jockey Club don't re-open the case it will be a disgrace. Jenny is always going on about the well-being of the horse. Carvill's Hill was mentally wrecked in the Gold Cup.'

Golden Freeze's owner Robert Hitchens added fuel to the fire. 'We played Carvill's Hill like a violin,' he chuckled.

Over the next few months I visited Pipe at his base on several occasions. From his office he gazed straight across his yard, and there was Carvill's Hill in his favoured box. I imagine the trainer must have pondered every single day what might have been.

Sadly, in March 1994 Pipe admitted that he had failed to get Carvill's Hill back in action on the racecourse due to recurrent tendon injuries, and he was retired. The glory days of the massive bay chaser were over. He had 25 runs, 17 wins, and three much-publicised falls. But the end probably started all the way back during those six excruciating minutes of the Gold Cup.

Carvill's Hill deserved an honourable retirement. The burden of expectation which surrounded him was immense. I prefer to remember his electrifying wins at Chepstow and Leopardstown rather than watching him clearly distressed and virtually walking over the line at Cheltenham, after one of the most controversial Gold Cups of all time.

Martin Pipe won his first Champion Hurdle in 1993 with Granville Again, but Make A Stand, his 1997 winner, gave him as much satisfaction as any. 'I claimed him for only £8,000,' he told me, 'after he won a race at Leicester for Henry Candy. His previous owner Peter Deal rang me and said he really didn't want to lose the horse. I agreed to sell him

Julian Wilson and I join the furore over the most controversial Cheltenham Gold Cup of all-time.

a half share, but later I secretly entered him for the Champion Hurdle. In those days the entries did not come out for three weeks and I was frightened to tell him. He was still a novice, but he had won the Tote Gold Trophy [previously the Schweppes] at Newbury.'

'Martin is an absolute genius,' Deal conceded later. Sadly, Make A Stand never won again.

In 1994 Miinnehoma became Pipe's sole Grand National winner. Third and seventh in the Gold Cup, and owned by the Liverpool-born comedian Freddie Starr, who had a working engagement that day and was not present at the National, he started at 16-1. 'He was on one knee after nearly falling at Becher's on the second circuit,' said Richard Dunwoody, who rode him, 'but he was very clever and got himself out of trouble.' On the Sunday morning I travelled to Pond House for Miinnehoma's homecoming. Pipe had sent his helicopter to pick up Starr to enjoy his moment of glory. I can only describe Starr's behaviour as zany in the extreme.

In 1991 Pipe appeared on the BBC's *Desert Island Discs*. For his favourite record he selected 'Oh Carol' by Neil Sedaka. His luxury item on the island was the winning post from Cheltenham. In 2000 he was awarded a CBE. 'It stands for "Carol's Behind Everything",' he grinned.

Despite all that Pipe had achieved during his magnificent career, 'he was still seen as an outsider,' wrote the *Racing Post*'s David Ashforth, 'and amid all his success, he evokes jealousy rather than affection.'

I remember talking to Carol at the time, and her confiding, 'The biggest shame with Martin is that, despite all the success, he still finds it hard to trust people. He's always been very suspicious. Our best friends are the people we have known the longest.'

Martin himself had a more simple explanation: 'I get on better with horses than I do with people.'

Martin Pipe had been smashing records and breaking through barriers and causing racing surprises for over three decades, but in April 2006 he really shocked racing. 'I'd like to make an announcement,' he told Channel 4's *The Morning Line*: 'I have decided to hand over the reins to my son David.'

'Winning races was always a drug,' Pipe reflected when I interviewed him for this book to bring the story up to date. 'I wanted to win every race I entered. My stables were run like a five-star hotel. If my horses wanted caviar, they could have it. In the end it was said that I had trained more winners than anybody else. I always point out that I also trained more losers than anybody else!'

I asked him if, after his fabulous career, he had any regrets. Typically, he took time to answer. Then he said, 'Yes. I definitely should have started earlier. I was 29 years old when I first got my trainer's licence. If I had started before I would have learned a lot more.

'My regret is that I never worked in another trainer's stables. I would love to have worked for Sir Henry Cecil and seen him working closely.' As I was leaving he said, 'David's at the Cheltenham sales today, so I'm in charge.' It would take an earthquake to keep out him out of the Pond House stables.

13

Darling Dessie and Dr Elzie

EVERY YEAR SPORTS WRITERS DESCEND ON the press room at Cheltenham to report on the Gold Cup. I still chuckle to think of one award-winning wordsmith who watched the horses parading that day in 1989 and then asked innocently, 'Which one is Desert Orchid?'

A few jumpers may have had more ability, but for sheer charisma Desert Orchid tops my winter gallop poll. He had bucketfuls of equine personality. He didn't have the awesome superiority of the triple Cheltenham Gold Cup king Arkle, or the Aintree iron of Red Rum when he won three Grand Nationals and was runner-up the two other times he ran in the world's greatest race. At Kempton the classy Kauto Star would have given Dessie a run for his money.

But darling Dessie was a flamboyant, often front-running white charger. He thrilled his fans with spectacular jumps and achieved great success over varying distances, often giving away lumps of weight.

That's the hallmark of a true jumping giant. He won 34 of his 71 races, was second 11 times and third on eight occasions. He was truly the people's champion.

I was at Kempton on 21 January 1983 when, ridden by Colin Brown, he fell at the last flight in his debut hurdle race as an unconsidered 50-1 shot. Fast forward to the King George VI Chase at Kempton on 26 December 1991, and Desert Orchid, this time partnered by Richard Dunwoody, was fading when he fell at the third last. Dessie might have started and ended up on the Kempton canvas, but in between, over nearly nine years, he scored many KO blows.

The Desert Orchid story was a fairytale, brilliantly told by his main owner Richard Burridge in his book *The Grey Horse*. When he was born he was called 'Fred' by his groom Ruth Jackson. One of his legs was the size of a small tree. 'Useless,' said a Leicestershire-based trainer. 'Send him to the sales.'

It could all have been so different for Dessie – even his name. The Burridge family wanted to call him Desert Air, but an official at Weatherbys made a mistake and said the name had already been registered. The horse was in fact called Desert Heir. So 'Fred' became Desert Orchid, and his career positively bloomed.

'It was agreed that I could choose the trainer,' Richard Burridge recalled. 'When I said "David Elsworth" my father Jimmy said, "Who?" I duly wrote a letter to David at Whitsbury with glowing phrases about Desert Orchid. But two months passed and I had not had any sort of reply. I eventually rang up, told him I was Richard Burridge and I had this three-year-old gelding. Elsie said, "Sure, send him down here, Robert."'

At this point I should inform readers that David Elsworth has always had trouble remembering people's names – Christian or surnames. For over 40 years he usually addressed me with a cheerful, 'Hello, Clive.' The only way I could get him back was to reply, 'Hello, Martin,' referring to his arch jumping rival Martin Pipe, whom he used to refer to as mischievously as 'Drain Pipe'. Elsworth had the last laugh one time, though, when his great socialising buddy Neville Callaghan, the retired Newmarket trainer, wound him up by claiming that I'd said his career was on the wane. (I'd said no such thing.)

'Hello, Clive,' came his West Country burr down the phone the next day. 'I just wanted you to know that I didn't believe a word of what that nasty Neville tried to tell me. I told him, "Clive and I have been great friends for nearly 40 years – Clive and I even robbed banks together."'

When the Burridge clan arrived at Whitsbury, Elsworth had looked askance at their battered old Citroen. 'That your car?' he enquired. 'I won't lower the training fees if you claim that you're poor. We're all poor here.' There followed a hilarious scene as Elsworth introduced all Dessie's four co-owners to his then wife Jane – and got all the names wrong. The Burridges became the Barrows.

Later, when Dessie started winning, Elsworth took Richard aside. 'You know something?' he said. 'You've got a bloody gold mine.' The talented trainer was not wrong. The white warrior earned £645,066, which in today's money would have been well over a million.

I regularly visited Elsworth at Whitsbury. Always accompanied by his beloved black labrador gun dogs, he carefully watched Desert Orchid's work-rider Rodney Boult putting the grey through his paces. My abiding memory is how obvious it was that Dessie enjoyed his daily routine. In all his hurdle and chasing races he ran over 170 miles – from London to Exeter and back.

In 1984 he won both the Tolworth and Kingwell Hurdles. But it was when he switched to chasing that he really hit the jackpot. He won the King George VI at Kempton four times, and became a traditional Christmas dish like roast turkey, with an annual stuffing for the bookies.

His epic Cheltenham Gold Cup win in 1989 sparked many mentions. But Desert Orchid very nearly did not run. 'When I arrived at the track I walked part of the course,' Richard Burridge told me. 'The ground was appalling. Rain was teeming down, and I secretly prayed that the meeting would be abandoned and the Gold Cup run on another day. I was very serious about pulling Desert Orchid out, although we realised that we would have been very unpopular.

'Then I bumped into David Elsworth. He would have none of it, and said, "Not only will Dessie run… but he WILL win."

'When Yahoo went clear I was convinced that Dessie would be beaten. But I never knew that he could call on such reserves of courage and stamina. David was in floods of tears as he tried to make his way back to the winner's enclosure through the joyous crowd. All the credit must go to David and his team.'

The Sun's ever-courteous John Sadler was an excellent general sports writer, and this is the memorable report he wrote of that historic race:

In precisely seven minutes and 17.6 seconds a horse became a legend and a national institution, in one of the truly great moments in British sport.

Desert Orchid, surely the most courageous and popular race-horse on earth, won the most thrilling Gold Cup of all time. He swamped the old racecourse with a sea of tear-filled emotion. The 50,000 on the course and millions of TV viewers were enthralled by the sheer guts and drama. It was a marvellous sense of theatre.

It was a privilege, an education, a glorious day in your life when you knew that you had watched history being made. I can only put up the Stanley Matthews Cup Final and Geoff Boycott's 100th hundred in a Test match for a sporting equivalent. They were sporting characters, destined for their finest hour on a given day.

But this one belonged to a horse. Desert Orchid looked like a child's favourite white rocking horse taken down from the loft and brought into life by magic.

But Dessie's triumph in the 1990 Jameson Irish Grand National, under a strength-sapping top weight of 12 stone, must rank as one of the greatest handicap jumping wins of all time – and he came home unchallenged by 12 lengths.

'Some people, not us, had compared Dessie to Arkle,' Burridge recalls. 'But Arkle was sublime, and it was almost considered blasphemy to compare any horse with him. Pat Taaffe, Arkle's jockey, came over to us in the paddock and wished us luck. With all the good wishes from the racing-mad Irish community I realised that we really did own a great horse. But David was unusually nervous and he knew that Dessie was on edge.'

From three fences out Richard Dunwoody had been worried. They ploughed through the last fence, and there was a mighty gasp from the packed grandstands. But they duly won and, says Burridge, 'Dessie got a better reception at Fairyhouse than the Pope.'

It was a truly great performance, but in the view of the much-respected *Timeform* his best-ever display was on 2 February 1991 when he won the Racing Post Chase at Sandown. He carried 12 stone, three pounds, including a three-pound penalty. He had to give a stone to the classy Delius, and two stone, three pounds to the rest of the field. He started as 5-2-on favourite, but had to pull out all the stops to beat Nick The Brief by three-quarters of a length. When you think that Nick The Brief was getting a massive two stone, you can understand *Timeform*'s rating of Dessie's victory.

The Burridges were adamant that their beloved hero would never run in the Grand National. But one year Elsworth persuaded them to enter him, to test what weight he would carry, and Christopher Mordaunt, the Jockey Club's handicapper, duly gave him 12st 2lb. 'He was never really going to run in the Grand National,' revealed Elsworth, 'but I'm convinced that he would have won. He always jumped like a cat, and the only problem may have been his over-flamboyance. But anyway,' he grinned, 'I got a good National weights lunch out of it.'

Ironically, Desert Orchid ran at Aintree twice, winning the 1988 Martell Cup over the Mildmay, not Grand National fences, making all to account for the 2-1 favourite Kildimo by eight lengths. A year later he started 5-4 favourite and carried 11st 13lb, but fell at the unlucky thirteenth fence. The victor? Yahoo, who had been beaten by Dessie in their previous famous encounter in the 1989 Gold Cup.

When he fell heavily in his final 1991 King George VI he lay motionless for over a minute. Racegoers feared the worst possible outcome. But suddenly he sprang to his feet and proceeded to gallop riderless past the winning post. It was a heartstopping moment, and Dessie received far more applause from the relieved crowd than Francois Doumen's winner The Fellow, who'd held off Docklands Express and Remittance Man.

A year after Desert Orchid retired in December 1991 he survived a life-threatening operation for colic. He spent the summers with the Burridges in Leicestershire, and the winters with Elsworth at his Egerton House stables at Newmarket. He led out the two-year-olds and made many public appearances for charity.

In 2006, after the Grand National weights lunch, a few thirsty journalists went for 'extra-time' refreshments to the famous old Cole Hole pub in the Strand. There, one wag sparked a rumour that the mighty Desert Orchid had passed away. As the rumour went round like wildfire the *Daily Telegraph's* 'Croc', Jim McGrath, was even contacted by his office. Ever the professional, McGrath rang Elzie in Newmarket and asked if the story was true.

'I don't think so,' the great trainer told him, far from pleased. 'It's dark up here now, but I did just see a big white face poking out of his horsebox.'

On 11 April that year I watched Desert Orchid celebrating his 27th birthday, charging around a paddock like a two-year-old. He could not have been happier in retirement, and almost seemed indestructible.

But by November it was clear that Desert Orchid was getting frail. He was having difficulties with his co-ordination. Elsworth, sensing that the end was near, summoned his owners to say an emotional farewell. A vet was on standby in case his help was required. Dessie was last seen by Elsworth at evening stables on Monday, 13 November. He was lying down in his box nibbling some hay. One hour later, at 6:05 p.m., he passed away in his sleep.

'He died in the same way he lived his life,' said David Elsworth the next day – 'always with dignity. There was no fuss, and it was almost as though he knew it was time to go.'

'He enjoyed his life to the end,' said Richard Burridge. 'We all dreaded having to make the decision one day to have him put down. But he made the decision for himself. He had always been in charge of his own life.'

In *The Sun*, opposite the main leader page, under the headline WHAT A GREY DAY, I began, 'These are the four words I have always dreaded writing – Desert Orchid is dead.

'Anybody who ever placed a fiver on Desert Orchid knew that he would run his heart out for you,' I wrote in my obituary. 'We will never forget that day at Cheltenham when, despite the mud, sleet and snow, his talent shone out like a diamond in the Steptoes' junkyard.'

Desert Orchid's ashes were buried in a private ceremony at Kempton Park near the striking statue of him erected to celebrate his four King George VI victories.

'He was a horse who transcended racing and got into the national conscience,' said John McCririck, a big Dessie fan. 'You always knew that he would run his heart out for you.'

Colin Brown rode Desert Orchid to seventeen of his wins. 'It was like driving a Ferrari rather than a Cortina,' he reflected. 'Basically, all I had to do was to sit on him. He was such an outstanding character. He wasn't especially well bred, but he proved that he was a totally class act.'

'He had the ultimate in courage,' said Richard Dunwoody. 'Just when I feared that he was going to get beaten he always found fresh reserves, and would always dig deep. Desert Orchid was the best horse I ever rode.'

'I'm glad that I trained Dessie,' said David Elsworth. 'I would have got bloody fed up with all his endless publicity and newspaper articles if anybody else had trained him but me. I have always trained from the heart and not the cheque book.'

And what of this mercurial personality himself? 'The press see me as a cantankerous old bastard,' says David Elsworth. 'I have always been very restless, and I get bored easily. As I've got older I've become more irritable. A lot of the young press guys really irritate me. But I'm not a bad old fella really.' I can certainly vouch for that. He is always the most entertaining company.

It would be easy to dismiss him as just a rather argumentative race-horse trainer. But that only skims the surface. Nobody can doubt that he is a genius. It is no coincidence that Elsworth has trained two of the most gallant racehorses in recent years: Desert Orchid and Jeff Smith's ill-fated Persian Punch, who won 20 of his 63 races, earning over £1 million and twice coming third in the Melbourne Cup in 1998 and 2001. 'I have always thought that he was the very best dual-purpose trainer,' says Smith in all seriousness.

At one time Elsworth had 143 horses in training at Whitsbury. He called it 'an equine public school'. But there was no silver spoon for Elzie when he was born. 'I was illegitimate,' he revealed. His mother was just 17. 'My father never showed up. It was a disgrace in those days, and all hushed up.' He was brought up by his grandparents on a council estate near Salisbury.

'I used to make money by catching rabbits,' he recalled, 'skinning them and selling them for half a crown each. I used to have a lurcher, a ferret and an air rifle. I used to take them all on my bike to Herridge, where the Hannons were later to train. But in those days Alec Kilpatrick used to train there and I was soon fascinated by the horses. I went to him for an interview and stayed for five years.

'I was out in the cold when I was assistant to Ricky Vallance and his licence was suspended. I had many jobs, including selling ladies' under-wear in Devizes market, and even as a night-watchman at Stonehenge. Then I worked for Toby Balding, who was a great man. I was called a journeyman jockey but I didn't get many rides.'

Behind all the bluster, though, there is a kind streak. During the 1987–88 jumps season Elsworth and Josh Gifford were going ding-dong for the trainers' title. They bet each other that the eventual winner would donate a case of whisky to the loser and his staff. Elsworth duly won, and arrived from Whitsbury to tell Gifford, 'I'm not going home until you and your lads have polished off all these twelve bottles.'

'I had a few stable lads non-runners the next morning,' Gifford confessed, 'but that was typical of Elzie. He'd spent every last pound in his pockets on his mates.'

'I'm not boasting about it,' says Elsworth, 'but I reckon I'm quite a good stayer. I've got quite a good carcass. I can go to bed at three o'clock in the morning and be first in the yard at six o'clock. Anyway, I could lay upsides Josh Gifford, and few people could ever say that.

'Luckily I've trained some outstanding horses, like Desert Orchid, the Grand National winner Rhyme 'N' Reason, Barnbrook Again, the Classic winner In The Groove, Indian Ridge, Seattle Rhyme and Persian Punch.'

Elsworth has had several brushes with officialdom. At Newmarket's July meeting in 2014 he was caught on camera having a pee in an equine sampling unit. It must rate as one of the most expensive pees ever – 'acting in an improper manner' was how the BHA phrased it – as he was fined £1,000.

He does not suffer fools at all. 'I have always found horses more honest than people,' he declares. 'I often find people bloody difficult, complex and sneaky individuals.' Certainly he has never been a candidate for a career in the diplomatic corps. At York in August 2015, after performing a typical miracle when his Arabian Queen, in Jeff Smith's purple silks, won the Juddmonte International Stakes at 50-1 (beating the Epsom Derby hero Golden Horn by a neck, the only defeat he ever suffered on British soil), he enraged York's top brass when he skipped the usual post-race interviews. 'Everybody would have made a bloody fuss of me,' he said defiantly. 'I thought, "Why should I let them patronise me?" Before the race everybody had been totally dismissive of the mare's chances?'

David's wife Jane Elsworth was a lively lass, and very much part of his success – it was often she who had to field the awkward questions from the racing press corps. My great friend Christopher Poole from the *Evening Standard* used to invite them to London for the Horserace Writers' Association's Lord Derby awards. 'Everything went well,' Poole told me, 'but then David and Jane would have a row. David would storm off and hire a black taxi back to Whitsbury. Jane would then find out he had gone and order a second cab. Can you imagine two separate cabs going back in the dark across Salisbury Plain to the same destination?' Sadly, David and Jane parted.

I have witnessed some sad sights on racecourses, but few could equal the raw emotion when, at Ascot in April 2004, Persian Punch collapsed from a massive heart attack in front of the grandstand just 100 yards from the line.

Many racegoers left the racecourse immediately, with no appetite to watch any more races.

Elsworth and Smith were in tears, but agreed to give Jim McGrath and me an interview. 'I loved Persian Punch,' said Elsworth. 'He was the most adorable horse. It's an awful thing to say in the circumstances, but he'd die for you.' Asked to compare Desert Orchid and Persian Punch, Elzie said, 'If I had been lucky enough to have been married to Sophia Loren and Marilyn Monroe, and endured the delights of both friendships, how would you compare them? It would be impossible, wouldn't it?'

In January 2016 the Jockey Club dropped their bombshell with the announcement that Kempton would be bulldozed for redevelopment with 400 houses, and the King George VI switched to Sandown, with an all-weather track created at Newmarket. In the *Racing Post* Tom Kerr was spot-on when he described this murky deal as a 'treacherous act of vandalism by racing's so-called guardians'.

But this wasn't the first act of vandalism at the track where Desert Orchid achieved his historic run of King George VI victories.

The Jockey Club invested millions in Kempton's all-weather, floodlit track, but it was never going to work, and laughable gimmicks like playing the 'William Tell' overture through the loudspeakers for the finish of a race didn't add a single punter through the turnstiles. Sometimes two men and a dog turned up for evening thrillers on the sand in January and February. Invading punters from Mars would have loved Kempton. They're used to tracks with no atmosphere.

But above all I hate to think of the cruel operation of digging up darling Desert Orchid's remains and moving his fine statue to Sandown or Ascot, or wherever the King George ends up. What a disgrace.

14

The Wizard of Wantage

DAVID GANDOLFO'S NICKNAME OF GANDHI COULD not have been inspired by any resemblance to the legendary Indian patriot Mahatma Gandhi, immortalised in Richard Attenborough's blockbuster film. That Gandhi was famous for his hunger strikes. The wizard of Wantage was a robust, jolly, 18-stone fun-lover who cheerfully acknowledged his two hobbies to be 'eating and drinking', and enjoyed many a happy hour drinking wine with his great friend the commentator John Hanmer at the Leather Bottle in Challow. His stables in Wantage stood on the site of a workhouse, he told me, 'where discipline was extremely strict. In my days it was more like a holiday camp.'

When Gandhi retired in October 2009 after nearly 50 years he was the second-longest serving trainer in Britain after Midlands-based Reg Hollinshead. When he started out as a trainer on the West Country circuit David Pipe was still at school. I was able to report his career from nearly start to finish. He trained over 1,500 winners, including 50 on the Flat. He had several big race successes: his Grey Sombero won the 1972 Whitbread and the Midlands National. Peter Scot was a popular chaser with punters, and won the 1979 Welsh Grand National and the Mildmay. Henry Kissinger won the 1971 Mackeson, now the Paddy Power, at Cheltenham. Mr Marlsbridge (the Topham), Trying Again (the Lanzarote Hurdle) and Coral Cluster, winner of 29 races including what is now the Pertemps Hurdle at the Cheltenham Festival, were other major winners. At the 1982 Cheltenham Festival Reldis won the Grand Annual.

In the 1960s and 1970s I used to follow Gandolfo's horses at Plumpton, when he was a frequent figure in the winner's enclosure. This tiny Sussex track staged its first race meeting back in 1884, and in 1998 it was purchased from Isidore Kerman by Peter Savill and Adrian Pratt, who have masterminded many fine additions to the facilities. Over the years many top-class horses have run there, including Nickel Coin, Anglo, What A Myth, Pendil, Docklands Express and Voy Por Ustedes. The locally-trained selling hurdler Manhattan Boy won 14 races at Plumpton but never won anywhere else. It also has the most impressive on-course announcer: Milton Johns.

'Milton has a marvellous voice,' says the commentator Simon Holt, 'and sounds almost Shakespearean even when he is announcing the results and starting prices.' Trained at the Bristol Old Vic Theatre School, the veteran Johns played a series of varying roles, and will be remembered for playing the *Coronation Street* shopkeeper Brendan Scott, who died of a heart attack while cycling down the cobbled street. A stalwart of the exclusive actors' Garrick Club in London, Johns recalled discussing the Swedish actress Ingrid Bergman with John Gielgud.

'She speaks in five different languages,' sniffed Gielgud, 'and can't act in any of them.'

It was Gales Cavalier who in the mid-1990s put Gandhi back into the big time after a spell in the doldrums. 'He was the best two-miler I trained,' said Gandolfo. One day I plucked up the courage to ask him, what was he suddenly doing right?

He smiled. 'Nothing at all. I'm still using the same training methods. I work 'em short and sharp, not long and steady. I was very superstitious, and I always made sure I stood in the exact spot at a racecourse where I had cheered home a previous winner! I admit that my career took a bit of a slump, but I always tried to use the best jockeys available, like Jamie Osborne, Mark Dwyer and Richard Dunwoody.'

The jockey Paul Barton gave Gandhi his angriest moment when he ran out on Master Upham at Newbury. 'I was absolutely furious,' laughed Gandhi – 'I took him straight round to an optician!'

'I won a chase at Market Rasen for David very easily,' recalls Barton, 'but for all the three-and-a-half-hour journey home he berated me, because at one stage I had been 25 lengths off the pace. He never stopped moaning for a minute – and I'd ridden a winner! Oddly enough,' Barton adds, 'if anybody else ever had a go at me, David was the first to defend me to the hilt. He was especially loyal.' Barton later became the BHA's much-respected senior stipendiary steward. He was not the first poacher to turn gamekeeper in racing circles.

'Racing is a tough old game,' says Gandolfo, 'and most of your dreams are usually shot down. You have to accept that 90% of the time you are going to endure disappointments. But you have to learn to live with the dark days, like when Grey Sombero was killed in the Grand National.

'I've never been a great PR man, and have never been any good at snaring owners. But those I have had usually stayed with me for many years. I like to be able to look them in the face and tell them the honest truth. I was always keen to tell owners quickly if their horses were no good – yesterday if possible! But at one time all my best owners seemed to be dying on me, and then I actually had an Arab owner who went skint on me. The best advice I was ever given was from Fred Winter, when he told me, "Never let go of your Irish contacts."'

One of Gandolfo's most loyal owners was Colin Mackenzie, the *Daily Mail's* racing correspondent from 1988 until he retired in 2008.

Colin had plenty of success as an owner, with 45 winners, some part-owned: his Welsh Oak won 16 races, Garryloch 7, Kirkstone Pass 7, Overall 7, Fleet Street 4 and All Right Jack 3.

Mackenzie was a worthy opponent. He started on the *Daily Express*, where his finest hour was the world exclusive that he had tracked down the runaway Great Train Robber Ronnie Biggs in Brazil. But Biggs evaded extradition by proving that his mistress was pregnant, and Colin and the *Express* executive Brian 'Vino' Vine's jubilation turned to horror on the plane back when they found Detective Chief Superintendent Jack Slipper sitting alone in first class. I always used to bait Mackenzie by pointing out that it was the 'Currant Bun' that managed to get Biggs back to England in 2001.

At the *Express*, Colin was always engrossed in the racing pages or on the phone to his bookmaker, to the extent that one day Brian Vine shouted, 'You won't find any exclusive stories in the Wye race card.' It became the standard refrain for a subsequent editor, Geoffrey Levy, to get Colin to concentrate on getting stories. Finally Colin got bored with this almost daily rebuke. 'I'd better tell you, Geoffrey,' he replied wearily: 'Wye closed down 15 years ago.'

Mackenzie joined the infant *Racing Post* in 1985 and was swiftly promoted to news editor. He never took no for an answer in his pursuit for exclusives, and claimed that many *Post* journos went on to better things having been taught everything they knew by him. He was so keen on exclusives that when he joined the *Mail*, the racing editor who subbed his copy every day thought he was actually called Colin Exclusive Mackenzie.

He certainly played a few shots, and if ever a story of his was knocked for six, the next day a casual 'I got my lines crossed yesterday' would appear in his copy. When Jim McGrath, later 'The Croc', was a down-table sub-editor in charge of the results on the *Racing Post*, he recalls, 'One day Colin spotted that there was an apprentice called Darren Biggs making his debut at Windsor. I was sent there specially to ask him the one big question: "*Are you related to the Great Train Robber*

Ronnie Biggs?" Colin was so terribly disappointed that the jockey had never even heard of his namesake.'

In 1991 we all had to follow up another of Colin's scoops when he revealed that the Irish owner-trainer Noel Furlong, a big gambler, had had to settle his debts with the Inland Revenue before he was able to enter horses for the Cheltenham Festival. And in 2008, just months before he retired, Mackenzie had another cracking exclusive, when he revealed that Kieren Fallon had failed a second drugs test on the very day he had been cleared of corruption at the Old Bailey. Racing exclusive stories have not come much bigger.

David Gandolfo came from a Swiss-Italian family, and his father Luigi owned a hotel in Madeira. But he was actually born in Southport, and brought up in the Lake District, before he came south to win his first race in June 1960 with Sunwood, in a seller at the old Buckfastleigh racecourse, when he was 21.

He named many of his horses after locations in the Lake District, including a remarkable horse called Hodge Hill, after a farm at Witherslack, near the unique Cartmel racecourse.

Hodge Hill was owned by a colourful character called Osbert Walter Pierce, landlord of the popular village pub the Peacock right down south in the Weald of Kent, on the outskirts of Goudhurst. I was lucky to be one of his regular customers. Between October and November in 1975 the gallant Hodge Hill rattled off six successive wins, starting at Fakenham, moving on to Worcester and then Cheltenham. He then scored again at Wincanton by seven lengths, Cheltenham again as 6-4 favourite, and rounded it off by making all at Kempton at 7-2-on. In *The Sun* I soon dubbed his owner 'Bert the Cert'.

When Gandolfo finally sold his stables in Wantage for redevelopment, many of the new houses built on the land were named after his horses, including one in memory of Hodge Hill. Hodge Hill was no worldbeater, but in the eyes of the Goudhurst gang he will never be forgotten.

Few racing characters could match Bert's enthusiasm for his horses, and his admiration for his great pal Gandhi knew no bounds. I accompanied Bert on many adventures at the races, thankfully before the days of the dreaded breathalyser. I recall one day at Warwick when we backed one of his horses off the boards and landed a monster gamble. After a happy, but long, journey home he rang me the next morning. 'I've woken up to find so much money in my pockets,' he said, 'I don't know whether it was my Warwick winnings or last week's takings from the Peacock.' All his horses ran in his familiar Peacock blue and yellow colours.

Gandolfo the gourmet had his own table every Saturday night at a Chinese restaurant in Oxford owned by one of his happy gang of patrons, Timmy Shang, who had a share in a horse called Lucky Runner. 'I remember he landed a nice little touch for us one day at Warwick at 33-1,' recalled Gandhi with a typically hearty laugh, 'but sadly he was killed in his next race at Bangor. I came back to the restaurant full of gloom, and was not looking forward to meeting Timmy. But he had already heard the news: when I was handed the menu there was an extra special dish pencilled in: "Curried Lucky Runner"!'

15

The Men Behind the Mike

PETER BROMLEY

'Get me the Director-General – *now!*' That is the sentence by which Peter Bromley will be remembered. If Sir Peter O'Sullevan with his silky tones was the king of BBC TV broadcasts, it was Bromley who for 41 years commanded huge respect with his unmistakable radio commentaries, which always crescendoed to a booming climax at the winning post. Being deaf, he usually shouted, and you could hear his views on life a hundred yards away. He shouted home Red Rum, Arkle, Desert Orchid, Shergar and Mill Reef into millions of households, calling 202 Classics before finally hanging up his binoculars after the 2001 Epsom Derby. 'It's the adrenalin which keeps us commentators going to such ripe old ages,' he used to say. He estimated that he drove well over a million miles during his career.

But his volcanic temper was likely to erupt at any unsuspecting moment.

At Royal Ascot in 1997 he was halfway through the Prince of Wales's Stakes when in his headphones he was suddenly told, 'Wrap it up.' Amazingly, the commentary was to be interrupted for a live newsflash on the verdict of the court case in America in which the young English nanny Louise Woodward was found guilty of causing the death of an eight-month-old baby by shaking him. (She was later released on appeal.) By the time coverage resumed at Ascot the race was over.

When Bromley came off the air he marched into the press room seething with rage, grabbed a telephone and yelled down it, 'Get me the Director General – now.' For once the press room was hushed as we listened to this maestro of the mike, who was used to getting his own way, lambasting an unfortunate BBC executive.

'I have never been so angry in all my life,' he told me subsequently. 'If the BBC producer had walked into my commentary box I would have been hard pressed not to have given him a punch on the jaw! I've been told to stop commentating before while I was live on air, but I never took any notice. Like Lester Piggott, deafness can come in handy on some occasions. I was so furious that day that I actually said on air, "Stop talking into my ear."'

Bromley started when there were no racecourse commentaries at all. A dentist's son in Cheltenham, he often used to skive off school to cycle to the local Festival jump meetings, and began a love affair with racing that was to last all his life. 'Raymond Glendenning was the voice of BBC sport in the 1950s,' he recalled. 'He was quite capable of doing a world boxing title fight, the FA Cup Final and the Derby all in the space of a few weeks. Racing was not his particular favourite, but he had a wonderful microphone voice and was an absolute gentleman.

'I did my first racecourse commentary at Plumpton in 1955. I was paid £20 and no expenses. I remember that I caused something of a stir when I said that Atom Bomb had fallen – luckily, it was the name of a horse. One race had twelve runners and they all fell. But one remounted and went on to win. The race took fifteen minutes.

'I was appointed BBC Radio racing commentator in 1960, after doing my first commentary for them at Newmarket in May 1959.' In 1961 Bromley commentated on his first Epsom Derby, and called home the shock 66-1 winner Psidium, trained by Harry Wragg and ridden by Frenchman Roger Poincelet. He had previously finished third in the 2,000 Guineas.

'Things were very different then, and some commentary positions were hopeless. At that time most of the clerks of the courses didn't have a clue what commentators required. We'd usually end up behind a pillar, or we were up on the roof of a grandstand and couldn't see the final furlong. The Stewards' Cup at Glorious Goodwood was very tricky. They started out of my sight, came galloping over the brow of the Sussex Downs and then... whoosh. One day at Brighton I opened the door to my position and was hit by a swarm of bees. I refused to commentate until some chap went down to the town and bought some spray. My best suit was once covered in pigeon droppings at Chepstow, and I was actually heard live on air saying, "I'm suing!"'

Bromley will always be remembered for his commentary on Dawn Run's epic win in the 1986 Cheltenham Gold Cup. At the top of the hill his voice went up an octave: 'Harden your hearts, gentlemen,' he shouted. 'You are about to have one of the greatest races of all time...' He was not wrong.

'I enjoyed calling home Lester Piggott's winners in his heyday. Of all the Grand Nationals, the commentary I remember best is Red Rum's win over Crisp in 1973. I cried for Crisp that day, as he was giving away 23lb, and was a gallant runner-up. Of all the Arc de Triomphe races, Dancing Brave's win in 1986 was the most memorable. I picked him up halfway in the straight, and was able to spot that Pat Eddery was going to win a long way before he hit the front. His finishing speed that day was sensational.

'Shergar's win in the 1981 Derby could have been very embar-rassing,' Bromley confided to me. 'I'd left my normal binoculars at home by mistake. I had to do the commentary wearing dark glasses, but luckily Shergar won so easily, and I was able to say, "You need a telescope to see the rest."'

Bromley enjoyed telling me about the highlights of his career, but was also honest enough to reveal his darkest hour. 'In the 1993 Cesarewitch, when there were 31 runners,' he told me. 'I called a fast-finishing horse in orange and green colours and named it as Martin Pipe's Balasani. Unfortunately it was Aasaylad, who won by a head. Balasani finished 20th. I could have cried. That taught me a lesson – never guess.' (I used to rather admire one well-known racecourse commentator until I heard Sir Peter O'Sullevan, the king of the men behind the mike, referring to his rival as 'Gus the Guesser'.)

'I survived ten Heads of Sport and nine Director-Generals. To the end I maintained strongly that big races should never play second fiddle to a game of bowls, or my pet hate of motor racing. I had furious rows with my superiors, but it never lasted for more than 24 hours.' He spent his all-too-short retirement training gun dogs. His loud voice must have come in handy.

When he died in June 2003 I was asked by *The Sun*'s news desk to prepare a 1,000-word tribute to him from the world of racing. The article was for a full two-page spread in the middle of the newspaper. I duly did the thousand words, but was asked for an additional 500. I thought that was odd. I was even more worried when a *Sun* executive rang me and asked, 'Why didn't you mention Attivo?' It then became clear to me: the paper's hierarchy had confused Peter Bromley with Peter O'Sullevan…

The Bromley spread duly appeared, and I was delighted with the big show. A year later at a racing cocktail party I felt sufficiently brave to tell O'Sullevan. 'I did a two-page spread when Bromley died – I imagine we'll do a 16-page pull-out when you go.' He wasn't exactly overjoyed at my macabre humour.

CLOUDESLEY MARSHAM

If Peter Bromley was well-known for his sudden outbursts of temper, one of the mildest men ever to look down a pair of binoculars in the commentary box was Cloudesley Marsham, whose Old Etonian flow of words could easily be picked out at the races. I can honestly say that he never had a single enemy in the world, and when he died in 2011 at 94 we all lost a most amusing friend.

The last time the Queen Mother ever went racing I was invited into the Royal Box for lunch at Sandown, and asked to bring a guest. We waited patiently for the lift to bring her up to the Royal Box. The moment she appeared she exclaimed, 'Oh, Cloudesley! My favourite commentator!' They ended up having a lengthy discussion about the time they had both spent at Fairlawne, Peter Cazalet's Kent estate, which was near the Marshams' family home.

He was never afraid to tell stories against himself. He struck up a friendship with the famous Lewes trainer Tom Masson, who took him aside at Newmarket one day and told him a new owner had splashed out a fortune on a two-year-old filly called Maid Of Sussex. 'Give her a few mentions for her debut and the owner will be pleased,' said the bow-tied Masson. 'It'll be worth a large bottle of brandy for you.'

The race duly started, with a big field scattered right across the Rowley Mile. 'Maid Of Sussex up there with the leaders, travelling well,' declared a confident Marsham. 'This is a very encouraging debut.' The race over, the course announcer came on the tannoy: 'Winner number three, Gone To Lunch. Twenty ran. Maid Of Sussex did not come under starter's order and did not run.'

On another occasion at the now-closed Birmingham racecourse he described a steeplechase and then attempted to climb back down the hazardous ladder from the commentary box. A racegoer yelled, 'They've got another circuit to go!'

'I can't believe that commentators now receive over £600 for a day's work,' said Marsham. 'I don't begrudge them a penny, but today's commentators don't know how lucky they are. In my early days there were no small monitor screens to show us the action. In 2005 the Lincoln Handicap at Doncaster was reduced from 24 to 22 runners for safety reasons, but I recall when Scobie Breasley won his second Lincoln on Riot Act in 1966, and there were *forty-nine* runners! In 1948 Bill Rickaby beat 57 rivals to win the Lincoln on Commissar!'

I used to go to Plumpton with him regularly, and I recall lunching with him in the directors' box there when he was introduced to the champion German jumps trainer Christian Von Der Recke, who was always known as the Baron. 'I was a guest in your country once for two years,' volunteered Cloudesley.

'Oh, when was that?' asked the Baron innocently.

'From 1943 to 1945.'

On another occasion at Plumpton a waiter asked, 'Water?'

'No, thank you,' replied Cloudesley. 'Water is for putting your teeth in.' And there was a third occasion when, after an especially well-refreshed trip, I dropped him off at his home where, unfortunately, he collided with a bird feeding table on his front lawn and went down in a heap like something out of *Ski Sunday*. For our future trips to Plumpton the bird table was removed so that he had a clear flight path to the front door.

For over 20 years Cloudesley and his wife Suzanne had lived in my tiny hamlet of Rolvenden Layne, near Tenterden in Kent, having moved into a house bang next door to the Ewe and Lamb pub. My father was thrilled, as Cloudesley's father CHB Marsham had captained Kent when they won their first County Championship title in 1906, and soon the pub was the venue for endless discussions about the old Kent cricket legends, including my father's idol Frank Woolley.

He joined the exclusive Rye Golf Club, and one day heard they were one short for a forthcoming match against another club.

'What do you play off?' barked the secretary, an ex-military man. 'Eighteen,' replied Cloudesley, only to be told, 'We're not that bloody short.'

Once he and I were playing there when we spotted an unshaven old tramp fast asleep by the hut next to the 14th green, dirty old ex-army overcoat tied with hop string, no socks or shoelaces, and an empty bottle of vodka sticking out of his pocket. When we got back to the clubhouse a concerned Cloudesley told the steward we should call Rye police. A crusty retired brigadier in the bar put down his *Times* newspaper and said in all seriousness, 'We had better check first that he is not a member.'

Late in life Marsham became an ardent bell-ringer at our local St Mary the Virgin church. When a bell-ringer dies, a colleague always tolls the bell for the number of years they have lived. One day, all alone up in the belfry, Cloudesley got rather confused when he reached 50 tolls. When he returned to the congregation the bell-ringers' leader said, 'I never knew he was 88.'

I was deeply honoured when Suzanne asked me to pay a tribute to Cloudesley at his service of thanksgiving. To be honest it was quite an easy task as I had countless stories about him, and few men went to make their maker leaving behind so much affection. 'He would be so proud,' I said, 'that in the congregation we have two Grand National-winning trainers – Nick Gaselee and Josh Gifford – and a Grand National-winning jockey, Marcus Armytage. The vicar tells me that today's packed congregation is a course record.'

A moving passage from Will H. Ogilvie's poem 'Galloping Shoes' was printed on the back of the order of service. It read:

And there with his peers we may leave him,
with all good men and true,
who have come to the Last of the Gateways
and laughed and gone galloping through.

JULIAN WILSON

If Sir Peter O'Sullevan was the 'Voice of Racing' on TV, there is no doubt that Julian Wilson, BBC TV's frontman for 32 years until 1997, was the face. In its heyday the Beeb covered nearly 100 days' racing a year, with 18 million tuning into the Grand National, and they were a formidable team. How times have changed – and I am not sure for the better. And though this Old Harrovian's deadpan countenance was often likened to that of an undertaker's assistant, behind his serious outlook on life was a genuine sense of humour, though John McCririck always managed to infuriate Wilson by claiming incorrectly that he was his fag at Harrow. He was also one of the very few colleagues in the press room who actually showed a healthy profit from his gambling.

The son of the *Daily Mirror*'s top sports writer Peter Wilson, who was dubbed 'The Man You Can't Gag', Julian got his break in broadcasting when four racing hopefuls took the train from Paddington to Newbury for trials as commentators, among them a little-known assistant trainer called Michael Stoute. 'We all travelled second class,' he later told me, 'but Wilson was seated in a first-class compartment. We somehow realised that we were all up against it, and Wilson duly got the job.'

There is little doubt that Wilson was just waiting for O'Sullevan to retire, as he always hankered for the commentating role and not that of presenter. Indeed, he had dreamed that one day he would 'call' the races on TV for the Beeb at the age of only nine! That was the position he always craved, but it never happened. 'The Voice' kept on until he was 79, by which time Jim 'Croc' McGrath had been shoehorned into the job. 'I felt totally betrayed,' he subsequently confided to me. He was less than pleased too when the BBC introduced Clare Balding, a rising star even in those days, as his co-presenter: 'I never felt happy that Clare and I were being presented as a Richard and Judy show.'

Very old-school, Wilson was pretty scathing about the rival TV coverage when it switched from the more sombre BBC. 'Channel 4 have trivialised it,' he declared. 'Talent and qualifications don't seem to count any more.' I dread to think what he would have made of C4 introducing a 'psychic pig' tipster feature at the 2014 Cheltenham Festival.

In his later years Wilson was a regular work-watcher on the gallops at Newmarket, often seen with his fellow cricket-loving friends William Haggas and Sir Michael Stoute. He also had a column in the *Racing Post* aptly trumpeted as 'Mr Angry'. He was one of the loud anti-Sunday-racing brigade, although I believe this was because it clashed with his cricket playing activities, and not on religious grounds.

Wilson's grandfather had played cricket for Kent in the era of W.G. Grace, and Julian inherited his love of the game. He had a home in South Africa and loved entertaining British friends during Test matches in Cape Town, among them the late Richard Merricks, a real cricket fanatic and worldwide watcher who, though disabled from birth, never let this spoil his love of cricket and was instantly recognised at Lord's and on Test match grounds in Australia, South Africa and the West Indies. He and Wilson had met at Rye CC when Wilson was on holiday in the area as a schoolboy with his mother.

Wilson also played, and often turned out for the Lord's Taverners. I played against him when he was guesting for Findon CC against the Josh Gifford-skippered Jump Jockeys XI. 'You wait until you see Wilson bowling his slow left-arm spinners,' Christopher Poole told me. 'He takes it all very seriously.' Indeed, Wilson claimed that he was 'the white Bishen Bedi'. When he came on to bowl he scattered virtually all his fielders to the boundary edges. I told Gifford, 'I don't go that far on my holidays.'

Wilson was also an enthusiastic member of the Newmarket Trainers' XI. With the opposition needing 32 to win off the last three overs, one game at Burrough Green, near Newmarket, was crawling to a tame draw when the captain threw the ball to Wilson. But a 16-year-old schoolboy belted him for six successive sixes in his over and the game was done. Wilson's team-mates, especially Michael Stoute, collapsed to the ground laughing hysterically. Further ignominy came when it was discovered that one of the sixes had dented Wilson's wife's car.

But nothing could dent Wilson's assessment of his own cricket ability. He knew he would get some ribbing from me the next time we met, but he saw me coming. 'I see you had to report my over in your Diary in *The Sun*. What you should have pointed out was that I actually coached that young Mark Ward to bat like that.'

In 1976 Wilson picked up a bargain when he paid 4,800 guineas for Tumbledownwind, who once set a course record at Glorious Goodwood, and later won York's prestigious Gimcrack Stakes. Wilson did the Radio 2 commentary, but flatly declined to be interviewed on television. A really proud moment came in 1996 when his colours were carried to victory by Tykeyvor in the old Bessborough Stakes at Royal Ascot. From 1953 he also started an unlikely love affair with Swindon Town, and in 1984 was largely responsible for the former Scottish international Lou Macari, a racing enthusiast, becoming their player-manager.

Wilson and I had one epic row. In the 1981 Irish 2,000 Guineas, Pat Eddery on Kings Lake had clearly bumped To-Agori-Mou several times but got home by a neck, and amazingly the Irish Turf Club, after the local stewards had reversed the placings – quite rightly, in my opinion – took the decision to reinstate Kings Lake as the winner. In the rematch in the St James's Palace Stakes at Royal Ascot, with feelings obviously running high, Greville Starkey on To-Agori-Mou adopted different tactics and Eddery was still a neck away as they flashed across the line.

In front of the Queen, and seen by thousands of trackside and TV viewers, Starkey looked across at Eddery after the winning post and gave him a very obvious V-sign. I contacted my sports editor Frank Nicklin, and he immediately saw the news potential. The next day *The Sun*'s back page led with OH GREVILLE – but for the 'V' in Greville, Nicklin inserted a two-fingered V-sign.

The next day Wilson opened his broadcast from Royal Ascot by holding up *The Sun*'s back page. 'This is an absolute disgrace,' he fulminated. 'It is a shameful, typical piece of red-top tabloid sensationalism.'

I thought that this was most unfair and sanctimonious, and challenged Wilson when he came off air. 'May I remind you that without the red-top journalistic jungle your father would never have had the fees to send his darling little boy to Harrow.'

'Fair point,' he graciously conceded, gave me a rare smile, and we remained friends to the very end.

16

The First Lady of Aintree

I HAD A LENGTHY LOVE-HATE RELATIONSHIP with the formidable Jenny Pitman: plenty of love on my part for the gallant horses she trained; oceans of hate from her when I had the audacity to criticise her.

She was unquestionably the first Queen of Aintree, after her two Grand National wins with Corbiere (1981) and Royal Athlete (1995), not to mention 50-1 Esha Ness finishing first in the 1993 void race fiasco. She also won the Cheltenham Gold Cup with Burrough Hill Lad (1984) and Garrison Savannah (1991), and became only the second trainer to win a full house of Nationals. After three wins in the Welsh National and two in the Scottish National, in 1997 Mudahim won her the Irish National on a memorable day at Fairyhouse to complete the set. 'I didn't do badly for a former stable girl working at weekends,' said Mrs P. She well deserved her OBE in 1998.

My admiration for her came from the way she continually produced a string of long-distance chasers for marathon races – I loved the way her horses, few of them fashionably bred, were trained to perfection to run their hearts out for her. Corbiere was bought in a field and won the Grand National: Mrs P. described him as 'a horse with a big arse like a carthorse'. Fairytales don't come much better.

Mrs P. was never afraid to get her cheque book out, and in the early 1980s she went to Ireland and bought the future Cheltenham Gold Cup winner Garrison Savannah, the Welsh and Grand National hero Royal Athlete, and the Midlands and Scottish National scorer Willsford, as well as the luckless Esha Ness. 'Jenny is more popular than the Pope when he touches down at Dublin Airport,' one wag commented.

'Depending on whom you listen to,' wrote Richard Griffiths in the *Racing Post*, 'Jenny Pitman is the biggest dragon since St George got his sword out, or the straightest, most caring trainer in the business. She is hugely motivated and never makes compromises.'

'When I was riding for her,' says John Francome, who at one time baby-sat her two sons too, 'she always knew before the races exactly how her horses would run. If owners wanted pandering and idle chat, Jenny was the last person you should send a horse to. She always played it straight down the line, and was black and white about everything.'

She was indeed, and she singled me out after I had the nerve to write one or two articles she absolutely loathed. Perhaps I should have taken heed of John Oaksey's famous assessment: 'Jenny Pitman is the most balanced person in the world I know. She's got a chip on *both* shoulders.'

Our relationship reached boiling point at a big awards lunch when she received a prize for her achievements. She spotted me at a table in the audience and suddenly, during her acceptance speech, hurled a roll of lavatory paper in my direction. 'That's for all the crap you've written about me!' she shouted. The individual sheets were even person-ally inscribed. She once threatened to sue TV's Julian Wilson when he described her as 'the Winnie Mandela of Racing', and on another occasion a journalist who questioned Pitman's abrasive approach was threatened with castration.

John McCririck always referred to Mrs P. as the 'Cuddly One'. It would not have been my ideal description. 'I had a few rows with her,' Big Mac insisted, 'but nobody could deny that she was a great trainer and a great personality. Her interviews with Des Lynam at the Grand National were great television. Racing needed characters like her, or it would all have been very boring. But I admit that whenever I bumped into her at the races I never quite knew what mood she was going to be in.'

The *Daily Telegraph* journalist Marcus Armytage, who in 1990 on Mr Frisk became the last amateur jockey to win the Grand National, still chuckles at the memory of riding Esha Ness for Mrs P. in the Hampton Court Amateurs' Handicap Hurdle at Ascot in December 1988. 'It was the second race of Esha Ness's career,' he recalls, 'and he had made an eye-catching debut. He was 6-4 favourite at Ascot, and everybody in Lambourn seemed to think that he was a "good thing".

'In the paddock Jenny was very clear about the tactics I was to employ. She looked me straight in the face and said, "This is the laziest horse I have ever trained. He doesn't do a tap at home, but I know he has plenty of ability. After you've jumped the second last hurdle, don't put your whip down. He'll respond to the whip, and it's the only way to ride him."

'John Oaksey's daughter Sara pissed off in front on the David Elsworth-trained Brandon Pier,' Armytage went on, 'but I was not at all worried, and travelling well. We jumped the second last flight, and I remembered Mrs P.'s explicit instructions. There were no whip-counting rules in those days, so I picked up my whip to get down to business – and dropped it! Sara was three lengths in front at that stage, and that was her winning margin on the line.

'For some naïve reason I thought that perhaps Mrs P. hadn't spotted my sheer stupidity. Some hopes... I came back into the runner-up spot trying to conceal my acute embarrassment. But I soon learned my fate, and in front of everybody within earshot I got the biggest bollocking of my career. She called me every name under the sun, and the language would have made a docker blush! Old Etonians like Marcus Armytage and all amateur jockeys all copped the verbal onslaught, Marcus dropped his whip and hoped Mrs P. hadn't noticed when he was beaten in a photo finish. I was relieved to escape into the weighing-room.' Ironically, Esha Ness was to win the 1993 void National, but, needless to say, Mr M. Armytage was not employed as the coachman.

The trainer Jamie Osborne, a former top-class jump jockey, incurred the wrath of Mrs P. at Ayr's Scottish Grand National meeting in 1990. He was accused of 'cutting up my son Mark', and a furious row erupted outside the stewards' room, with Mrs P. subsequently being fined £1,000 for hitting Osborne in the face. 'Jenny has a marvellous left hook,' he confirmed ruefully.'

'That £1,000 fine was a bit harsh,' said Mark Pitman. 'But Mum said, "It was the best grand I ever spent!"'

My lowest placing in Mrs P.'s popularity poll came in January 1991, when I had a tip-off that some of her stable superstars were injured. James Stafford, later to mastermind the Thurloe Thoroughbreds racing syndicate, was working part-time on *The Sun*'s racing desk as a casual sub-editor, and on his way into work one day he stopped off in a betting shop and saw, on the new Racing Channel, Pitman's assistant David Stait (later to become her second husband) being interviewed and revealing that indeed some of her biggest names, like Toby Tobias (poor blood count), Garrison Savannah (muscle problems) and Royal Athlete (septic foot) were all on the sidelines. Stafford telephoned me and repeated the interview. I duly wrote up my article, and my then racing editor, Noel Wilson, never a man to hide a controversial story, splashed an exclusive under the huge banner headline, JENNY IN THE PITS.

The moment I saw it I sensed trouble. I was off playing cricket for Sussex 2nd XI at Hove that day, but warned my wife that Mrs P. would be on the phone. Sure enough, when I walked through the door Fiona said, 'She's already rung four times.'

The phone rang again, and I was subjected to a wholesale slagging. Mrs P. was not interested in how I had obtained the story, and her language got progressively worse. At one stage I tried to stall her by saying, 'Hold on for a minute – I'm putting my cats in another room. They're not used to language like this.' But the torrent of abuse went on.

Finally Mrs P. said, 'I am going to sue your ghastly little rag for every penny it's got.'

'I suspect, Jenny,' I replied, 'that, like most of the horses in your yard, you haven't got a leg to stand on!' Her phone crashed down and my cats came back to snuggle up on the settee.

Days later at Plumpton, Jenny went up to Chris Poole and said, 'I'd given up smoking for months, but after one furious row with your great mate I'm now smoking forty a day.'

Many more racing figures received the Pitman ear-bashing. I suspect if you got all of us together we could easily fill the Albert Hall and they'd be still be queuing outside to get in.

'She started with just eight horses,' wrote the *Racing Post*'s Richard Griffiths, 'and said her stables were the last place they went before the knacker's yard.' After she had taken out personal loans and an overdraft

I knew there would be trouble... my exclusive over Jenny Pitman's sidelined horses.

to acquire the 16th-century Weathercock House stables in Upper Lambourn, it was Corbiere, winning the 1983 Grand National by just three-quarters of a length over Greasepaint, who was giving him ten pounds, who really put Mrs P. on the map. The horse had a great Aintree record – first, third, fell and 12th in the world's greatest race – and had previously won the Welsh Grand National at Chepstow.

Burrough Hill Lad, named after the Leicestershire village of Burrough-on-the-Hill by the local owner-breeder Stan Riley, was the best chaser to pass through Mrs P.'s jumping academy. Amazingly, early in his career the dreaded green tarpaulins were on standby when he suffered a crashing fall over hurdles at Kempton in 1980. Thankfully, the vet was not required to put him out of his obvious misery.

He won 17 of his 27 races, the highlight being the 1984 Cheltenham Gold Cup. His potential was shown at Haydock, when he took on Michael Dickinson's Gold Cup hero Silver Buck and only went down by two and a half lengths, although he was getting 21 pounds. Before the race Jenny joked, 'I gather Michael is more worried about Burrough Hill Lad's trainer than the horse himself.'

He proved he was a typical Pitman-trained long-distance slogger when he won the Welsh National at Chepstow, oozed with class when he won the Gold Cup by three lengths at 7-2, and produced one of the greatest weight-carrying displays of all time when he won the 1984 Hennessy at Newbury carrying twelve stone, despite giving 21lb to the runner-up Canny Danny. The 'Lad' made a horrendous mistake at the seventh last fence, and a mighty groan erupted from the packed Newbury stands, but John Francome did well to stay on before winning easily by four lengths. Burrough Hill Lad had triumphed in the Hennessy, where even the immortal Arkle had been beaten by the unforgiving handicapper. The 'Lad' also won three Gainsborough Chases, the Charlie Hall Chase and the 1984 King George VI Chase at Kempton on Boxing Day, defeating Combs Ditch. He sustained an injury in early 1985 and was hit by several leg injuries, so was never able to defend his Gold Cup crown.

Nobody who had seen Royal Athlete being beaten by 37 lengths in a Doncaster hurdle race could have got very excited by his prospects. But Mrs P. worked her magic on the horse, who she claimed had made her old before her time, and in 1995 Mrs P. was back in the Aintree winner's enclosure when he won the National at 40-1, partnered by Jason Titley, who at 24 was having his first ride in the race. At the joyous Upper Lambourn homecoming on the Sunday she hugged her hero and said, 'Every year I've had him in training he's cost me five years of my life. I was glad when he had a year off from racing – it gave me time to recover.' It was Royal Athlete's first and last run in the National.

Despite our rows Mrs P. warmed to me and *The Sun*, and in 1996 the newspaper leased her horse Superior Finish for the day to run in the Grand National in our red and white silks, and be 'owned' for the day by a lucky reader. (Unlike poor Blackie, of course, I'd escaped the firing squad back in 1982, and indeed, when I'd pointed out to Kelvin MacKenzie that I'd insured Blackie for the maximum £15,000 of my budget, so we'd actually made a profit on the whole business, his response had been, 'Well done! Perhaps we should do this every week?')

I drove our prize-winner, Peter McGrane, a retired fork-lift truck driver from Wiltshire, to Weathercock House and, to be fair to Jenny, she could not have been more charming to him. We watched our big-race jockey, the champion Richard Dunwoody, put Superior Finish through his last serious schooling session, and were made to feel very welcome. *The Sun* columnist John Francome was there to add to the occasion, and his banter with Mrs P. and Dunwoody was hilarious. 'The first Grand National I saw was Merryman II's race in 1960,' Mr McGrane told me, 'but it was so crowded that the only horse I saw was a police horse.' He was thrilled that Mrs P. was training 'his' horse, 'but I won't be calling her the "Cuddly One" – I'm not that brave!' Sadly, there was no fairytale ending with 9-1 Superior Finish, but he ran a blinder and finished a very respectable third behind Mick Fitzgerald on Rough Quest, the 7-1 favourite.

Spurred on by Peter McGrane winning over £23,000 place money with Superior Finish, for the 1997 National *The Sun* again leased a Pitman-trained horse, Nahthen Lad, who had won that year's Sun Alliance Chase at the Cheltenham Festival. The competition attracted postbags galore of entries, and the winner was a delightful granny called Pearl Hemmings, who only the day before the National was due to retire after working for ten years at Newbury's postal sorting office. 'I have a lucky horseshoe hanging on my front door,' she told me, wiping away tears, when I knocked on her door in Berkshire the Sunday before the big race to give her the news, 'but it's never brought me much luck – until now.'

Grand National day 1997 was one I will not forget in a hurry. A professional punter had just handed me a magnum of champagne to say thanks for my confirming with the trainer of the horse he'd tipped to win the first race that he was good for a win, when a burly, charmless Liverpool policeman, carrying a nasty-looking baton in his hand, came into the press room, grabbed my shoulder and shouted, 'Out!' It was the first we knew of the course being evacuated and the meeting abandoned because of an IRA bomb threat.

I found myself with fellow journalists Richard Evans and Julian Muscat in the middle of the course. Nobody, apart from the BBC's Des Lynam, was allowed to get into any of the car park areas. Even Ginger McCain, Mr Grand National himself, was not allowed to drive his car away. One frantic woman was screaming at policemen that she had a bitch dog in her car about to produce puppies, and she was terrified she would die of dehydration. It was a crazy situation – cut off from the outside world, but still holding the magnum of champagne. We decided to take the small branchline train from bang opposite the course to Ormskirk and re-book into our hotel. There, the magnum of champers did not last long with three thirsty scribes, and we learned later that the race had been rearranged for the Monday.

On the Sunday I had one simple order from *The Sun*: 'Get Mrs Pitman.' Luckily I bumped into a colleague who told me that Mrs

P. always stayed at the same hotel at nearby Ormskirk, where I found her having a coffee with Pearl Hemmings. She gave me a brilliant interview.

'I sensed there was going to be a drama on Saturday when I heard a police announcement saying, "All officers, Code A". The horses were looking at me and seemed to be asking, "What the hell is going on?" Nahthen Lad made me cry – he looked at me as if to say, "Please don't go, Mummy."

'We were invited into complete strangers' houses for mugs of tea. The Dunkirk spirit really kicked in. We saw some jockeys, still in their riding silks, walking down a road near the racecourse, eating fish and chips. You had to see it to believe it.' I also recall how wonderfully Jenny dealt with Pearl Hemmings, who'd been thrust into a world she could never have envisaged.

Over 60,000 racegoers had been evacuated from Aintree on the Saturday, and officials thought there would be a huge drop in the attendance for the Monday. But over 20,000 turned up, and newspapers encouraged people to take no notice of the IRA threat. One headline I loved was: WE SHALL FIGHT THEM ON THE BECHER'S. Lord Gyllene, jumping like a stag, made all to win for the popular owner Stan Clarke. Nahthen Lad did not let us down: he started at 14-1 and finished ninth. At least Pearl Hemmings had three days to remember.

Mrs P. would never have let Burrough Hill Lad run in the Grand National, especially when he was given a stamina-sapping 11st 9lb, but it was one of the few times she didn't give the handicapper a verbal volley. Virtually every year she would barnstorm the Grand National weights lunch in London and give Christopher Mordaunt, the Jockey Club's mild-mannered and gentlemanly senior handicapper until 1999, a scathing view of his assessments. Only the fabulously outspoken Ginger McCain topped her outbursts. In 2017 the British Horseracing Authority appointed Mrs P. to join their disciplinary committee. Eyebrows might have been raised, but she said, 'I shall add a bit of common sense.'

Like many Jockey Club officials, Mordaunt came via the army route, in this case as a former captain in the 9th/12th Lancers. He was especially proud of the Queen Mother's Special Cargo winning a three-way photo-finish to the 1984 Whitbread Gold Cup at Sandown – a handicapper's dream result. The year before his passing, at the age of 82, I had my last conversation with him over a quiet glass at the Gimcrack dinner at York.

'I bet you don't miss your annual encounters with Jenny Pitman,' I ventured.

'Oh, she wasn't all that bad,' said Captain Mordaunt. 'I got far worse on the telephone from some famous trainers. Her bark was far worse than her bite. But I didn't enjoy it much in 1984 when I put up her Grand National winner Corbiere ten pounds for winning the previous year. That was the normal hike for a National winner, but she really went on the warpath.'

'What does that man know about racing?' Mrs P. had stormed at that year's London weights lunch. 'He's never worked in stables!'

'I told Mrs P.,' Mordaunt recalled, 'you don't have to have a baby to be a top-class gynaecologist!

'When a fancied horse gets beaten,' he went on to reflect, 'the owner complains to the trainer, and the trainer complains to the jockey. All three end up kicking the stable cat. There's only one person left to kick – the poor old handicapper. If you have a hundred runners at one six-race meeting, 94 connections go away obviously disappointed. The other six probably celebrate for a few minutes, and then go down in the dumps when they work out how much the handicapper is going to bump them up.

'When I retired I was innocently leaning over the rail at Aintree one day, when Jenny Pitman came up behind me and caught me totally unawares. She gave me a parcel and said, "Don't worry – it's not ticking." When I got home I opened it up, and inside found a lovely framed photograph of her first Grand National winner Corbiere. On the back she had written, "From one old handicapper to another."'

So maybe many of us had got it all wrong about the ex-stable lass. Behind the battleaxe exterior perhaps there was a genuine heart of gold.

17

'That's the Way with the 'Oss'

IN JANUARY 1994, I WAS AT Leopardstown with BBC Radio 5 Live's long-serving racing correspondent Cornelius Lysaght. There we watched a horse called Danoli finish second at 12-1 in the AIG Champion Hurdle to Dermot Weld's much-fancied Fame And Fortune. It was only the horse's fourth run over hurdles, and the first time we'd encountered his virtually unknown farmer-trainer Tom Foley, who had his base in the remote hamlet of Aughabeg in County Carlow, in the shadow of the Blackstairs Mountains and the peak of the snow-splattered Mount Leinster.

Now we listened as, in his charming, unaffected way, Foley outlined his plans for Danoli. 'I picked out Danoli when he was an unraced three-year-old, and it changed our entire lives,' he told us. 'I bought him because he already had the head of a champion. When he first ran in a bumper race at Naas I knew he might be a bit special, and we were prepared to have a few good bets. But when we looked around at the calibre of the other horses and their well-known trainers, we chickened out. We didn't have a shilling on... and Danoli won at 16-1!

'This horse has never been extended. The value is watching him run,' Foley went on. 'This is one horse in Ireland which money simply could not buy. Danoli will run in the Sun Alliance Novices' Hurdle at the Cheltenham Festival,' he concluded.

That evening Lysaght and I enjoyed a drink in Jimmy's bar at Dublin Airport, having plunged hefty bets at 10-1 for Danoli to win the Sun Alliance. We realised this was Grade 1 fairytale material. Danoli went on to win the Deloitte and Touche Hurdle at Leopardstown in February as 4-5 favourite. By then everybody in the Emerald Isle was proclaiming him as the Irish banker for the 1994 Festival.

Three weeks before the Festival, Lysaght and I journeyed to Aughabeg, five miles from Bagenalstown, after stopping at some unmarked cross-roads amid winding country lanes to ask the way. When we eventually turned up at Foley's white farmhouse and 24-horse-power stables he could hardly believe that two journalists had travelled all the way over from England to see his stable star. But Danoli would soon be carrying the hopes of an entire nation. A local estate agent was even advertising a property as 'Only eight miles from Danoli'.

The trainer with his trademark bearded stubble proudly paraded Danoli in his yard for us. Then his phone rang in the farmhouse. 'Just hold him for me for a minute, please,' said Foley. Lysaght was quick to take a snap of us both: if I look rather nervous it was because it occurred to me how easily Danoli could have galloped off in the direction of the faraway Blackstairs Mountains and ruined all the Cheltenham plans. I was greatly relieved when Foley walked back into his yard.

'I wasn't making any money out of farming my 62 acres,' he told us, 'and decided to train a few jumpers. I couldn't have done any worse. I started in the Eighties with six horses. I still farm a bit, and I've got some beef cattle. But horses have taken over my life. The problem when I started was that if the horses were any good they were always sold on.'

He described how he had picked up Danoli from the Tipperary owner-breeder Willie Austin for just 7,000 guineas at Goffs, for the first-time owner Danny O'Neill, who wanted a suitable store horse. The horse had failed to reach his reserve, but cutely Foley persuaded the breeder to accept a much lower price. He was named for 'Dan' as in Danny and 'Oli' for his daughter Olivia. The Danoli fairytale was under way, and soon the horse, already a gelding, had rattled off a hat-trick of bumper race wins at Naas, Punchestown and Fairyhouse for the Wexford amateur rider Padraig English.

On that first visit Foley could not have been more hospitable. His lovely wife Goretti provided Irish scones, and we were introduced to his daughters Sharon, Adrienne and Goretti junior, plus son Pat. A large and striking portrait of the Virgin Mary gazed down on this incredibly happy family. The following day, confirmed Foley, the local parish priest of Bagenalstown, Father Dowling, was coming to bless Danoli with the sign of the cross for his Cheltenham adventure.

'Danoli has had countless prayers in church said for him,' grinned Foley. 'I always seem to have a microphone thrust in my face since the Danoli bandwagon started to roll. But it is better to have one stable star than a hundred also-rans.'

We had one last glimpse of Danoli in his box, and I commented on how relaxed he looked. 'That's the way with the 'oss,' replied Foley in his gentle voice. I would come to hear that expression another hundred times or more.

Lysaght, armed with his tape recorder, and I were soon knocking on Father Dowling's door. He cordially invited us in, and seemed just as excited about Danoli's Festival challenge as the rest of this part of County Carlow. I recall him pouring me a hefty gin and tonic. 'Don't spill any,' he said. 'The bishop will be sitting in that same chair in an hour and I don't want him to get his pants wet!'

It was rumoured that every priest in Ireland on the annual Cheltenham pilgrimage, including the wonderful Father Sean Breen from his Naas and Punchestown diocese, had backed Danoli. 'Sure,' grinned Foley. 'We've got the Good Lord on our side. Somebody said after Mass the other evening that even the Pope was on!'

As a small, down-to-earth trainer, Tom Foley was loved by his local community. 'By far the two biggest trainers in this part of Ireland are Jim Bolger and Willie Mullins,' he told us, 'but they could not have been more helpful. Jim has a generous heart, and he has allowed Danoli to work on his all-weather gallop. Willie has been on hand with all sorts of advice about the travelling arrangements.'

Foley did not enjoy the prospect of making his maiden flight to England with his beloved Danoli. 'I've never been on a plane before,' he confided, 'and never left Ireland. I can also confirm that the only day I have ever worn a tie was for my wedding. I have lived in the same three-bedroom house all my life and I wouldn't swap it for Buckingham Palace. You couldn't put a price on the views I wake up to every morning.'

His fears were soon realised. It was only a short flight from Dublin to Bristol, but flying conditions were terrible, with high winds buffeting the aeroplane. 'I looked out of a window and had to dash to the loo to be sick,' he subsequently told me. 'Then I decided to go and hold Danoli for the rest of the journey. I don't know whether he was giving me confidence or the other way round. I was mighty glad when we landed. I still had not worn a tie, as when I fasten the top button on my shirt I always feel dizzy.

'I had been booked into a hotel in Cheltenham, but I decided to sleep in the stable lads' hostel, as I wanted to be as close to Danoli as I could. Each time I visited him in the night he was fast asleep, just as he was at the Goffs sales when I first saw him in his box.'

Wednesday, 16 March 1994 was D-Day for Danoli. 'I knew that Danoli had already become a very popular horse in Ireland,' Foley recalls. 'Even after his second in the Irish Champion Hurdle as a novice virtually all the flights from Dublin to England were fully booked.

'I was very nervous as I saddled him. The pressure was mounting for the second day of the Festival, as all the Irish horses on the first day had failed to strike. We had one second with The Committee in the Fulke

Walwyn Kim Muir Challenge Cup, but all the other raiders were beaten out of sight.'

George Ennor in the *Racing Post* summed it up perfectly. 'They cheered Danoli the moment he stepped into the parade ring,' he wrote. 'They cheered him all the way to the start. When the announcer said that Charlie Swan had driven Danoli up four flights from home and had gone into the lead three out, a mighty roar went up, and when he won by two lengths from Carl Llewellyn on Corrouge the cheers nearly took the roof off the grandstands.'

Danoli had eventually started 7-4 favourite at Cheltenham and beat 22 rivals. Some massive bets were struck on him, and JP McManus is rumoured to be the punter who plunged in with a £130,000–£80,000 gamble. There were endless bets of £40,000–£20,000.

The Irish in the crowd went mad. Foley, now wearing a tie provided by his wife, was carried shoulder-high into the joyous winner's enclosure. But he was still wearing his old pullover. Arkle and Dawn Run were given a similarly wild reception. But there was something unique about Danoli. His fairytale success was already deeply etched in Irish folklore. And it came on the eve of St Patrick's Day.

Who could ever have dreamed that a small-time trainer, who had never left his native Ireland before, would have been summoned by the Cheltenham supremo Lord Sam Vestey to the Royal Box and ended up having tea with the Queen Mother? The next time Foley and his entire family attended Mass in their local church, the whole congregation rose to their feet, and they were given a lengthy round of applause. Magic moments.

Next stop that season for Danoli was the Martell Hurdle at Aintree. Flakey Dove, winner of the Champion Hurdle, headed the betting as 9-4 favourite, and Fame And Fortune was 3-1. Danoli was a generous 9-2, and for once Foley rang home and asked Goretti to have £50 on him. The Foleys backed him at 5-1.

I played up my Cheltenham winnings. Danoli belted the fourth last hurdle but, as at Cheltenham, he led at the last obstacle and stormed home by a runaway eight lengths from Mole Board. From his eight career starts Danoli had won six races, and been second and third. Who says that racing dreams never come true?

I had doubled up Danoli to win the Sun Alliance Novices' Hurdle and the Champion Hurdle the following year. The odds were terrific as I'd plunged immediately after his second in the Irish Champion Hurdle as a novice. I was not too worried when he was second on his reappearance as 2-1-on favourite in the Christmas Hurdle at Leopardstown behind his new arch-rival Dorans Pride, trained in County Limerick by Michael Hourigan.

He then ran third in the Champion Hurdle at the Cheltenham Festival, having started 4-1 joint favourite, to Kim Bailey's Alderbrook (11-2). My Danoli double never really looked like coming off, but I was lucky enough to have a saver on Alderbrook, as a few weeks earlier at Warwick Kim Bailey had told me I should have a few quid on him at 50-1.

I had not lost faith in Danoli, who duly returned to winning form with a half-length success over Boro Eight in the Martell Aintree Hurdle as 2-1 favourite. His preparation for Cheltenham had been interrupted, but at Aintree he was back to his best.

But Foley says he knew something was wrong with Danoli at Aintree. 'I could read him like a book. I soon discovered that his off-fore leg had blown up like a balloon. He had broken a fetlock joint, and how brave he must have been to have even finished in the race. The local vets told me his leg would have to be pinned together with screws. The Liverpool police did a great job, and Danoli's horse ambulance was rushed through the streets to the vets for his operation with a police escort in front and behind.

'I hated saying goodbye to him. It was like leaving him with strangers. I had missed my plane and had to cadge a lift in one of the horseboxes going back to Ireland. It took twelve hours.' People started sending postcards simply addressed: 'Danoli, Liverpool'. Foley confided that at one time he thought Danoli would never run again.

Miraculously, Danoli did come back, and finished fourth in his second Champion Hurdle attempt. In my very biased preview I wrote, 'Screw the lot of 'em!'

Now Danoli started out on a chasing career, and won at Clonmel and Naas. But his moment of glory was when he won the Hennessy Cognac Gold Cup at Leopardstown on 2 February 1997. 'The scenes which greeted him after injuries threatened his career,' reported George Ennor, 'will live long in the memory.'

Danoli's last public appearance came in the Cheltenham Gold Cup on 13 March 1997. As usual Father Dowling blessed Danoli: 'May the Holy Spirit shine down and bless and protect you.' But for once the heavenly guidance did not work. Watching anxiously, Foley knew that the old sparkle had gone, on ground unsuitably fast. Perhaps the old fetlock injury was creeping into his mind. But Danoli was still as brave as a lion. He simply wouldn't give in, but fell at the second last as Tony McCoy roared to victory by nine lengths on Mr Mulligan. Later it was found that Danoli had suffered an additional fracture to the same fetlock. There were dreams that he would return for the 1998 Cheltenham Gold Cup, but it was not to be, and he retired having won £320,759.

In April, 2006 Danoli was put down after a severe attack of colic at the Irish National stud in Kildare, where he and the 1993 Melbourne Cup hero Vintage Crop had become unlikely but inseparable friends and the main tourist attractions. 'Danoli's life achievements from a small stable will rarely ever be matched,' reflected Tom Foley. 'Whenever he stepped onto a racecourse, he was all heart. I am sure he was very intelligent. Often Goretti showed him photographs of himself in newspapers, and he just whined at her. That's the way with the 'oss.'

18

A Gold Cup Fairytale

IN JANUARY, 1996 CORNELIUS LYSAGHT RETURNED from a Sunday race meeting at Leopardstown, and was soon on the phone to me, 'I've been told about a trainer from deepest County Cork,' he said excitedly, 'who thinks he'll win the Gold Cup. Apparently, he drinks a pint of Foster's lager for breakfast every morning, mixed with two raw eggs… and he's got a wooden leg!'

Then, just days later, David Nicholson prodded his finger in my chest in his characteristic way and announced, 'All my Irish contacts are telling me that Imperial Call will win the Gold Cup.'

We soon identified the trainer with a live Gold Cup hope in Imperial Call, who had been backed down from 33-1 to 5-1 second favourite, as Captain Fergie Sutherland, an Englishman. He had lost his leg, apparently, during the Korean War. I confess I had never heard of him.

But then in the February, Imperial Call burst onto the scene by running away with the Hennessy Gold Gup and beating the previous Gold Cup winner, Master Oats. He led from start to finish, made a bad mistake at the last fence, but still won by six lengths.

'I don't give interviews to the press' – Captain Sutherland was quick to point that out. 'Never have done.' But he knew a relation of Lysaght's from his army days, and was a fellow Old Etonian to boot. That swung it, and we were granted an audience at his four-horse stables at Killanardrish, high in the mountains above County Cork's River Lee. Cornelius Lysaght was a good travelling companion – we often teamed up for trips to Irish racing, and when I was researching for Tony McCoy's first book, we were the first to visit his parents in Northern Ireland.

Tracing the Captain was easier than locating Tom Foley in the wilds of County Carlow, but we still had problems. I knocked on the door of an impressive house. A rather strange-looking woman who would not have looked out of place in Alfred Hitchcock's *Psycho* opened the door a few inches and said, 'Mr Fergie lives in the stables down there.' When we got there it transpired from Fergie's wife Ann that they were expecting us the next day. We were told to wait in his stable office until he returned 'from the mountains, where Imperial Call had been taken for a day out.'

Half an hour later we heard the distinctive sound of a man with a wooden leg approaching the office. It was almost like something out of *Moby Dick* with Gregory Peck playing the one-legged Captain Ahab.

'I was serving with the 5th Royal Inniskilling Dragoon Guards in the Korean War,' he explained, when a land mine exploded in 1952 and I lost the lower part of my left leg. I was 21 years old, and had been in the army for just six months.

'I never let losing a leg impede my great love of sport. I won the formidable Melton cross-country ride in 1957, and hunted with the famous Quorn hunt in Leicestershire five days a week. I have a wooden leg for real life, dancing, riding and shooting.'

We soon learned that Sutherland, who had been born in London but raised largely in Peebles, did not suffer fools easily, and was very outspoken. 'Any bloody fool can train two-year-olds,' he said. 'But placing horses to win handicaps is a far more difficult art. I trained Fox King to win 16 handicaps – four each year for four years.' He smiled: 'That took a bit of management!'

He had started training on the Flat from Newmarket in 1958, he explained, having served as Geoffrey Brooke's assistant for the previous four years. His first winner was with Tribune at Wolverhampton in 1958, and his biggest success up to then had come when A.20 had won the Queen Mary Stakes at Royal Ascot later that summer.

Fergie and Ann were excellent hosts, and Irish smoked salmon was readily produced. A half-empty port decanter was proof that Fergie and I had started a fond friendship. 'I've got no money, you know,' he told me. 'I spent it all on a misspent youth.' One story about Fergie in his younger days at Newmarket has survived the passing years. He was staying with a lady friend, and the next morning the woman's young daughter came into the breakfast room and said, 'Look what I found in mummy's bed!' It was a wooden leg.

Then we got on to the horse that was going to win the Gold Cup.

'Imperial Call is a natural jumper,' he told us. 'I got him as a three-year-old from the famous Irish horse dealer Tom Costello. I took him into his indoor school and popped him over three really hairy obstacles. He flew over them, and I could tell that he was really athletic. I paid £20,000 for him, and the deal was all over in ten minutes.

'At first I used to gallop Imperial Call after the local point-to-points, when most of the people had gone home. Sometimes it got so dark that I used to get friends to position their Land Rovers by the fences with the headlights on. Even in the half-dark I could see his immense potential.

'He won his second hurdle race at Limerick by fifteen lengths. In his second season he won at Limerick, Gowran Park and Leopardstown, and finished a short-head second to Dorans Pride when he was carrying ten pounds more.

'To make ends meet I usually ended up selling horses. I sold Ebony Jane, who went on to win the 1993 Irish Grand National. I've never been able to keep anything decent until Imperial Call came along.

'His owner liked to be mysterious, and runs his horses in the name of Lisselan Farms Ltd. He just walked into my yard and bought Imperial Call. How lucky was that for him – and me! Imperial Call could have won a string of point-to-point races and hurdles, but the owner only had eyes for chasing and the Cheltenham Gold Cup.'

Fergie's wife Ann told me they always used Jack Russell terriers as guard dogs. 'One was so weasel-faced and mean that we called him Lester. Anybody who tries to get into Impy's horsebox will get a terrifying welcome from Lester.'

When the 1996 Gold Cup came round Imperial Call, ridden by Conor O'Dwyer, started 9-2 second favourite, with One Man as 11-8 favourite. One Man, as widely expected, did not stay and finished sixth. But in contrast Imperial Call stayed on strongly, and won by four lengths from the future Grand National winner Rough Quest.

As the Irish sang 'The Banks of My Own River Lee', Sutherland made his way with his stick through the joyous supporters to the packed winner's enclosure. When he spotted me he said, 'There's my man. I shall have to be careful what I say...' Later he told me he hadn't liked my exclusive about Imperial Call jumping in the dark after point-to-point meetings. But now Fergie said, 'He put them all in his place, didn't he? I made no secret that he would win, and all the locals in our nearby Angler's Rest pub were on at 100-1 and 66-1. I've always thought he would win a Gold Cup one day, since he was five years old, and he has never stopped improving.

'Horses like Imperial Call only come along once in a lifetime. I just let him gallop three times a day up a sharp gradient nearby. There are no petrol fumes or pollution on my cinder gallop.

'I am a simple man, but the Irish have accepted me as one of their own. I like to sing all their favourite songs. They know that I can produce one correctly for the big day, but I've never had a horse with real class."

After his moment of glory at Cheltenham, Imperial Call was never quite the same force again, although he did once slam the mighty Florida Pearl by fourteen lengths. His strengths were that he had no weaknesses,' said Conor O'Dwyer. 'He jumped for fun, had speed and guts to burn. Fergie did a great job with him, considering that he only had three other horses in training at the time. Imperial Call was his first-ever runner at the Cheltenham Festival!'

So that was two magical Irish racing stories Cornelius Lysaght had pointed me in the direction of: the silver-haired gentleman Tom Foley and the extrovert Fergie Sutherland. No Hollywood scriptwriter could have penned that pair. He's still on the lookout for the one-legged Irish nun riding a Cheltenham Festival contender.

19

The Romford Foghorn

'YOU OUGHT TO GO TO PITCH number 88 in the Silver Ring,' I was told by a contact one day in the 1970s – he was talking about Ascot. 'It's well over a furlong away from the winning post, and half way back to Windsor Castle. There's a bookie there who has a big notice on his board reading "NO DOGS – NO WOMEN".' So, for Royal Ascot that year I persuaded *The Sun*'s Royal photographer Arthur Edwards to briefly give up his German hunting assignment and join me on this venture deep into the Silver Ring. This was my first sighting of Barry Dennis.

The next day we published our photograph of this unique spectacle, and suddenly Dennis was attracting mountains of publicity. Looking back, I often wonder whether, in these ridiculously PC days, he would be locked up for causing distress to female racegoers – not to mention dogs.

Barry Dennis – whose full name is actually Barry Dennis Middleton; not a lot of people know that – rose from being a barrow-boy urchin at his local market to become arguably the most colourful independent on-course bookie racing has ever known, as well as famous for tipping losing '*Bismarck*' fancies on Channel 4's *The Morning Line* programme for 14 years. *The Sun* and I played a significant part in creating the legend of the man I christened the Romford Foghorn.

The Barry Dennis legend has always been centred on Romford in Essex. 'My stepfather used to post bets to a firm called McLaughlins in Glasgow,' he recalls, 'in the days before there were any betting shops. I would post the bets on the way to school, but one day I clean forgot, and came home terrified that the horses had won. But his bets that day had all been losers. He was thrilled that he'd got his money back!

'My mind started whirring, and I thought it was quite a big deal to lay horses. So in 1954, as a 13-year-old schoolboy, I made a book with my school chums on the Derby. I had no idea about hedging bets, and realised that if Lester Piggott won on Never Say Die I was really in trouble. He duly won at 33-1, and I *was* in trouble. I was skint, and couldn't pay my debts. The only way out was to skive off school and work doing any jobs on the stalls in Romford market. I played truant for two months, earned the £15 I owed, and paid everybody off. Teachers from the school used to come round, but my mother always convinced them that I was unwell.

'I started making a book at Romford greyhounds in the sixties, but got warned off after a spot of fisticuffs. I started at the races at Brighton in 1968. I was in the fourth ring, and in the four-shilling enclosure in the middle of the track. If I'd taken a step backwards I would have fallen arse-over-head down the hill behind me.'

In my early years I always liked the little bookie Jackie Levy, who at southern tracks like Lingfield and the now defunct Wye could be heard shouting in his high-pitched voice, 'Anybody want a big 'un?' I was soon assured that he was more likely to lay an egg than a reasonably big bet. But men like these were the fabric of the tracks, and added to the colour of the pitches.

Gradually Dennis progressed into better pitches. 'I decided one year to bet on the hill at Tattenham Corner. I was miles back in the back row, and never dreamt that one day I would have one of the best pitches in Tattersalls, in front of the Queen's grandstand.

'The Derby was run on a Wednesday in those days. The only way you could get a pitch on the Hill was to go down there and bung a few quid to one of the travellers who controlled who could bet on the Hill. After I had greased somebody's palm I turned up on the Wednesday and was shown my allotted pitch. All I had were my board, my chalks, a duster, a satchel for the readies, and a few tickets. But the margins were so big on the Hill, and I made big money for years and years. The only way I could lose money was if it fell out of my pockets. Sir Ivor and Lester Piggott won my first Derby in 1968 as 5-4-on favourite.

'In 1974 I moved up the scale and took over pitch 50 in the four-bob ring. I was still miles back, and realised I had to go up 50 places in the Silver Ring and then another 50 in Tattersalls. Working from the back row of the pitches I had to do it all myself. The dead man's shoes rule dominated the way pitches changed in those days. If a bookie died, some obscure relation would take over the favoured pitches. Most of these men had second professions and were not real bookmakers. It was a disgrace. It was totally unfair to bookies like myself in the back rows trying to lay proper bets, and also attempting to get punters a better deal.' A friend of mine didn't go racing at Folkestone for over 20 years. When he finally went again and I asked him how he'd found it he said, 'Same bookies – different mugs.'

'Snow Knight won the 1974 Derby and we all cleaned up. If you back to figures there is no way a bookie should lose. But the late great William Hill always laid horses subject to his opinion. He was outstanding, and was always prepared to back his judgement. I was beginning to get a feel for racing – I knew a bad favourite from a good favourite. That's what made my '*Bismarck*' selections pretty easy for me.

Like William Hill, I started to back my opinions on form.

'In 1976 I was quite certain that Wollow, who had won the 2,000 Guineas for Henry Cecil, was not going to win the Derby. He showed so much speed at Newmarket, and I was prepared to gamble heavily that he wouldn't stay at Epsom. Even from the back row in the Silver Ring I was able to lay Wollow at bigger prices than most of the bookies, and I cleaned up when Lester Piggott won on Empery. Wollow had no luck in running and finished fifth. But they were not all good years. Willie Carson cost me a bomb when he won on Troy and Henbit in 1979 and 1980 at 6-1 and 7-1.

'Entrepreneur's Derby in 1997 was another turning point. When I arrived at the track at 11 o'clock he was 10-11. By 2.30 I had my book nicely sorted out and was laying 8-11. I didn't think anybody would back him at those odds. But Stephen Little' (a fellow bookmaker) 'came over to me and wanted me to lay him a bet of £11,000 to £8,000. But Entrepreneur's part-owner Michael Tabor, a notable gambler, is alleged to have had a bet of £200,000 on his horse with him. Tabor had other bets and was flooding the ring. I'd laid Entrepreneur to lose over £20,000, which was never my intention.

'I was suddenly looking down a gun barrel. It was far more than I had laid one horse in my life! I watched the race on the big screen, but I was in another world. I tracked Entrepreneur all the way round Epsom. Benny The Dip won the race, and Entrepreneur finished fourth.

'After the race I sank into my chair at the back of my pitch. I was totally drained. I simply couldn't bet on the next race.' But Barry's wife Marion claims that when he walks through the door she can never tell whether he's had a good or bad day.

Barry's whole situation changed in 1998, when he borrowed £250,000 from his fellow Essex man David Johnson, the shrewd financial wizard who had horses in training with Martin Pipe. Barry splashed out £40,000 to have pitch number 4 at Epsom, and £50,000 to have pitch number 7 at Ascot. Quickly he became Britain's most recognisable bookie, and his hoarse bark reminded me of Victor Chandler, father of the Gibraltar-based bookmaker, who always stood out at the races for his gruff-voiced 'Six to four the field!' Dennis repaid Johnson's loan within two years, and saw his annual turnover rocket from £100,000 in 1996 to £18 million in 2005.

But it was still the Derby that caught his imagination. 'There are Derbys all over the world, but the Epsom Derby is really the only one which matters. The others are just tame imitations.' He had a Derby-day ritual. 'I used to get up at 5.30,' he reveals, 'and open up my outdoor swimming pool. I'd do a few lengths, and that would put me in the right frame of mind for the battle ahead.' Barry Dennis has been making a big splash for most of his life – and, unlike the original *Bismarck*, he has seldom looked like sinking. 'In 2003 most bookies were clobbered by the Kieren Fallon factor when Sir Michael Stoute's Kris Kin was backed off the boards down from 12-1 to 6-1 on the day. Again I took a view and decided to lay the first three in the betting, and Fallon did me a favour and I won £25,000.'

I once caused the great man to display a major lack of humour. My son James and a few friends were having an outing to the Epsom Derby. 'Go to Barry Dennis's pitch – the green-coloured one – just before the big race,' I told him, 'and say, "Claude Duval is my father and he says you'll give me five points above the odds on any horse I fancy in the Derby."' The ancient betting ring on the Epsom Downs never reverberated to such explosive language.

In October 1998 I teamed up with the outspoken Essex man on his front-line pitch for a typical Monday meeting at Plumpton. As the London train pulled into Plumpton's tiny station, Barry surveyed the sizeable crowd making their way over the footbridge straight into the course. 'Aye-aye – here come the mugs. Let's hope they've got plenty of money with 'em,' bellowed Dennis. Things had been going well at Newmarket the previous Saturday, and coming into round six that day he had been £10,000 ahead, though he'd lost £3,500 of it when the locally-trained Prince Babur roared in having been backed from 10-1 to 5-1.

At Plumpton, however, Dennis's mood soon darkened when the 6-4 favourite Auburn Boy won the first race. Then two more 'jollies' skated in – Townley Hall at 8-11 and the 6-4 chance Torduff Express. Then the much-fancied Just Nip won at 7-2. What had started out as a journalistic scoop was now turning out exceedingly sour.

'Four winning favourites! – no wonder you're bloody Punter's Pal. This isn't a *Bismarck* but a tragedy like the *Titanic*, and there'll be few survivors if this keeps up.' I watched Dennis handing back fistfuls of readies, and his demeanour was turning decidedly unfriendly. 'Come on, you horrible lot!' he yelled. 'You've won the first four rounds – let's see how lucky you really are.'

'God is a bookmaker,' Mike Dillon of Ladbrokes always claims: 'He usually comes to our aid when things are getting sticky.' And so the gospel of Plumpton came to pass: Tony McCoy ended the winning streak of favourites, and Barry actually won £186 on the last race. By trading off some of the earlier bets on favourites Dennis had turned over £12,079 on the day... and lost £3,179. 'The next time you want to stand on some bugger's pitch,' a grim-faced Barry told me as we made our way to the car park, 'I'll pay money to make sure it's not on mine.'

The picture became even gloomier when a punter, clearly the worse for drink, told Dennis, 'You're just a loudmouth. You'll get sorted out one day.'

'It's half-term again,' replied the Romford Foghorn. 'Does your mum know you're out?' To another similar insult he replied, 'What's your village doing for a village idiot now you're having a day out?'

'This game would tame tigers,' reflected Dennis in the car. 'One minute you're on terrific highs; the next you hit rock bottom and imagine you'll never win another penny.

'I have no illusions. I am the most loathed and detested man on the racecourse. Over 90% of on-course bookmakers never speak to me. On a hate-scale of 0-10 in racing I am on 15. Other bookies dislike me because I am an extrovert, and punters queue up to try and knock me off my perch. I don't have any real friends at the races.'

The next day I rang him to thank him for my day out. 'I had the perfect end to a perfect day,' he said: 'watching my beloved Spurs on the telly getting thumped again.' I've never forgotten my day on the Dennis pitch at Plumpton. Curiously, he never invited me to share the experience again.

Those were the days when *The Morning Line* was full of wonderful spontaneous banter between John Francome and Alastair Down, topped off by Barry Dennis's *Bismarck* input, and viewing figures soared. When the trio departed the ratings plummeted. 'At one stage 98 of my *Bismarck* bets – all morning favourites in *The Sun*,' he was quick to point out – 'resulted in 81 of them being stuffed. They all went down quicker than the *Bismarck* in 1941.'

But with the internet revolution early this century, storm clouds were assembling on the horizon, to change the whole landscape of on-course betting... Now effectively in semi-retirement, Dennis explains, 'My turnover went downhill from when betting exchanges started, and then firms went offshore in places like Gibraltar. I lost all the roller-coaster punters. Previously I was at the centre of one big, mad, gambling circus. Because of the margins I would be offering evens on a horse, but punters would stand in front of my pitches looking at my prices and, by using their mobile telephones, they could get 11-10. The exchanges don't have my expenses and can offer better prices.'

'I went to Brighton in 2016,' he told me, 'but I won't be going again. I was so bored that I went home after seven of the eight races. My turnover on the seven races was £2,856. By the time I'd paid my entrance, my staff and petrol I made £240. Windsor on a Monday night used to be a big earner. But in 15 years my turnover dwindled from £70,000 to £6,000. Years ago I used to scrape into the back row of bookies. Now there isn't even a full front row of bookies.

'In 2016 I did 130 days, mostly at Lingfield on the turf and the all-weather during the winter. But in my heyday I did over 350 meetings a year, often getting helicopters going from Ascot, to Newmarket, and Goodwood to take advantage of two meetings in a day. It was very viable in those days and I didn't want to miss anything.' Because at the races he was always likely to be making big cash payouts, he once confided to me, 'If I don't have 20 grand stuffed away in my pockets, I feel naked.' But nowadays, he said, 'I'm well over 70, and I don't get the buzz any more. It won't be too long before on-course bookies are like dinosaurs. The exchanges have killed the game.'

These days the great racecourse characters in the betting ring are almost non-existent. Unless JP McManus strides into the hectic cross-fire of betting at the Cheltenham Festival, most of the gambling giants are operating via the exchanges. 'Bookies are in the entertainment business,' says Dennis, 'and members of the public like the mystery and magic of it all. Standing up shouting the odds makes us like comedians. Racecourses in America and France have no atmosphere, but my motto was always to make punters smile as you take their money.'

Dennis remains great company at cricket matches. He once had a party at the Oval during a Test match against Australia, and his generosity knew no bounds. He has watched England around the world with the Barmy Army. I can vouch for how much money he has donated to charity, particularly for cancer research. Where charity is concerned, behind the gruff, often offensive posturing he is as soft as a kitten.

What the loud-mouthed Dennis is, never, though, is lost for words. One day his lovely wife presented him with a dozen choice Colchester oysters. Unfortunately, while he was opening one of them his special sharp knife slipped, and he cut himself badly. Blood was pouring everywhere, and Marion nearly passed out. The great man managed to dial 999, and asked for an ambulance.

'Where are you actually bleeding from?' asked the woman at the other end.

'I'm from bleeding Romford!' shouted Dennis.

20

The Press Gang

WHEN GEORGE ENNOR PASSED AWAY ON New Year's Eve, 2005, at only 65, horse racing's press corps lost one of its greatest characters. It had already been a bad autumn, as we had also lost jumping's superstars Best Mate and Rooster Booster. Now the press room would never be quite the same again.

How could you not be captivated by this smiling character, always in his trademark trilby at the races, cheering on his beloved Portsmouth FC at Fratton Park, and enjoying the odd glass of wine or three watching Hampshire on the county cricket circuit? In plain, simple words, we all adored him.

It was sneaking away from his public school at Malvern to Worcester races that sparked his lifelong love of racing. 'The form book took a bit of a knock when Colin Mackenzie [later the *Daily Mail*'s racing correspondent] was made head boy,' he used to say with an impish grin.

He joined the *Sporting Life* in 1960, and stayed there until in 1986 he was headhunted for the newly launched *Racing Post*. The *Post*'s editorial director Brough Scott assembled his new staff and issued the strict order that his reporters were only allowed one drink at the races. 'That's fine,' said Ennor. 'I'll only drink gin.'

Ennor had a fund of nicknames for racing personalities: the Sardine, the Dwarf, the Bounder and Scarface. In snow-hit March 1989, while over 60,000 Cheltenham Festival racegoers roared the great Desert Orchid up the hill to win an epic Gold Cup, up in the press box Ennor, with an each-way ante-post betting voucher for 66-1, was a lone voice cheering on the runner-up Yahoo.

Unbelievably, after twelve years at the *Post*, and despite all his invaluable contacts and knowledge, they cancelled his contract. No moaning from Ennor; in the words of Norman Tebbit, he got on his bike and explored pastures new, joining Mark Popham's *Racenews* team for the big Festival meetings, and playing a vital role. I would often give him a ring about some obscure statistic, and he always came up with the answer. His memory was outstanding. He always reported on racing fairly, and without a hint of bias. I can recall only one disagreement. I was once extolling the virtues of Captain Ryan Price. Ennor shook his head violently: 'I wouldn't have him.' I never quite discovered how these two men had fallen out.

For over 20 years Ennor was president of the Horserace Writers' Association, and entertained us at the annual Derby awards just before Christmas with quick-fire, often slightly slurred speeches which often left the audience puzzled by his rhyming slang. He was a very caring president: when the Yorkshire journalist Keith Rogers was left paralysed by a freak accident after slipping on some ice, within days Ennor had arranged for a cheque to be sent from the Association.

He was a great traditionalist, always displaying the perfect manners that harked back to a yob-free society. When things were not going his way, one of his pet sayings was, 'How incredibly impertinent!' I lost count of the number of times he used that line. How he fitted in among Fratton Park's beer-bellied regulars, who loved to take their shirts off even on the coldest of winter days, I could never quite understand. I once asked him how often he used his season ticket. 'I don't go unless they are three o'clock kick-offs,' he replied.

Ennor used to love recalling his Hampshire cricketing idols: the swashbuckling West Indian opening batsman Roy Marshall; Derek Shackleton, the classic swing bowler; and Colin Ingleby-Mackenzie, their cavalier captain who, asked for the reason for their success after they'd won the county championship in 1961, replied, 'Wine, women and song. Plus all the players have to be in bed in time for breakfast.'

Traditionally, Kent CCC played Hampshire at the St Lawrence Ground in Canterbury over the August Bank Holiday. Ennor used to stay with me, and we spent hours enjoying the matches from the Buffs cricket tent, which was always full of retired military men from the famous Kent Regiment and their wives, one of whom made me chuckle by asking innocently, 'Which one is Carl Hooper?' The West Indian all-rounder did rather stand out from his Kent colleagues.

In the end the cards were not dealt too kindly for George. His neighbours introduced him to Jan, a fellow divorcee, and it was a match made in heaven. (I don't think I won many bonus points with my wedding present, though: a framed photograph of Portsmouth's well-known Northern Ireland international goalkeeper Norman Uprichard.) But no sooner had they married than cancer crept upon him like a stranger in the dark. Still, they had ten good years together – 'the best years of my life,' said Ennor.

I never heard him complain. Once he even rang me and said, 'This chemotherapy lark is such a bore...' Those who attended the 2005 HWA lunch will never forget Ennor, just weeks before his passing, walking with a stick, his voice affected by the drugs he'd been given to ease the acute pains in his spine. 'I'm a goner,' he told me, still bravely smiling. 'Don't take evens that I'll see the New Year.' Sadly, he got his final result spot-on.

THE *EVENING STANDARD'S* CHRISTOPHER Poole was a larger-than-life character: eccentric, choleric, bearded – a cross between Henry VIII, Burl Ives and Robert Morley. The trainer Arthur Stephenson, on the other hand, called him Rasputin.

He had a huge appetite for life – and food. Born in Derbyshire, he started his path in journalism with the *Sussex Express and County Herald*, as their Rye correspondent. Every year he made a fortune from the national newspapers with his reports of massive jellyfish invasions at nearby Camber Sands.

Later he moved to the *Sheffield Star*, before joining the *Evening Standard* via the *Daily Telegraph* racing desk, where for many years his racing editor had been Adrian Hunt, who gained notoriety after a boozy lunch at Ascot the *Telegraph* had organised for their amateur jump jockeys' championship. After the first race a well-refreshed Hunt had stumbled into a packed lift with the *Telegraph*'s main guest of the day, the great Seb Coe. As we came out of the lift Hunt turned to Coe and stammered, 'You made me the happiest man in the world when you beat that shit Coe in the Olympics.' He had mistaken Coe for Steve Ovett.

Because of the urgent need for afternoon deadlines, Christopher Poole's special talent was to ad-lib his reports from the track to copy-takers at breakneck speed, via his faithful telephone assistant Max Read. In those days all three London evening papers had telephone men; it seems another world from today's instant transmission of copy from a laptop.

After racing at Newmarket, Poole and I often visited the former five-times champion jockey and trainer Doug Smith at his home in Hamilton Road. Smith was not averse to a gin and tonic or two, and his wife Pat produced splendid cucumber sandwiches, which Poole readily attacked. Smith was a good contact for Poole, who broke many exclusive stories from their conversations, notably on Sleeping Partner, whom he saddled to win the 1969 Oaks. One day Poole phoned the Smith household and Pat told him that Doug had flown to France, and was about to sign up the jockey Sandy Barclay, the one-time wonderkid who had won the 1968 1,000 Guineas on Caergwrle and the 1970 Oaks on Lupe for Noel Murless. Poole duly launched the story, with an Exclusive tag on his back-page lead.

But Barclay was perfectly happy re-launching his career with the top French trainer Francois Boutin, and had turned Smith down flat. Imagine Smith's anger, then, when he arrived back at Heathrow and spotted a huge *Evening Standard* placard reading, BARCLAY SIGNS FOR SMITH – EXCLUSIVE.

The next day we were in the old press room at Ascot when the door flew open, and in walked the diminutive, trilby-topped figure of a furious Smith. He marched up to the 20-stone-plus Poole wagging his little finger. 'You've made me look a bloody fool' – he had to look up to speak to him – 'I shall never speak to you again.'

'Can I have that in writing?' Poole flashed back. Gin and tonics and cucumber sandwiches were off our Newmarket menu.

He was a stickler for the correct use of the English language. At the Old Bridge Hotel in Huntingdon, a scene of much revelry where Poole and I always stayed for Newmarket meetings, a youthful barman served him with his usual Campari and soda, and handed him his change with an innocent, 'There you go.'

'If I was going anywhere,' snapped Poole, 'I would not have ordered this drink.'

Or there was the time in the tree-lined paddock at Longchamp before an Arc de Triomphe when Poole spotted His Highness the Aga Khan and the well-connected *Daily Express* scribe Charles Benson walking towards us. 'Watch out,' he murmured: 'Here comes the Prince of Princes and the Pounce of Pounces!'

He had two strangely divergent interests: his beloved Wolfgang Amadeus Mozart, and Eastbourne Eagles speedway team. Poole was adamant that no proper music was ever written after Mozart's death. But he also loved musicals, and would hurtle up and down the motorways singing:

Everything is up-to-date in Kansas City
They've gone as far as they can go…

But for some obscure reason he also had an aversion to Vera Lynn, the Forces Sweetheart. We were speeding through Ditchling on our way from his home in Ringmer to Glorious Goodwood when a woman in a huge sunhat suddenly stepped off the pavement, and Poole had to swerve to avoid her. 'You do realise,' I told him: 'that was the one and only Vera Lynn?"

'Bugger!' he replied. 'Missed her!'

He was no stranger to a good row. Over the years I watched some splendid ones in the press room. When the *Daily Mail* took over the *Evening Standard* I had a feeling we were in for some fireworks. Sure enough, no sooner had Poole and I arrived at Newmarket the very day the merger was announced than he spotted the *Mail's* Colin Mackenzie on his *Standard* phone, and the blue touchpaper was lit. A big row erupted, and Mackenzie was physically threatened by Poole.

'I wouldn't try anything,' warned Colin. 'I was an Oxford University boxing blue.'

'That won't do you a lot of good when I kick you in the balls,' countered Christopher.

Poole had an aversion to racecourse jobsworths in white coats attempting to organise the press car parking facilities – especially at Doncaster, in the socialist state of South Yorkshire once dominated by Arthur Scargill. Over the years I witnessed many a heated row.

But the most vivid memory concerns the Cheltenham Festival. One day we dashed out before the last race to beat the crowd, only to find ourselves almost blocked in. Poole's temper quickly rose. I managed to guide the great man out, but he identified the offending car, which he was certain had been left by a bookmaker. Minutes later I heard a hissing noise… and then another. Poole was letting the car's tyres down. Why the need for two? I asked him as we drove away. Poole chortled. 'He won't have two spares.'

When it came to cigarette smoking I witnessed ructions galore, from England to France, and even America. Poole strongly objected to the strict PC 'no smoking' bans in public places. Once, when we were in a shop in Cambridge, he bought a packet of cigarettes and lit up, only for some little jobsworth to tell him, 'Please put that cigarette out.'

'So it's OK to sell cigarettes but not to smoke them?' retorted an angry Poole. 'Anyway, I didn't realise we were in an ammunition factory.'

As I mentioned, Poole was a Group 1 eater. One afternoon during a Cheltenham Festival he suddenly keeled over and collapsed on the floor. 'Bring him a double brandy!' yelled a colleague.

The great man gazed up at us. 'I'd rather have a pork pie.'

We were in Chicago for a Breeders' Cup meeting, which Poole adored, when he spotted a sign reading 'Maine lobsters, $10'. I was ordered to swing the hire car I was driving across a busy motorway, and minutes later he was polishing off an enormous lobster thermidor.

At the Old Bridge Hotel in Huntingdon one evening, I was enjoying a glass of wine on the veranda. 'Lovely wine,' I said.

'Yes,' said Chris. 'Twelve pounds.'

'That's good value for a bottle.'

'No,' he chuckled – 'it's twelve pounds a glass.' I was a quantity drinker; he was in the quality camp.

We went on a cricket tour of Devon, and Poole was umpiring one day when I came back on the field after a call of nature. 'You should see the spread the wives have laid on,' I told him – 'tons of local cream.'

At the end of the next over, still ten minutes to go before the interval, he took the bails off. 'That's tea, gentlemen.'

The night before Poole's funeral service at Hastings crematorium his son Simon rang me to say the vicar had stressed that my speech must be no longer than five minutes. I'd rehearsed it, and knew it was well over ten. Undaunted, I gave the packed congregation my full oration, which raised some laughs on a sad, sad day. 'You spoke for far too long,' the vicar told me as we were leaving the chapel, 'and now we have hearses stretching back to Bexhill… but I would not have missed your tribute for the world.'

OVER 47 YEARS I enjoyed nine racing editors at *The Sun* – all very different in background, enthusiasm and approach. The first was John Kendrick, a true Fleet Street legend who hailed from Leamington Spa in Warwickshire; any talk of the town's boxing hero Randolph Turpin would result in endless stories.

Kendrick could not have been more helpful when I became the new *Sun*'s racing correspondent. 'Make it swing, my son,' was his ever-cheerful message when I rang in each day at noon. Sometimes when I made my check call back in at six it was hard to believe I was speaking to the same man. By then refreshment had always been taken.

He addressed every barmaid in Fleet Street as 'Miss World'. His favourite ploy with Jock Hardie, then a sub-editor on *The Sun* before he became the columnist 'Templegate', was to enjoy a few pints in the Albion, or the Bell, or the Tipperary, and then tell the hapless Hardie, 'Pay the bill, Jock, and make sure you get me the receipt.' Those were the days, when many top journalists lived on their expenses, and never touched their wages.

But Kendrick's great flair, before he wandered down to the Albion pub at the bottom of Fleet Street for lengthy lunch sessions, was his ability to scheme pages. He was a great lay-out artist: many of my early racing features were enhanced by his magic touch. He could make pages come alive.

Jock Hardie had been taken on by Frank Nicklin from the *Greyhound* newspaper because he'd been a Bevin Boy during the war. He always seemed to be languishing at the bottom of the *Sporting Life* naps table, however, and Kelvin MacKenzie summoned him to Fleet Street with the intention of downgrading him back to the subs' desk. How long has Hardie been 'Templegate'? he enquired.

'Five years.'

'Well, it's not good enough,' said MacKenzie. 'Why should *The Sun*, with the biggest circulation in the country, be at the bottom of the naps challenge, while some unknown tipster from the *Blackpool Gazette* is top?'

But Hardie had been primed. 'It took Sir Gordon Richards 28 years before he finally won the Derby.' The answer earned him a year's stay of execution.

In the early days of *Sun* Racing we carried a daily cartoon with a tip for a horse, and Hardie was detailed to give the cartoonist, Gay Gordon, a selection of names he'd be able to draw. For the King of Clubs, for example, Gordon would draw a playing card of the Ace of Clubs with a crown on top. One day John Kendrick and I adjourned to the Albion pub for a two-hour lunch, to find on our return a frustrated Gay Gordon still looking at his brushes and inks and Hardie still engrossed in his formbook. An angry Kendrick ordered our hapless sub-editor to come up with a tip – any tip.

Eventually Hardie said, 'Can you draw Cala Mesquida?' – and Kendrick exploded. But Hardie had the last laugh – the next day Cala Mesquida won the Schweppes Hurdle at 33-1!

I liked Hardie: he was as honest as the day was long. He had trouble writing eye-catching intros, though, and on the eve of the 1976 2,000 Guineas he called me up for help. I asked him what his tip was. Predictably he had chosen the evens favourite Wollow, trained by Henry Cecil. I jotted down an intro: 'Whichever way you look at today's 2,000 Guineas it's got to be Wollow.'

Hardie was baffled.

'It's a palindrome,' I said: 'Wollow is spelt the same backwards.'

He still didn't get it.

'Tit,' I told him, 'is another palindrome.' Cue much laughter in the press room.

John Kendrick's first lieutenant, Roy Swann, an engaging character who went back to the days of the *Daily Herald*, once shared a room with him at the Adelphi Hotel on the eve of a *Sun*-sponsored Grand National. Kendrick's snoring could nearly be heard in Southport, and Swann decided to push his bed out into one of the vast corridors.

The next morning, a slumbering Kendrick still snoring his head off like a tractor, *The Sun's* editor Sir Larry Lamb was going down for breakfast. As he walked past, he turned to his wife and said, 'That bloke is the spitting image of my racing editor.' A few more paces, and he turned round and gasped. 'Christ – that *is* my racing editor!'

Kendrick's reign came to a sad end in 1973. Those were the days of hot metal newspaper production, and while he and a few like-minded revellers were up at Newmarket on the Friday afternoon to watch the Champion Stakes, a compositor on the stone reacted to a literal in a turn line by taking out two lines of copy, and *The Sun* was published on the Saturday without Harry Harriet, whose trainer Paddy Mullins had engaged the ace French jockey Yves Saint-Martin to ride it in the big race, in the race card.

It was Kendrick's ill fortune that the Irish raider duly won the Champion Stakes at 33-1. At the course I was buttonholed by angry *Sun* readers asking how a horse had won the Champion Stakes that was not even in the race. It was a fair question. In Fleet Street all hell broke loose on *The Sun/News of the World's* switchboard. Frank Butler, the *News of the World's* feisty sports editor, ran his Saturday afternoon copy times with military precision, but all his football scribes could not get through because of irate *Sun* punters blocking the lines.

In a subsequent *Sun* stewards' inquiry Kendrick was downgraded from the racing editor to a sports desk sub-editor. It didn't seem to worry him too much. Often he would catch a train up to London from his home in Peacehaven, get into a session in the buffet car with the barman, and decide to return to Sussex on the same train pleading a sickie. One morning, by virtue of a few sports desk absentees, he was promoted to attend the editor's 11 o'clock conference. Unabashed, he breezed in and announced, 'Well, you've had all the milk. Today you've got the cream.'

Noel Wilson had a short reign as racing editor. I always referred to him as 'My Hebrew friend', and it was very hard not to like him, although our partnership would surely have led to libel cases galore. I once did a story about the top trainers Richard Hannon, Michael Stoute and Luca Cumani winning all the big three-year-old Classic trials with horses that were not even entered in the Classics. On my way home from Newbury I made a check call, and Wilson said, 'I'm afraid your copy is a bit light – I've had to add a bit.' He sure did: before the names of all the big trainers in the intro he'd only added the word 'Dopey'. The last time I saw him he was leading round a horse he trained at my local Charing point-to-point.

From 2004 to 2014 the racing editor was Trevor Clements, who died tragically young in 2015 at the age of 51. We all loved Trevor, although he regularly drove us mad. He arrived at *The Sun* after serving the traditional journalist's background on the local paper, the *Whitehaven News*, in his native Cumbria, moving on to become sports editor of an Aberdeen evening newspaper, and then an award-winning reporter on Newcastle's *Sunday Sun*. He was a very talented journalist who excelled in writing splash headlines in our Favourite racing pull-out on a Saturday. On Monday I would put up an idea for a Saturday feature, and he would fire back immediately with a headline. Some of them were quite stunning.

For many years he ghosted the jockey John Francome and the top on-course bookie Barry Dennis for their popular columns in *The Sun*. Ghost-writing is quite an art, and when you read the Francome-Dennis articles you could actually hear them saying those words. 'He knew exactly what I was thinking about racing's big issues,' said Francome when he spoke at the thanksgiving service for Trevor, 'and made my words come to life. I trusted him totally.' Not that these columns were produced without a few scares.

For he was not the greatest timekeeper. Once he turned up in the office at three o'clock and a colleague asked, 'Are you late for the early shift, or early for the late shift?' He was famed for his Reggie Perrin-style excuses for the late trains he caught each day into London. 'Leaves on the line at Lingfield' or 'Staff shortages at Oxted' were often quoted. But his best was surely, 'Lions loose on the line at Chessington'. Yet the kind and ever-smiling Clements could be forgiven for almost anything.

Barry Dennis, therefore, always wanted Trevor to ring him early on a Friday morning. He was even keen enough to make a few notes through the week on various topics of the day. But often he'd find himself on his pitch at Newmarket or Sandown, surrounded by queuing punters about to bet on the first race, and his mobile would jingle into action. 'Hey, Barry!' would come a cheerful voice. 'Ready to do the column?'

Trevor used to tell his racing desk colleagues that he was just popping out to the local Waitrose supermarket. This was a coded message that he was going for a few pints in the nearby Cape pub. One Grand National day he nipped out as usual to 'the supermarket'. Actually he was in the Cape watching his beloved Liverpool on TV. Around five o'clock he wandered casually back to the office and asked, 'What won the Grand National?'

Sadly, Trevor never quite fulfilled his promise, and died suddenly of a heart attack at his home in Lingfield after watching Liverpool on TV in a nearby pub, leaving an ex-wife and two daughters. At his service of thanksgiving the famous journalists' cathedral St Bride's echoed to the strains of 'You'll Never Walk Alone'. 'He'd even have a funny line about his own funeral,' John Francome told the congregation. 'He should have been a comedian, and at one stage was brave enough to take part in stand-up pub competitions. Only a week before he died he sent me some cracking jokes on my mobile.'

But Jim 'Croc' McGrath summed up the story of Trevor's life best. 'In cricket terms Trevor played a lot of exciting shots when he was batting,' he said. 'He had tremendous flair. But, sadly, in the end he threw his wicket away.'

One *Sun* racing colleague I was never a fan of was the late Sir Clement Freud, whom I considered to be a highly odious creature. His son Matthew married Rupert Murdoch's daughter Elisabeth (they later divorced), and *Sun* Racing's Favourite pull-out was forced to use Freud's ghastly weekly racing column. Soon racing desk colleagues were being asked to accept reverse-charge calls from him from all over the world. He greeted the Grand National-winning amateur jockey Marcus Armytage for the first time with the words, 'You're a c***.' The ever-courteous Armytage still cannot get over the effrontery.

The racing editor entitled the column 'A Freudulent Slip', but the veteran politician and entertainer was quick to complain. 'If you carried a column from Michael Parkinson,' he protested, 'you wouldn't call it "Parkinson's Decease".' It had to be changed to 'A Knight at the Races.'

I once joined Freud at a pre-Christmas rugby club dinner in Dublin. The party revellers were soon getting pretty outrageous, and bread rolls were hurtling across the restaurant. Freud's after-dinner speech was not going well against this raucous din, and finally he turned to the chairman and moaned, 'I haven't been able to hear myself speak for the last twenty minutes.'

'Don't worry,' the chairman replied.' You haven't missed anything yet.'

When Freud died in 2009 there were countless fawning appreciations of him. I was persuaded to pen a glowing tribute in the Favourite, but the words did not come easily. His halo completely slipped when it was later alleged that he had been a child-abusing paedophile and rapist. He went from TV hero to zero, and his reputation was completely wrecked.

WHEN I ENTERED THE inner sanctum of the press room in the seventies, one of the greatest characters was Dickie Onslow, a much-admired journalist who, more importantly, became the sport's finest historian.

Bred in the purple himself, Onslow started work as an assistant to the keeper of the archives at York Minster. But years later, at his home at Windlesham, near Ascot, Onslow told me, with his memorable grin, 'the call of the local betting shop proved more vocational than the Minster.' He joined the staff of the northern-based *Sporting Chronicle*, and was then promoted to become the paper's important resident Newmarket racing correspondent, 'Old Rowley'.

When he first arrived, a mischievous local racing scribe approached the great trainer Sam Armstrong and told him, 'Did you know that Dickie Onslow comes from a very, very rich background and is dying to be asked to ride out for one of the major Newmarket strings?' Sadly, Armstrong took one look at a completely uncoordinated Dickie on one of his horses, and he was never invited to ride out again.

Armstrong, subsequently Lester Piggott's father-in-law, was known to have never missed a trick. Onslow referred to him as 'Slippery Sam'. In an imaginary world, ran one of his oft-repeated tales, if Adolf Hitler had won the Second World War, Armstrong would have been there at the White Cliffs of Dover to greet him with, 'I will train your horses, *mein Führer.*' He loved that story.

Onslow enjoyed the life in Newmarket, which was not confined to just one of the town's numerous pubs. Henry Cecil and his half-brother Arthur Boyd-Rochfort became lifelong friends, and together they all realised there was more to life than the 4.15 at Yarmouth. Tales of Onslow in Newmarket at this time were legion.

One of my all-time favourite racing stories came from Onslow, about a drunken session at Newmarket's Bushell pub, tucked away just off the high street. Much refreshment had been taken, and the landlord willingly agreed to an after-hours session. Around one o'clock in the morning a group of well-refreshed writers came up with the jolly jape – why don't we phone Sir Cecil Boyd-Rochfort?

Sir Cecil Boyd-Rochfort was not just any trainer. Eton-educated, from 1943 to 1968 he'd trained royal horses, and his lordly manner had earned him the nickname 'the Monument'. In his heyday Boyd-

Rochfort never gave press interviews, and nobody had the courage to even try to get an exclusive. As for being approached while riding his hack on the Newmarket gallops by modern media men, or in-your-face Matt Chapman with a microphone in his hand, he would surely have had a major heart attack. He was simply a total no-go area.

So picture the scene in the saloon bar of the Bushell well after midnight when, after a lengthy delay, the great trainer answered his telephone.

Boyd-Rochfort had several very wealthy American owners, which is why he fell for it when he was told, 'We have a transatlantic call from New York. To test the line will you please say, "My spotted dick hasn't got any custard."'

'My spotted dick hasn't got any custard,' muttered Boyd-Rochfort. He was asked to repeat it twice more. Then the hacks collapsed with laughter and put the phone down. Onslow dined out on that story for many years.

The PA's chief reporter Dai Davies loved to get under people's skin and had few friends and admirers, though his constant travelling companion, the *Sporting Life*'s top writer Len Thomas, an ex-Army major, was one of the most popular, sincere and helpful colleagues you could have wished for. They made an unlikely double act. 'Ah, Len,' Davies said as soon as he met me, 'here comes the bloody Frenchman.' When I laughed it off each time he soon got bored with it.

A staunch (or in certain matters not so staunch) Roman Catholic, Christopher Poole was a more formidable butt of Dai's waspish, so-called Welsh humour. This time it was, 'Hey, Len, here comes His Holiness. Forty Bloody Marys all round...' Poole put up with this almost daily insult for many months, until one especially hot day, in the tiny press room at Salisbury, he boiled over. He grabbed the Welshman by the collar and, until one or two of us spoilsports dived in and wrestled them apart, was about to throw him forcefully out of the window.

Robin Gray, the racecourse commentator, who also worked for the barmaids' bugle, the *Morning Advertiser*, and then the *News of the*

World, was a sitting target. An ex-male model, whose beaming face used to gaze down on us from a giant Guinness advert in the old Arkle Bar at Cheltenham, Gray was always immaculately turned out. He was happily married with children and seemed to trip through life. One day in the old Kempton press room he came dancing up the steps in his usual flamboyant style. Davies heralded his arrival with, 'Hey, Len, here comes the great ballet dancer Nijinsky.' That was too much for Gray, who proceeded to floor Davies with a right-hander Muhammad Ali would have been proud of.

I liked Gray, although he drove me mad by arriving so early at the races to hog *The Sun*'s telephone, claiming he was using it for early *News of the World* copy – 'Sorry, old Claude, but they want a big feature this Sunday.' I was never impressed.

Once, he was asked to name six jumpers to follow for the 1987–88 jumping season. He proudly picked out Neblin, whom Toby Balding had trained to win the 1987 Schweppes Gold Trophy at Newbury. 'We have not seen the best yet of Neblin,' he wrote. Unfortunately, Neblin had died some months earlier. Thereafter, Gray's best pal in the press room, John Garnsey of the *Daily Express*, nicknamed him Neblin. I thought it was terribly unkind – but bloody funny.

21

My Best Mate

TUESDAY, 1 NOVEMBER 2005 WAS TO be one of the darkest days of National Hunt racing I had to report on in my 47 years with *The Sun*.

Best Mate, the most popular chaser since the darling grey Desert Orchid, had started his fairytale career over the biggest obstacles back in October 2000, at the friendly Devon circuit of Exeter, where that day he beat the subsequent Grand National winner Bindaree.

Five years later over 5,000 – twice the normal attendance – packed into Exeter's grandstands for the William Hill Haldon Gold Cup Chase, as Best Mate, by now the magnificent triple Cheltenham Gold Cup hero, thought by some to even better than the immortal Arkle, off the course for ten months since his third Gold Cup win and looking superb, walked around the parade ring in his usual lordly fashion.

On a crisp autumn afternoon I stood with Best Mate's owner Jim Lewis and his charming wife Valerie as the large crowd only had eyes for one. 'Best Mate,' the racecourse announcer informed the excited racegoers, 'has won the prize for the best turned-out horse.'

I can clearly recall Jim Lewis's response: 'That's the kiss of death.'

Starting a generous 12-1 after his lengthy lay-off, Best Mate looked very comfortable in second place, and for most of the two-and-a-quarter-mile race there were no alarm bells ringing. But in the long back straight at Exeter his jumping, by his own immaculate standards, began to look a little ragged. Somehow I sensed that something was not right.

Paul Carberry, riding Best Mate for the first time, must have had a sixth sense that our one-time hero was not at his best. They went back in the field but, to his credit, Carberry did not press him, and eventually he pulled him up before the second last.

Best Mate walked in the direction of the last fence, but then suddenly staggered, and went down like a heavyweight boxing champion. It was all so quick. The dreaded screens were soon put up. Over the years I have witnessed many horses emerging from behind them to heartfelt applause from relieved racegoers. This was not such an occasion.

Best Mate's trainer Henrietta Knight could never watch him in his races. It became a big superstition. She only came out of her hiding place at Cheltenham to witness him galloping up the hill to clinch Gold Cup glory when she was sure he was going to win. At Exeter she had sneaked away and was watching from near the last fence.

The vets tried hard to revive him, but Best Mate literally died at her feet.

I recall walking down towards the stricken horse as Henrietta Knight's husband Terry Biddlecombe was coming back to the shocked grandstands. Tears streamed down Biddlecombe's rosy cheeks. This was the great tough guy, known as the Blond Bomber during his cavalier days as a champion jump jockey, who had broken 47 bones and suffered over 100 concussions. He just uttered, 'He's gone.'

In contrast, Henrietta Knight, the ex-schoolteacher, could not have been more stoical. I was amazed how she rose to the situation and dealt with the most difficult media attention of her life. That took real guts.

'I was thinking in the parade ring how well he looked,' she told me. 'Terry and I agreed that we had never had him looking better. Sadly, I have seen incidents like this in eventing. Horses wobble, and they go straight down. I knew the moment I dashed down and saw him that I was looking at a dead horse. I remember Major Dick Hern telling me, "When you've got livestock, you've got deadstock." Thankfully, Matey didn't suffer – he didn't die in a fall or break a leg. That would have been too terrible. He died doing what he enjoyed best.

He was truly a great horse, and we will all miss him terribly. He was chasing perfection.'

If Henrietta Knight put on an extremely brave face, Jim Lewis was equally controlled. 'I am the proudest man ever in racing,' he said with trembling emotion, fighting back the tears, 'just to have owned Best Mate.'

So many memories of that fateful day at Exeter come flooding back. Just 30 minutes after Best Mate's death, Henrietta Knight's Racing Demon won the next race, and she was cheered into the winner's enclosure like an Open champion approaching the 18th green. 'I have had so many good winners at Exeter over the years,' she told me, 'but I've never had such a reception as that.'

A double sadness emerged from that day. It was also the last time I chatted with Jim Lewis's wife Valerie. In June that year he had written to tell me she had been diagnosed with cancer of the pancreas. 'It's a bugger, isn't it?' she told me in her lovely Brummie accent when I met them at Exeter. Before the end of the year she had passed away.

The day after Best Mate's death a *Sun* editorial, under the headline, A LOST MATE, read:

Best Mate was one of those rare horses who captured the affection of millions. Not just because the triple Gold Cup champ put a few quid in our pockets – but because he showed character, and refused to be beaten.

In Henrietta Knight he also had a trainer who had the knack
of communicating her love of her wonder horse to millions on TV.
Mate's death left Henrietta distraught. Sun *readers share her tears.*

Jim Lewis asked for Best Mate's body to be buried at the course, on the outside of the track where he finally fell. Disgracefully, some health and safety jobsworth on Exeter Council blocked the idea. What a crazy world we live in.

It was in Newmarket-on-Fergus in County Clare in Ireland that the legend began. It is well documented that, after seeing Best Mate at Tom Costello's stables there, 'Hen' and Terry sent a fax to Jim and Valerie Lewis that read, 'We have just seen the horse of our dreams. He is the perfect racehorse and we would train him for nothing.'

Tom Costello was the legendary breeder who produced six Cheltenham Gold Cup winners: Midnight Court, The Thinker, Cool Ground, Cool Dawn, Imperial Call and Best Mate. Best Mate had been born unexpectedly in a field near Trim, County Meath on 28 January 1995 – his owner Jacques Van't Hart found him in a thin layer of snow, a tiny black foal amidst the white – and Costello had bought him as a foal at Fairyhouse in the November.

A one-time Birmingham newspaper boy, who even as a ten-year-old used to keep his customers waiting as he made his racing selections before putting the papers through their letterboxes, Jim Lewis had made his fortune importing pine and upholstered furniture from South Africa, where at one time he had as many as 20 horses in training. When he bought his first horse, Pearl Prospect, in the mid-1960s, he registered his colours of claret and blue stripes, as worn by his beloved Aston Villa when they beat Manchester United in the 1957 FA Cup Final. He always wore the claret and light blue scarf of Aston Villa when Best Mate ran.

It was a chance meeting with the French agent Pierre-Charles Le Metayer in the Newmarket sales car park that had started Jim's association with French-bred horses. In 1994 his Nakir won the Arkle

Chase at the Cheltenham Festival, and in 1998 Edredon Bleu the Grand Annual Chase, and two years later the Queen Mother Champion Chase. 'I was the last owner to receive the trophy from the Queen Mother,' says Lewis, 'and she was 100 years old.'

Best Mate eventually ran in a point-to-point at Lismore in County Wexford in February 1999. Short of work because of Ireland's rain-lashed gallops, he was pulled up by Tom Costello's son Tony. But Henrietta and Terry were there. Henrietta remembered 'a strange day in very heavy ground. Best Mate stood out in the paddock before the race, but had failed to finish. We had never been to Tom Costello's establishment, but made a point of viewing Best Mate on our next visit to Ireland.' A week later, in a two-horse point-to-point at Tuam in County Clare, Best Mate beat Michael Hourigan's much fancied Well Then Now Then by a runaway eight lengths.

'We flew to Ireland,' Lewis recalls, 'and I could see why "Hen" and Terry were so excited. He looked superb. I went off with Tom Costello, and I remember saying to him, "I know you're going to break my heart – and my bank balance." Tom stressed, "I will only sell Best Mate to you if you never disclose the final price." We shook hands on the deal, and I never told even "Hen" and Terry what I paid. Tom said to me the only reason he sold him to me was he thought nobody would train Best Mate as well as Henrietta. It was a tremendous gamble, really.'

On 1 April 1999 Best Mate arrived at West Lockinge Farm in Oxfordshire, a unique place full of chickens, ducks and horses... and racing's Odd Couple: the former girls' school teacher, and the blunt-talking, ex-alcoholic, three times champion jockey who rode 908 winners, including the 1967 Gold Cup winner Woodland Venture. Henrietta, six years younger, had stood by the last fence at Cheltenham and watched her idol fearlessly delivering the goods so often before his adoring Gloucestershire public; Terry was Hen-pecked for years and loved every minute until his death at 72 in January 2014. 'They were not the Odd Couple at all,' Jim Lewis always said. 'They were simply madly in love with each other.'

It may have begun on April Fools' Day, but from then on it was only the bookies who were made to look fools by the majestic chaser's succession of big race wins. Best Mate made his debut at Cheltenham in November 1999 and won a bumper race at 10-1. 'He ran at Cheltenham a total of six races,' his cool jockey Jim Culloty was honest enough to admit, 'and I think he should have won them all. I still maintain he should have won the Supreme Novices' Hurdle at the Festival in 2000.

'We crawled for a mile and a half, so it became a sprint finish. I got tapped for toe. Best Mate was a bit slow over the third last hurdle and I should have been handier. Then I had nowhere to go and I was caught a bit flat-footed.' In the end Best Mate went down by half a length to give Noel Meade his first Festival winner with Sausalito Bay. Sporting as ever, Henrietta Knight refused to blame her jockey.

Culloty never had to worry about Best Mate at Cheltenham again. In 2002 he won his first Gold Cup by a length and a half from Commanche Court, and with his background became very much the people's horse. Afterwards Ladbrokes made Best Mate 12-1 to win the next two Gold Cups.

After Best Mate won his first Gold Cup, Doug Ellis, the chairman of Aston Villa, invited Jim Lewis to parade his glittering trophy at Villa Park. 'Can you imagine,' he smiles: 'an old age pensioner running around the ground like a kid with the trophy in front of all the Villa fans! I loved it, and I got a terrific reception. When I paraded in front of the Holte End of the pitch, where I used to stand on the terraces as a child, I spotted a huge banner which read, "Best Mate is a Villa Fan".'

'If I was confident that I would win in 2002,' says Culloty, 'I was absolutely certain Best Mate would win in 2003. I told everybody that Matey would win – quite simple. On the day he was brilliant, and was as easy a winner as I have ever ridden.' He beat Truckers Tavern comfortably by ten lengths.

Before the 2004 race nearly 800 good luck cards arrived at Knight's stables for Best Mate. He was a red-hot, odds-on favourite to bridge the 38-year gap since Arkle won the third of his three Gold Cups, but he still had 22 fences to negotiate. On 18 March a sell-out crowd of 60,000 roared Best Mate on as he strode up the famous Cheltenham hill to pip Andrew Thornton on the 33-1 outsider Sir Rembrandt by half a length. He had joined Arkle (1964–1966) and Cottage Rake (1948–1950) as hat-trick winners. Between 1932 and 1936 Golden Miller, of course, had triumphed five times. 'I went round the inside,' said Jim Culloty, 'which is always a gamble, because you are not guaranteed a clear run. This was the Gold Cup, and no quarter was given at any stage, but Best Mate showed great battling qualities to win.'

The reception Best Mate enjoyed brought back memories of Dawn Run and her excited Irish supporters after the mare won the 1986 Gold Cup. 'Coming to the last fence I was certain he would be beaten,' Henrietta Knight confessed, 'but his win is the biggest relief in the world.' Amazingly, Best Mate's third Gold Cup win made him only the fifth winning favourite in the previous 22 years.

Jim Lewis described himself as 'walking in paradise. We saw another side of Best Mate this time. He is a streetfighter.'

Sadly, Best Mate was denied a fourth crack at the blue riband when he broke a blood vessel on Mick Channon's gallops shortly before the 2005 Gold Cup, and did not run. I rang Henrietta, and as usual she was very calm. 'It was better that it happened on the gallops and not at Cheltenham. At the time I thought the world had come to an end. But he's like my husband Terry – he frequently has nosebleeds but keeps coming bouncing back.' Yet again I reflected on how Henrietta's 'kid-glove' tactics had contributed hugely to Best Mate's success. Some other trainers would have over-raced him, and no doubt paid a big penalty. Manifesto, the greatest jumper in the Victorian era, raced for 13 seasons. But in all he only had 35 races – less than three a season. Best Mate won 14 of his 22 races, and was second in seven of them. The only time he was out of the first two was that finale race at Exeter.

After Best Mate's third Gold Cup triumph, the *Racing Post* devoted much space to the old question: who was the better chaser – Arkle or Best Mate?

Terry Biddlecombe, who loved being controversial, soon weighed in. 'Best Mate would have beaten Arkle out of sight. He had much more class and speed. What's all this bloody fuss about Arkle anyway? He was nothing more than a relentless galloper. Best Mate won three Gold Cups and beat 400 other horses. Arkle may have also won three Gold Cups but he beat a total of only ten rivals, and the biggest field he ever took part in was the five-runner race for his last Gold Cup win in 1966.'

'It's very hard to compare horses from different generations,' reflected David Elsworth, who was involved in racing all through the Arkle era. 'Henrietta Knight was often criticised for never running Best Mate in handicaps and subjecting him to conceding lumps of weight. That was her style, and I don't believe any other trainer could have produced Best Mate to win three successive Gold Cups.'

'Arkle was always the first consideration of his trainer and owner,' observed Sir Peter O'Sullevan. 'It's exactly the same thing with Best Mate. It is very seldom that you get perfect marriages in racing between owners, trainers and horses. They have both been lucky in that respect.'

Last words are with Jim 'Lucky' Lewis, for whom 'Matey' won over £1 million: 'Arkle was a jumping god, and I hope that Best Mate will now be standing up there next to him – two gods together.'

I wouldn't bet against it.

22

Characters

'ISN'T GOD GREAT?' SAID Father Breen to me once: 'I am the only parish priest with two jump tracks in my parish.' He meant Punchestown and Naas.

Ireland's racing priest, Father Sean led the annual pilgrimage to the Cheltenham Festival. 'Only the lid of my coffin will stop me from coming over,' he declared. 'All my parishioners know that each March I will be away for four days visiting my Gloucestershire diocese.' In the old days the holy fathers in their dog collars almost outnumbered the punters. 'It isn't like that now,' noted Breen ruefully. 'Once the bishops thought it was wrong and evil for us to go racing. I bought a horse with another priest, but we didn't want the bishops to know anything about it. So we called him Nobody Knows. Our secret was kept for years. But there is nothing in the Bible to say you should not gamble.'

Services at the Church of the Immaculate Conception at Ballymore Eustace in County Kildare were always packed, and, a canny tipster, Breen even gave the congregation at Mass every Sunday the benefit of his betting forecasts. 'If you have a bet,' he always stressed, 'stick to your first choice. Never change your mind. It's fatal. And always gamble only what you can afford to lose.' His knowledge of the form book almost equalled that of the Bible. 'Many people think I have a hotline to heaven,' he said, claiming that, over 40 years, most of his Cheltenham Festival ante-post selections ended up in the winner's enclosure. 'Everybody thought the Good Lord was on our side when Prolan won the 1976 Kim Muir. I told all my congregation to back him, and he was heavily gambled down to 3-1 second favourite. But he made a terrible mistake at the last fence, recovered and just held on by three-quarters of a length to hold off Gylippus. God was definitely on our side that day.' In 2004 he also told everybody that Hardy Eustace would win the first of his two Champion Hurdles at 33-1. 'I once nearly won a £1 million pound jackpot at Cheltenham,' he told me. 'I had five winners and the sixth horse finished second.'

In 2005 he recommended his congregation to back Cardinal Ratzinger at 13-2 to become the next Pope. 'Quite a few lads were on, and I was very popular when the white smoke finally filtered out of the Vatican chimney. But, of course, I did not back him out of reverence.'

When St Patrick's Day (17 March) fell during Festival week, Breen always said Mass for Irish punters at Cheltenham's nearby Golden Valley Hotel. One year, sensing that Irish horses would have several winners, he even prayed that the English bookies would have enough money to pay out the shamrock punters. 'I always used to bless horses for Ted Walsh, Willie Mullins and Dessie Hughes before they left for Cheltenham,' he told me. 'I blessed Kicking King for Tom Taaffe before he won the Cheltenham Gold Cup in 2005. Perhaps my prayers were answered, as he'd been second in the 2003 Supreme Novices' Hurdle and the 2005 Arkle Chase. But I don't do that now – you feel a bit of a fool if they go and get beaten. I just pray now that they will all come back in one piece.'

Breen was a very engaging character. I first met him in the late 1970s at Dublin's Burlington Hotel. At the time he was very friendly with the local trainer Bill Durkan, who combined a successful construction firm with running horses from his Carrowkeel Stud at Sandyford, high in the hills above Leopardstown. I recall one splendidly convivial dinner when Durkan studied the menu and said, 'I'm thinking of having the sole.'

At the other end of the table Breen grinned: 'I'm looking after your soul, Bill.'

Durkan struck gold in the Dublin hills with his top-class mare Anaglogs Daughter, who made all to win the 1980 Arkle Chase at the Cheltenham Festival by an unchallenged 20 lengths. She was some performer, never looked like a novice, and Tommy Carberry was able to absolutely throw her at the fences. It was quite a party that evening at the Queen's Hotel, and Breen was much to the fore, having advised everybody to back Anaglogs Daughter when she was a generous 7-1 in the ante-post market.

Breen was so popular in racing circles that he even had a horse named after him – The Breener, which became the first winner trained by Oliver Sherwood, who won the 2015 Grand National with Many Clouds. The Breener won the Challow Hurdle at Newbury, and finished third in the Supreme Novices' Hurdle.

I once had a spot of trouble getting into Leopardstown races – despite my displaying my English press badge a female jobsworth was being as unhelpful as she could. Thankfully, at that very moment I spotted the beaming face of Father Breen behind me in the queue. The dog-collared priest saved the day. 'I can vouch for him – it's *The Sun*'s devil himself.'

The Father was no horseman, though. On one occasion he did ride out at Phoenix Park for the trainer Joanna Morgan, wearing a large black mackintosh: the horse bolted and threw his passenger, who suffered a broken leg.

I rarely heard Father Breen criticise anybody, but in one of my annual pre-Cheltenham Festival interviews with him he claimed that Cheltenham's managing director Edward Gillespie wouldn't give him his usual free badges that year – 'after all the publicity I have given the meeting. The devil. I shall be having a word with my guv'nor about him!'

When he died in 2009 at the age of 72, a huge congregation turned out. The Mass lasted over two hours. There were 37 priests concelebrating.

TIM BROOKSHAW

'I'll sign all the expenses,' my sports editor Frank Nicklin used to say when *The Sun* took its usual table at the Horserace Writers' Association lunch at the Dorchester – 'but only if Tim Brookshaw is there.' Nicklin was an ex-fighter pilot who had shown great bravery in his younger days but, having met Brookshaw many times, he rated him as one of the most heroic sportsmen he had ever come across.

In 1964, at the age of 34, Brookshaw had been stretchered away from one of Aintree's minor meetings after a horror fall from the inaptly named Lucky Dora. He had already broken his collarbone six times, both legs, and his nose and ankles twice, but breaking his back meant his career was over. He was paralysed from the waist downwards; doctors told him he would never walk again. But they did not know the inner strength of Tim Brookshaw.

In those days there was no compensation for jockeys whose careers had come to an abrupt and sad end. It was Brookshaw's injury, and that of Paddy Farrell, which inspired the then John Lawrence, later Lord Oaksey, and the ex-jump jockey Jack Berry to form the Injured Jockeys Fund.

Even though Brookshaw was wheelchair-bound he took out a trainer's licence, and in the early 1970s I visited him at his stables at Tern

Hill Farm in Shropshire. He used to have a strange habit of greeting you with a cheery, 'How now, brown cow?' I can still recall watching in a barn as Brookshaw, brave as a lion, arranged for a pulley and hoist so he could be lifted aboard his horses. It was a fascinating manoeuvre. Despite his cruel disability he was quite determined to ride again. He even took part in a jockeys' showjumping competition in Ireland and rode in a veterans' charity race there. 'I was actually stopped for speeding the other day,' he told me once. 'The policemen didn't realise I was using my walking stick on the accelerator pedal and it had got stuck.'

So no man ever walked into the Dorchester, with the aid of a walking stick, with his head held higher. He beamed across the room; he was so proud of his annual reunion with Frank Nicklin.

Before his career-ending fall he displayed wonderful talents as a jockey. Many top riders like John Francome, Stan Mellor, Jeff King, Terry Biddlecombe, Jonjo O'Neill and Peter Scudamore never won the Grand National despite numerous attempts. But arguably Brookshaw was the unluckiest jockey never to win the National.

Six times between 1950 and 1958 he rode in the race. But in those days he was usually partnering a no-hoper, and he completed the course only once. In 1959, however, he seemed destined to end his hoodoo when he partnered the 10-1 fourth favourite Wyndburgh, who had finished second behind Sundew in 1957 and fourth in 1958, when the race was won by the Irish-trained Mr What.

Brookshaw and Wyndburgh, a little brown gelding trained in Scotland by Ken Oliver, were travelling like a dream, challenging with Michael Scudamore and Oxo for the lead, until they reached Becher's on the second circuit. On the landing from Becher's, Brookshaw's off-side stirrup iron snapped. 'With no control of the off-side I had to take my legs out of the other iron,' he told me years later, with not a hint of self-pity or bitterness, 'or I would have had no balance at all. I was determined to keep going, and Wyndburgh was a very safe jumper.

'But I can remember shouting across to Michael Scudamore, "Look! – no feet!" plus a few choice words. I asked what I should do, and he replied, "Please yourself!"'

'I then had to ride over eight fences and a mile and a half without the use of stirrups. In the end Michael and Oxo just pipped me by a length and a half. I can't believe there was an unluckier loser than Wyndburgh. To get so close with my legs out of the irons was a miracle.' Brookshaw then produced the shiny broken stirrup, still chortling away.

That same season, to ease the pain of Wyndburgh's heartbreaking National, Brookshaw was crowned champion jockey with 83 winners. 'At the height of my career I was riding for £6 a race,' he told me. 'I used to love meeting the Irish priests at Cheltenham and Aintree – they always had the funniest dirty stories. In my day there was great camaraderie in the weighing-room, and there was only one jockey who would try to pinch rides by ringing up trainers. One day I was asked to ride a two-bob blighter down in the West Country. The trainer said if I didn't take the ride he would ask the number one ride-nicker. I was so determined to outdo him that I accepted and travelled hundreds of miles for the one ride. Ruddy funny, really – I fell at the first and broke my leg in four places.

'I really loved the National, and I remember crouching in Becher's Brook after a fall while half the horses were flying over my head. I was just happy to take part.' In 1961 he was sixth on Wyndburgh; a year later, eleventh on Eternal. Wyndburgh was the only horse to finish third in three Grand Nationals. Ironically, Brookshaw had previously partnered Nicolaus Silver, but warned Fred Rimell that he thought the grey was too cautious for the dreaded Aintree fences. In 1961 the grey won it with Bobby Beasley on top. But two years later Brookshaw did win the 1963 Scottish Grand National on Pappageno's Cottage.

At our last London awards lunch I asked him if he would like to ride in one final Grand National. 'I'd be daft enough to do so,' he said immediately. 'Even now.' My last memory of this bravest of brave men was his ever-cheerful figure waving his walking stick in Park Lane to hail a taxi.

JOHN MANNERS

There can hardly ever have been a bigger character in horse racing than 'Good Manners'. In a sometimes over-stuffy sport John Manners was a breath of fresh air. During my long and always fascinating career in racing, this eccentric trainer was one of the funniest characters I ever encountered. After hard days spent working and socialising at the Cheltenham Festival, one morning spent with the colourful Manners was like a tonic. I drove home still chuckling at his antics.

Born in 1926, he was only six months old when his father bought the 400-acre Common Ground near Highworth, on the Wiltshire outskirts of Swindon, where he remained to his dying days. John's father was convinced that Adolf Hitler would invade Wiltshire, and often went on guard with a shotgun in the clock tower.

Manners bred many horses for himself, and called them names like Fox John, No John No, Dashing John, Hi Johnny and Rustic John. John McCririck was brave enough to interview Manners on TV at Windsor one day and call him Rustic John.

He had several quirky traits. He would always give his horses their main feed between midnight and 1 a.m., and was often seen mowing his grass in the middle of the night wearing only his long johns and guided by a torch attached to the front of the mower. A Cognac-lover, he used to have porridge in bed every morning, and never got up before ten o'clock. I was fascinated by him.

In 1982 the splendid Audrey finally persuaded Manners to marry her at Swindon Registry Office. Under his suit, Manners was in full hunting gear. Mrs Manners' first job as his wife was to drop him off at a nearby pub, where the Vale of the White Horse Hunt was meeting. His hunting hat was full of confetti, and the happy gathering realised that at long last Manners had tied the knot. Manners was always late for hunt meetings.

After one Cheltenham Festival I arranged to see him at his stables on my way back to Kent. It was a meeting I will take with me to the grave.

The stables looked more like the setting from *The Darling Buds of May*. Manners emerged from a rather dilapidated barn, put his hand to his mouth and dashed off into his farmhouse without saying a word. *The Sun* photographer and I were somewhat confused. Eventually Manners re-emerged. 'Sorry, Mr Claude Duval, but I didn't have my teeth in.' For years he always hailed me as 'Mr Claude Duval'.

He was no bad trainer. His beloved horse Cavalero ran 30 times, winning eight races worth £63,456. In 1998 he won the Fox Hunters' Chase at Aintree at 33-1, beating the 3-1 favourite, JP McManus's Elegant Lord. In December that year, Manners was out in the pitch dark with Cavalero when he dismounted to open a gate and the horse bolted. There was a serious search for him before he was found by torchlight grazing innocently by a stream. Two years later Manners had his finest hour when the same horse won the Foxhunter Chase at the Cheltenham Festival at 16-1 by three-quarters of a length from Real Value.

In the 1998 Grand National, Killeshin, whom Manners had bought for 1,200 guineas, was sixth behind Earth Summit at 25-1, having been seventh behind Lord Gyllene a year earlier at 33-1. He won five of his 43 races, earning £61,186, and his greatest achievement was winning the 1994 Fox Hunters' Chase at Aintree at 8-1, beating 27 rivals. These three big race wins were the pinnacle for the extraordinary Manners.

But predictably he had his own maverick take on it all. 'The way some of the trainers prepare their horses is a joke,' he told me. 'I just gallop them myself round our 400 acres, and sometimes I gallop them on neighbours' farms when they're not looking. I used to take my horses to Lambourn to jump a few fences. It does horses good to have a ride in a lorry.' He used to ride all his horses himself, but 'it was like my riding career in point-to-points,' he confessed: 'I rode them until they got tired, and then they'd fall arse over head.'

He loved his nickname. But more often he was known as 'Bad Manners'. He had constant battles with the iron fist of the Jockey Club, and went to their then Portman Square HQ on frequent occasions. But he was able to laugh about it all. Of course he sailed close to the rules, but no lives were ever lost, and unlike some silver spoon merchants he never took a pot of gold out of racing. 'I'm a farmer who had just trained a few horses for fun,' he told me, seated in his kitchen surrounded by pictures galore of his point-to-point triumphs. 'I'm not a rogue, Mr Claude Duval. You interview far bigger villains than me every day.'

In 1982 he was fined £82 by the Cheltenham stewards for running onto the course after his horse Knight Of Love had cleared the last fence to win. 'I jumped over the running rail and followed him up the straight, waving and tossing my trilby into the air.'

He once tried to name a horse Bigandard, claiming that it was the name of a romantic Austrian village where he had met his wife Audrey, but the Jockey Club saw through this jolly jape and it was rejected. The JC spent many hours trying to keep up with the mercurial Manners.

'I admit I had a spot of bother in 1989 fiddling around with the weights,' he went on. He had trained a horse called Voices Of Spring to win a point-to-point at Siddington, near Cirencester. 'I didn't want the horse to win, and I didn't put any weights in the weight cloth. It all went horribly wrong – the bloody horse won, and they discovered afterwards the horse wasn't carrying weight. The Jockey Club warned me off for three years. I was stupid. I'd been fiddling about for years with horses' weight cloths but this was the first time I was found out.

'I later named a horse Spambruco after the three top Jockey Club officials who had warned me off. Spam was for the Dewhurst meat baron Lord Vestey, Bru for Bruce Hobbs, and Co for Robert Waley-Cohen. I got the name through Weatherbys, and the snooty Jockey Club officials didn't realise it was all a leg-pull.

'When I won the first of my two Fox Hunters' Chases at Aintree in 1994 with Killeshin, many people came up to me to congratulate me in the winner's enclosure. Then I realised that three of them were the same buggers who had previously warned me off! I thought that was a bit bloody rich.'

In this particular interview Manners was firing on all cylinders, and I could barely keep up with his quickfire quotes on virtually everything in life. He barely drew breath, except to say to his wife Audrey, 'Pour Mr Claude Duval another large gin.' When I suggested that my photographer had been waiting quite some time for a snap of the great man, he disappeared again.

Minutes later, he emerged in his yard dressed fully in his hunting outfit. In red hunting jacket and black cap, the shabby old farmer had been transformed into a vivid incarnation of what Oscar Wilde famously described as 'the unspeakable chasing the uneatable'.

His last stable jockey, Alex Charles-Jones, used to drive him to the races. 'He would say he was going to fall asleep and would not be a very entertaining passenger. Yet he always talked the entire journey – and all the way back. He had so many hilarious stories, and he never repeated himself. He was an excellent trainer, and an outstanding stockman.'

He was still riding out on his beloved horses until six months before his death in September 2009 at the age of 83.

The last time I saw him was at Towcester, where he was his usual playful self. The previous race had been a selling hurdle, and we stood by the edge of the winner's enclosure as some poor beast was put up for auction. Once again I was somewhat baffled by Manners, who seemed to have developed a strange facial twitch. He kept it up for some minutes before I twigged that he had the secret eye of the auctioneer, and was making hidden bids for the selling race winner. 'Stop it!' his long-suffering wife Audrey told him after countless twitches. 'Don't you think we have enough horses already?'

HUGO BEVAN

Hugo Bevan was a class act as clerk of the course at several tracks, including Worcester and Huntingdon. One day an attractive woman, a permit trainer in Suffolk, telephoned him on his mobile to find out the likely going at Worcester for a jumping fixture. 'My pride and joy is a hunter-chaser,' she said, 'but he must have some give in the ground.'

'Oh, there are no problems at Worcester,' Bevan reassured her in his usual gushing way. 'It's right by the River Severn, and we can always water the track to take any possible sting out of the ground. I look forward to your horse running at my track.'

What the trainer did not know was that when Bevan answered his mobile he was actually up to his chest in the River Tay fishing for salmon. But his reply worked, and the meeting at Worcester duly kicked off.

Unfortunately, the predicted watering had not taken place, and after just one race Bevan was forced to change the official going from good to soft, to good to firm. Chaos reigned, and several soft ground specialists were withdrawn.

I was in the weighing-room when the Suffolk trainer stormed in. 'You are a total disgrace!' she shouted at an embarrassed Bevan. 'I shall be reporting you to the Jockey Club for your complete incompetence. I shall also be suing Worcester and demanding that all the sizeable horsebox transport charges will be refunded to me. I can't believe you could have got today's official going so blatantly incorrect! You have not heard the last of this fiasco.' By now a large crowd had gathered in the weighing-room to see Bevan on the end of a very one-sided ear-bashing.

Eventually the woman had no more insults to hurl at him. There was a moment's silence. Then Bevan said, 'I suppose a blow job's out of the question?'

NEVILLE CRUMP

My attempt to interview Neville Crump in 1970 – one of the first racing personalities I approached – did not start well.

'I'm Claude Duval of *The Sun*', I said when I telephoned him.

'Never heard of you,' barked Crump.

Having overcome the terrors of Captain Ryan Price, I was determined to win over another ex-army captain, and especially one who had trained three Grand National winners, with Sheila's Cottage (1948), Teal (1952) and Merryman II (1960). So eventually I made the long journey to his Warwick House stables at Middleham in North Yorkshire and, once you had broken through the initial armoury, Crump, like Price, was kindness itself. Their bark was far worse than their bite.

Vincent O'Brien won the Grand National with three different horses – Early Mist, 1953, Royal Tan, 1954 and Quare Times, 1955. But trainer George Dockeray won it four times, including the first running with Lottery in 1839. Fred Rimell and Ginger McCain trained four National winners.

Born in Kent, Crump went to Marlborough and Balliol, Oxford before joining the cavalry section of the 4th Hussars. After Sheila's Cottage became the first mare to win the Grand National since Shannon Lass in 1902, four years later he followed up with Teal, whose claim to fame is that the radio commentator announced that he had fallen at the very first fence. When his 13-2 favourite Merryman II won the first televised National in 1960 by a runaway fifteen lengths as the first Scottish-bred winner, Crump had trained three National winners in twelve years. 'This is the best Liverpool horse I have ever trained,' he insisted.

Up on his windswept gallops in 1970 I could sense Crump's immense pride as he prepared Permit to attempt a fourth Grand National win. (The horse was subsequently brought down.)

Then suddenly, to our complete surprise, over the brow of the hill came about 200 camera-clicking Japanese tourists. Their spokesman approached the great trainer. 'Captain, can you please tell us the way to Middleham Castle?'

'You found bloody Pearl Harbor,' roared Crump, 'so you can find f***ing Middleham Castle on your own!'

23

Fergie's Great Relaxation

IT WAS A CHANCE INVITATION FROM Mike Dillon into Ladbrokes' private box at the Cheltenham Festival in March 1997 which sparked Alex Ferguson's love affair with racing. He went with his wife Cathy, noticed that Sparky Gayle was trained in Scotland, backed him as 3-1 favourite for the Cathcart Chase, and the horse won easily by four lengths.

Ferguson enjoyed the Cheltenham experience so much that he told Mike Dillon he would one day like to own a horse of his own. '"Don't do it," he said,' Ferguson told me later. '"It's the quickest way to tear £50 notes in half." But I used to see the trainer Jack Berry at Manchester Airport, and I asked him to buy a yearling for me. Nothing happened, but later, when we were off to Europe one day, I bumped into him again at the airport.

'What about that horse for me? I said. He replied, "I thought you were joking." Later Queensland Star became my first horse – he was named after a ship my father helped to build – and he duly trotted up on his debut at Newmarket in 1998. Then I had another winner, Candleriggs, who was named after a neighbourhood in Glasgow. I later sold him for 40,000 guineas and he was trained in Ireland by Dermot Weld. I was tempted to buy back a share, but there must never be any sentiment in racing – or football. You must always take a profit when you can.'

Then the Coolmore boss John Magnier offered Fergie a part-share in his flying two-year-old Rock Of Gibraltar. The horse won the 2001 Gimcrack Stakes at York, and Fergie was due to be the speaker at the famous dinner in front of the local landed gentry like Lords Halifax, Grimthorpe, Manton and Zetland.

I flew up to Manchester with Mike Dillon, watched United play an evening European Cup tie, and arranged to meet the great manager afterwards at the Manchester Airport Hilton. I was surprised by the change in character of the man I had just seen parading on the touchline at Old Trafford. Fergie was famous for his after-match dressing-downs after lacklustre performances – what the former United striker Mark Hughes called 'the hairdryer'. 'There's nothing worse,' confirmed Wayne Rooney. David Beckham had once had to duck to avoid a flying teacup. Fergie even named a horse Hairdryer, who knocked at the door but whose only early victory came on the Chelmsford all-weather in November 2016.

So I asked Fergie why he looked so angry during United's games. 'Unlike some other managers I've never taken notes during matches,' he explained. 'I have to get everything into my head, so I really have to concentrate. If I only get 99% right at the half-time team talk, then I've failed. It's not a time to get it wrong.'

Sir Alex seldom got it wrong. Scotland produced legendary football managers: Jock Stein, Bill Shankly, Matt Busby – and Fergie, who managed Manchester United from 1986 to 2013 and is widely accepted as the most successful football manager of all time. In his 26 years at Old Trafford he won 38 trophies, including 13 Premier League titles, five FA Cups and two UEFA Champions League titles.

He was knighted for his services to football in the 1999 Queen's Birthday Honours list, and turned up at Buckingham Palace proudly wearing a Ferguson tartan kilt.

Memories still come flooding back from when I was lucky enough to be invited to Fergie's private 'holy of holies' room after many European Cup evenings at Old Trafford, when he was surrounded by his old friends from Aberdeen, who always flew down from Scotland. 'When Fergie managed Aberdeen, it was like Christmas every day of the year for us,' one of them told me. 'We worshipped him.'

Now at the Hilton he was relaxed. 'When I was growing up in Govan I never dreamed that one day I'd be making the Gimcrack speech,' he confided. 'Back in those days the only horse I ever saw was a one-eyed beast called Fletcher who pulled the coalman's cart. My father did a tenner on the horses every Saturday. So did my mother. She would get me to find out which horses my father had backed and then select different horses. That was my first involvement with racing.' It's no surprise that a working-class background like his has left him with a socialist outlook. He was embarrassed, he told me, when his jockeys used to doff their caps to him before races. 'It reminds me of the bad old days when people's employees were so subservient.'

He was taking his Gimcrack speech very seriously, he said, 'as I know that every word will be well documented. I feel a bit like the Christmas turkey – I just hope I don't get stuffed. My biggest worry is that I shall be delivering my speech in Scottish. I hope they understand me...'

Then he went on to reveal how finding an interest in horse racing had helped his managerial career. 'A lot changed for me in my final years with Manchester United. There was a time when I was totally and utterly obsessed with Manchester United, but when I got into racing it became my great relaxation. It was only because of my racing hobby that I was able to stay at Old Trafford for all those final years.

'At the races I am usually left alone. People don't want to talk to me about football, but about which horse is going to win the next race.

When I was a manager and we had suffered a bad defeat, going to the races got the disappointment out of my mind.

'It's funny to think back to the days when Bryan Robson was our star player. One year he begged me to give him the afternoon off so he could go to the Cheltenham Gold Cup. I was far from happy, as we had a big game on the Saturday. I delayed the training session in the morning on purpose, so that by the time we finished it was too late for him to get to Cheltenham. Later we would have been in the same car dashing off to the races!

'Football is all wrapped up in emotion and the rivalry between supporters, which is often very fierce. Fans love chanting. That's what it's all about – tribalism. It's been handed down from fathers to sons. But racing is different. We're all there to enjoy the spectacle, but we're all united in trying to beat the bookmakers. There's a wonderful camaraderie between people in racing. I absolutely adore it. I'm very pleased to be a new boy in racing. Often a newcomer can spot the most obvious. I have found that there's more heart in jump racing than the Flat. I never thought you could beat Cheltenham for atmosphere until I came to Aintree!'

At one stage Fergie even dreamed of a Manchester United Supporters Club racing syndicate buying yearlings and having a set of horses in training. I gave his ideas some publicity in *The Sun* with an exclusive interview, under the headline, I CAN WIN THE DERBY – AND I'M NOT TALKING ABOUT MAN CITY. As Sir Peter O'Sullevan once said to me, 'You don't do things by half on the *Sun*.'

In September 2002, the day after one of my midweek visits to Old Trafford, John Francome, Mike Dillon and myself were invited by Sir Alex Ferguson on an exclusive tour round Manchester United's ultra-modern Carrington Road training centre. It was a real privilege to see Fergie's superstars being put through their paces, under the ever-watchful eye of their track-suited manager in his see-all office, and fascinating to see the special health foods being provided for the millionaire players. In the medical block Paul Scholes was being treated for a recent knee injury, and was quick to ask the three racing enthusiasts if the boss's horse (Rock Of Gibraltar) was worth more than Rio Ferdinand!

It was a good question. Rio had cost Manchester United £30 million, but it was estimated that Rock Of Gibraltar would earn far more in his forthcoming stud career. That obviously amused Scholes quite a bit.

Rock Of Gibraltar had duly won a record seven Group 1 races on the trot. His victory in the 2002 Prix Moulin at Longchamp Fergie described as 'one of the biggest thrills of my life'. That was to be the penultimate race of the Rock's fine career, however, and he was later retired having won £1.1 million.

But in buying a share of Rock Of Gibraltar, the seeds of a monster, high-profile fall-out were sown, and Fergie and John Magnier became involved in the famous dispute over the stud ownership. The colt may have won a million, but his potential stud earnings would have been over £100 million.

Sir Alex threatened to sue, but in the end the case was settled out of court. Mike Dillon and Fergie were two of the closest friends I have ever known, but the Rock Of Gibraltar case meant they never spoke to each other again. It's a shame when you see two likeable people break off all contact. But Dillon decided to side with the Coolmore boys, and Fergie never forgot that.

Chatting with Fergie at York races in 2016, I was disturbed to hear that even nowadays the great ex-manager could not travel on trains to watch United on away match days: 'There would be too many people trying to bend my ear,' he explained. But up on the gallops at Newmarket – 'there's no better place to be early in the morning. There are very few mobile phones on the gallops, there's the lovely fresh air, and I have come to love those Newmarket sausages. I think I'm in heaven.'

24

The Nicest Guy

WHEN SIR HENRY CECIL DIED IN June 2013 at the age of 70 it was not unexpected. We had seen him at the races in the farewell days with Frankel, his body ravaged by the drugs he was taking to combat the inoperable stomach cancer first diagnosed in 2006. The day after he died I penned his obituary in *The Sun*:

His statistics were incredible, and he set records which may never be beaten. He was champion Flat trainer ten times, saddled more than 3,000 winners, won 25 British Classics and 11 overseas. There were 73 winners at Royal Ascot, four Epsom Derby triumphs, over 350 Group successes.

He trained for royalty, lords and sheikhs, but was equally at ease chatting with a down-and-out punter in Newmarket's high street. No kindness was too much for him. From Warren Place, perched high on a hill outside Newmarket, he ruled racing as King Henry.

During the 1990s the Cecil-Steve Cauthen double act was unbeatable. Together they had an unheard-of winning strike rate of 40 per cent.

After Henry won the 1999 Derby with Oath, owner Ahmed Bin Salman said, 'Winning Classics is easy. Just send the horses to Henry and he will do the rest.'

But it was not all plain sailing for Cecil. In his heyday he trained over 200 blue-bloods, many provided by his owner-breeders. But suddenly he fell out with Sheikh Mohammed, and he was left with just 40 horses. In 2005 he trained just 12 winners and slumped to 97th in the trainers' championship. But in 1987 he had saddled 180 winners and was the first trainer to break the £1 million prize-money barrier.

But at his lowest point Cecil said, 'I've always been a winner and I will bounce back. I am determined to be a winner again. I hate being defeated, and I get very depressed when things go wrong, but just get on with it.'

Arguably the greatest racehorse trainer of all time, he was certainly the most truly loved. He had grace and class in buckets. When I was told of his passing so many stories and memories came flooding back.

Cecil was wonderfully approachable. Anybody could address themselves to him. 'If a punter seeks a word with me at the races,' he said, 'I will always stop and talk. I take the view that if I snub that person it might spoil his whole day, and I'd hate to do that.' I interviewed the aristocratic Cecil, born in a Scottish castle but a friend to every racecourse lord or lout, many times. He was so self-deprecating: in one lengthy session at Newmarket's Warren Place he was deadly serious when he said, 'I've never been much good at anything really. I was a little spoilt in the past. But things don't always go right, do they? It's all supposed to be good for the character.' His father had been killed in the war at 28 just before he was born.

He always had the ability to laugh with you. On a visit to Warren Place, the Queen noticed the complete sets of lead toy soldiers Cecil had collected. 'Oh, Henry,' she shrilled, 'you've got all the knights!' Quick as a flash Cecil replied, 'Sir Michael Stoute is the only one missing.'

But, more importantly, he could laugh at himself. He spent much of his life doing that. 'I failed an entrance exam into Eton,' he recalled, 'and went to Cirencester Agricultural College to study gambling and drinking.' Once a heavy drinker, at one stage Cecil had been 'warned off' from driving on the Queen's highway. But he later gave it all up: 'My mother and brother were alcoholics,' he confessed, 'but alcohol is like poison to me.' When his twin brother David died of cancer in 2000 he admitted, 'It was like losing half of me. I hate the thought of death, and I'm not ready for it yet.'

When his numbers were greatly reduced, his winners drying up and he was having his worst ever season, he was leaving Nottingham races one day when a man asked him to sign his race card. Ever courteous, Cecil duly signed his autograph, only for the racegoer to say, 'Thank you, Sir Michael.' He definitely was the aristocrat with the common touch.

I remembered when he had started training in Newmarket in 1969. He was one of the young brigade then. I enjoyed many happy hours with his step-brother Arthur Boyd-Rochfort and their great pal, the journalist and ace racing historian Richard Onslow. They were carefree days. Of his first winner, Celestial Cloud, at Ripon in May 1969, he said, 'It was before the days of photo-finishes, and I am certain that in fact we finished second. I had 30 losers before my first winner, and one day in the stands a racegoer behind me said, "This chap Cecil couldn't train ivy up a wall."'

In his early days Cecil's famous father-in-law Sir Noel Murless took him aside and said, 'Your horses are galloping like a lot of old gentlemen.' 'It was the best piece of advice I was ever given,' Cecil acknowledged in later years: 'Sir Noel thought I was a bit of a playboy, and after that remark I was determined to prove him wrong.' One ritual of Cecil's career was that after any Group One winner his family flag was always hoisted above Warren Place, where he liked nothing more than smelling his beloved roses.

In early March every year I would venture to Warren Place to get the lowdown for *The Sun Guide to the Flat* on all Cecil's chief hopes for the coming season. He could not have been a better host, and spent hours going through his leading horses and their targets. He already had a campaign plotted out for them all, and I was able to enjoy some juicy ante-post vouchers.

I once asked him to name his favourite horses. He immediately singled out Frankel. 'He's so exciting, isn't he?' he said with that familiar grin and nod of his head. 'Bosra Sham was a very good filly, and won the 1,000 Guineas and Champion Stakes in 1996. The less said about her defeat for Kieren Fallon in the 1997 Coral-Eclipse the better.

'Reference Point won the Derby and St Leger in 1987. Steve Cauthen had a remarkable clock in his head, thanks to his American upbringing, where sectional timing is so important. The way he made him settle to win the Derby was fantastic. He was always going to win once he got into his stride. He was the first horse to make all to win the Epsom Derby since Coronach in 1926.

'Oh So Sharp pulled off the fillies' Triple Crown in 1985 of the 1,000 Guineas, Oaks and St Leger. Again, Steve Cauthen played such a major part in her success. Kris was only beaten twice in his 16-race career, while Ardross was my best stayer – he won Cup races galore, and was a gallant head runner-up in the 1982 Arc de Triomphe.

'I've never performed any racehorse training by the book,' he reflected. 'Few horses were ever weighed or had blood tests. I did everything simply by instinct. I have grown to have an understanding with my horses. The good ones always have a special grace and air about them.'

The much-publicised falling-out with stable jockey Kieren Fallon was another low point for Cecil. But in 2007 tears of unbridled joy trickled down our faces when Cecil won the Oaks with Light Shift, ridden by Ted Durcan. It was his eighth Oaks: he had been in the wilderness for seven years since training his previous Classic winner, Love Divine in the 2000 Oaks.

It was a supreme irony that Henry Cecil had to wait until the last days of his career to train his greatest horse – Frankel. Born on 11 February 2008, Frankel was an Aquarius, famed for being 'truly the trailblazers of the universe'. With four white feet, he defied the old racing adage of 'Four white feet go home without him'. He only started odds-against on his initial racing debut at Newmarket, when he went off 7-4 favourite. His shortest SP was 20-1-on, when he won the Sussex Stakes at Glorious Goodwood in 2012. A £1 accumulator on all his career wins would only have paid a meagre £89.83. Over 300,000 racegoers gathered to watch his entire career – three times more than the crowd who watch the FA Cup Final at Wembley.

He was unbeaten in 14 races, and won almost £3 million. He won ten Group 1 races, including his unforgettable siex-length romp in the 2,000 Guineas in 2011 in 97.30 seconds. Clock watchers estimated that he was travelling at a Group 1 sprinter's speed. He covered the length of a cricket pitch (22 yards) in a mere second. In York's International he reached 43 mph, and his length of stride was 22 feet. After his fabulous 2,000 Guineas win, one notable Flat judge, whom I will not embarrass by naming, told me in all seriousness, 'Frankel will never win another race. He has blown his brains away by being allowed to run that way down the Rowley Mile.'

The much-respected *Timeform* rated Frankel as the best they had seen since starting their records over 60 years ago. That made him superior to Ribot, Sea Bird II, Brigadier Gerard, Mill Reef, Shergar and Sea The Stars. After Frankel's retirement the World Thoroughbred rankings were altered, by moving the goalposts to downgrade previously highly-rated wonder horses like Dancing Brave, Shergar and El Gran Senor. Our top handicapper Phil Smith was not prepared to raise Frankel to 147, which is what *Timeform* did.

One theory claimed that Frankel had a larger heart than other horses, and a wider windpipe, which enabled him to absorb more oxygen to fuel his giant strides. Weighing half a ton, he was the biggest scoffer in Henry's yard: he ate 23lb of Canadian oats every day – the equivalent of 600 Weetabix. He also ate 30lb of English hay, as he found the American hay too rich.

The big question mark forever hanging over fabulous Frankel's career was what would have happened had he been allowed to run in the Epsom Derby over a mile and a half. Would he have had the stamina to go that extra half a mile? Or was he simply a great miler who showed immense speed, but would not have had enough petrol in the tank to last home in Epsom's punishing final four furlongs?

I have heard arguments for and against. After his romp in the Juddmonte International Stakes at York it was openly suggested that Frankel might make his career farewell in the Arc de Triomphe, and not the Champion Stakes at Ascot. But Lord Teddy Grimthorpe, Khalid Abdullah's outstanding racing manager, KO'd that: 'Following discussions with all parties, it has been decided that the Champion Stakes will be his finale.'

So Frankel duly retired, leaving a few questions unanswered. He never raced beyond a mile and a quarter, and missed the Arc, Europe's most prestigious race. He also skipped the challenge of a Breeders' Cup autumn invasion, and therefore never raced outside England. We will never know what could have been.

But Cecil's fellow top Newmarket trainer John Gosden assured me, 'I honestly don't believe that anybody else apart from Henry would have trained Frankel to win 14 races on the trot. Frankel was his own boss, but Henry spent hours teaching him to settle, and in the end he became the perfect racehorse.'

Seeing Sir Henry Richard Amherst Cecil's gaunt figure at York in 2012 was heartbreaking. He wore a brown fedora hat to hide his almost bald head, the result of his cruel medication. He looked like the ghost of the man who had previously adored flashy, colourful clothes, loud socks and Gucci loafers. He had virtually lost his voice but, patting Frankel in the winner's enclosure at York, he whispered, 'That win has made me feel 20 years better.'

Sadly, that was not to be true, and he died the following year. Lady Jane Cecil, his third wife, stood by him to the very end. He never lived to see the magnificent start the sire Frankel has made to his breeding career. He was charming and patient, and in the end, a very brave man. 'He had a knack of knowing precisely what every single horse needed,' said Lester Piggott. 'He always put the needs of his horses first.'

Sir Michael Stoute echoed his sentiments: 'I do not believe that England has produced a better trainer than Henry. I know that there has never been a man so much loved. And then there was the courage and strength to continue to train horses when he was struggling health-wise. He was some man.'

'I have been through rough times,' Henry Cecil reflected in my very last interview with him, 'and it has not always been a bed of roses. But I like a challenge, and I would never be pathetic, walk away and retire. Life is not about what you have done in the past, but what you will do in the future.'

25

Exclusives

'WRITS,' KELVIN MACKENZIE ONCE TOLD ME, 'are the Oscars of our profession.' Over the years I produced a good few scoops, but not always without some hesitation and self-doubt, and though exclusive horse racing stories always drove me to go that extra inch or two, I tried not to go that far.

I always admired the Epsom-based Reg Akehurst as one of the best dual-purpose trainers, and happily recall backing his 1989 Lincoln Handicap winner Fact Finder at 40-1 ante-post, before he actually won at 20-1. He had a string of good jump winners, too, and trained Cool Ground to win the 1990 Welsh National and the 1991 Anthony Mildmay Chase before he was switched to Toby Balding to win the 1992 Cheltenham Gold Cup. Inlander was another popular Akehurst winner when he took the 1987 Imperial Cup at Sandown, and also the Ascot Stakes on the Flat the same year.

One of his greatest handicap coups was in 1993, when his owner Stuart Aitken won £500,000 after Sarawat had won the Ebor at York. Once when we were up on the Epsom gallops near his base at South Hatch, I asked Akehurst what his secret was for winning big handicaps with seemingly moderate horses. 'They all say that I'm giving 'em some drug or other,' he smiled. 'I feed 'em well and I train 'em hard. It works with the wife.'

Akehurst had told me more than once that he had no intention of retiring, so I was mightily surprised when a long-time contact of mine in deepest Cornwall rang me on a Sunday morning in August 1997 to inform me that Akehurst had told his staff that he was retiring and handing over the licence to his son Jon.

I tried to contact Reg, but he was playing golf – this was long before the days of mobile phones. But later that afternoon I did speak to Jon Akehurst, who could not have been more dismissive. 'I don't know where on earth you got that from,' he told me. 'If you print that you'll be made to look very stupid.'

I went back to my contact, who stuck to his story: 'Reg had all his staff in. I know because I've got to rearrange one of his apprentice's indentures.'

After agonising over what to do I decided to take a chance. Sometimes you have to play a journalistic hunch and back your informers. As my pal Chris Poole would say, 'It's a very windy day, and a good one to fly a kite.' But I awoke several times in the night, terrified I'd made a terrible error. The next morning I saw the Exclusive splash across six columns of SunSport, with the headline, AKEHURST QUITS.

Later that morning I tuned into the *Sporting Life* online, and my spirits rose dramatically when I saw their headline: AKEHURST CONFIRMS RETIREMENT. I poured myself a large glass of wine.

An exclusive early in my career on *The Sun* came my way in April 1970 when Willie Robinson quit as Fulke Walwyn's jump jockey in Lambourn, and returned to his native Ireland at the relatively young age of 36. Robinson had ridden the giant 18-hands Mill House in his epic battles with Arkle, and indeed to victory the first time, when they beat the great horse by eight lengths in the 1963 Hennessy. 'Arkle slipped that day,' recalled Robinson, 'and we were never to beat him again, in two Cheltenham Gold Cups, a Hennessy and a Gallagher Gold Cup.

'I just can't keep up with it any more,' he told me. 'I've had a lot of falls, and my doctor says that I can't take many more. There is always the element of anxiety every time you walk into the paddock – you know you could come back on a winner... or in an ambulance.' Even the day of his greatest triumph, Robinson revealed, riding the pony-sized Team Spirit in the 1964 Grand National, had been marred for him by Paddy Farrell's career-ending fall.

But he was fascinating on Arkle. 'I suppose I was the only Irishman on the planet who cursed Arkle's greatest triumphs,' he told me. 'I have always claimed that if Mill House had stayed 100% sound it would only have been necks between him and Arkle. But Mill House had a massive frame, and it put a lot of strain on his legs, and his jumping occasionally suffered. When he was spot-on, Fulke Walwyn simply could not believe that any horse would beat him.'

At the end of 1971 another good exclusive came when I revealed that Arkle's great trainer Tom Dreaper was handing over the reins at his

Exclusive stories are the name of the game. Here I reveal Epsom trainer Reg Akehurst retiring.

famous stables at Kilsallaghan, near Dublin Airport, to his son Jim. But Tom retired before achieving his greatest goal – to win the Grand National. In 1971 his Black Secret was pipped into second place in a photo-finish by Specify, and the year before his Vulture had finished second to Gay Trip, who, ironically, was ridden by Pat Taaffe, associated with so many of Arkle's memorable victories.

I was not quite so on-the-ball with the top Newmarket trainer Sir Noel Murless. A close friend of his family told me that he was definitely going to retire. Unfortunately for me he decided to stay on for another year. Twelve months on, when he did finally retire, *The Sun*'s racing editor John Kendrick sent me a telegram: 'Well done. You got Murless right in the end.'

Another less-than-happy episode for me came in the autumn of 1999, when *The Sun*'s racing editor Mark Maydon was adamant he had an exclusive tip from a Newmarket bloodstock source that Aidan O'Brien's top two-year-old Aristotle had been sold to a new mystery owner for £10 million, and would be joining the rookie Newmarket trainer Eoghan O'Neill.

I checked with two of my Coolmore sources, and was told quite firmly that the Ballydoyle brigade thought the world of Aristotle, and were not in the habit of selling on their brightest prospects. I relayed my information to Maydon, but he was quite sure we had a terrific exclusive. I double-checked my Irish connections, and they all denied any Aristotle sale.

It all seemed so unlikely – at the time Aristotle was ante-post favourite for the Derby, and being described by a super-confident Aidan O'Brien as 'the best Derby horse we've ever had' and 'perfectly made' for Epsom. (Sadly, he didn't perform as expected, finished fifth and was later sold to race in Singapore.) But Maydon decided to run the story, and it duly appeared the next day with 'Claude Duval Exclusive' splashed all over the racing page. I must have been bonkers.

The next day the Ballydoyle and Coolmore giants of the turf completely knocked down the story. Trevor Clements, later to become

The Sun's racing editor, was dispatched to an address in east London where the mystery owner was alleged to live. He came back with the revelation that the address was like something out of Tony Hancock's hilarious radio series: Flat 2a, Railway Cuttings, Canning Town.

'We've really pissed on our chips,' the sports editor Paul Ridley said to me. So the ever-caring *Sun* went to town, and I wrote a piece – exclusive, of course – about how the poor, unfortunate Eoghan O'Neill had been terribly duped, and then kept my head well down for a few days. Eoghan O'Neill went on to become a successful trainer in France, and years later I bumped into Mark Maydon, a perfectly pleasant individual, in a box at Aintree during the Grand National meeting. I greeted him with a cheery, 'Ah, Mr Aristotle!' but he was not in the mood to relive the episode with any humour. Thankfully, Aristotle was a rare blunder in *The Sun*'s racing history.

Kieren Fallon, on the other hand, was, I soon realised, an especially good source of tips that could be relied on. In 2002 I was writing a series of articles with the six-time British champion jockey, and he was cursing the fact that he would have to miss the St Leger because of a 13-day ban. 'Bollin Eric will win,' he assured me on the eve of the race – 'no doubts. I rode him in the Great Voltigeur last time out at York, and the race was not run to suit me before we finished third. I definitely should have won. The extra trip of the St Leger is made for him, and I'll be amazed if he doesn't win.' I took Fallon's advice, tipped Bollin Eric in *The Sun*, and sent the selection to 'all clients'. Kevin Darley deputised as the jockey, and won commandingly at 7-1 by one and a quarter lengths.

I had a string of contact mobile numbers for the elusive Fallon, whose roller-coaster career has few equals for highs and lows, and seemed to be plagued by one disaster after another – dawn arrests, heavy drinking, divorce, failed drugs tests, and countless fines and bans. He had top jobs with Sir Michael Stoute, Sir Henry Cecil and Aidan O'Brien, and managed to lose them all for one reason or another. It all started in September 1994, when he was banned for six months for pulling his fellow northern jockey Stuart Webster off his horse after a barging match at Beverley.

But nobody could ever question his genius in the saddle. He rode three Epsom Derby winners, and his 2003 triumph on Kris Kin saw a monster morning gamble from 12-1 to 6-1. Bookies moaned about the 'Fallon factor'.

His greatest ride? I think without doubt his head victory in the 2007 Arc de Triomphe on Dylan Thomas. He was never beaten on him, and that day at Longchamp he rode a magical Group 1 treble. Amazingly, the next day he was in the dock at the Old Bailey on race-fixing charges. I gazed across the courtroom, and saw Fallon boxed in. It seldom happened on racecourses, and his whistle when he scented victory was the one noise rival jockeys never wanted to hear inside the final furlong. He and other jockeys were cleared, but the 53-day trial fiasco heard of 40,000 pages of police evidence, costing in all a staggering £13 million.

He gave me several exclusive interviews, and in 2002, on a quiet afternoon at Lingfield, he opened up to me about his lengthy battle with alcoholism. 'I know every off-licence within a few miles of every racecourse in Britain,' he confided. 'They're all like pit stops to me. But race riding is all I know. If I keep failing I'm hardly likely to get a job as a nightclub bouncer.'

He finally retired in 2016 at the age of 51, blaming depression. The tiny muscleman rode 2,577 UK winners, and had already made more comebacks than Sinatra. Among the many tributes none was more glowing than that from the Coolmore-Ballydoyle supremo John Magnier. 'If Ireland reached the final of the World Cup and had a penalty to win in the dying seconds,' he said, 'I would get Kieren Fallon to take it. He doesn't know what nerves are.' Fallon is now seen work-riding in Newmarket for William Haggas and Saeed Bin Suroor. I doubt we've heard the last of him.

With Ryan Moore I got into trouble for revealing something I thought he'd be proud of. I have the greatest appreciation of him as a rider – he can rightly claim to be the world's number one big-race jockey (although Frankie Dettori might disagree) – and in 2014 he won £10,200,352 from 19 Group and Grade 1 winners. I wrote a glowing article in which I observed that his rich percentages must have made him a multi-millionaire.

A furious Moore buttonholed me one day at Doncaster. 'How dare you say I'm a millionaire?'

'Well, if you're not,' I could not resist replying, 'you must have a bloody great hole in your pocket.'

I ended my *Sun* career with the scoop of the end of the 2016 Flat season – the sacking of Paul Hanagan as first jockey to Sheikh Hamdan Al Maktoum.

On Friday, 23 September a friend I much respected tipped me off that Hanagan's five-year reign as Hamdan's number one rider was over. I was quite surprised, but the source was so insistent that I simply had to follow it up. Over the years nobody has been more loyal to his trainers and jockeys, many moderate performers, than Sheikh Hamdan.

I got hold of Hamdan's racing manager Angus Gold on his mobile in the paddock at Newmarket. 'That's all news to me,' was his response when I asked him whether my story was true. 'I wouldn't write that if I were you.'

At times like these you have to weigh up the situation. We decided to run the story, but included Gold's firm denial. The racing editor, Dave Cook, produced one of his typically eye-catching headlines – IT'S PAUL HANA-GONE.

At Newmarket the next day, after my story had been published, some of my rivals were queuing up to knock it down. They loved printing the firm denials of Hanagan's sacking. 'I don't know where this story came from,' Gold was still maintaining, 'but it isn't true.'

'Why didn't Claude ring me?' Godolphin's supremo John Ferguson was quoted wondering. 'I could have put him straight.'

Even Hamdan Al Maktoum was asked about the story. 'You are telling me something,' he mumbled. 'It's the first I've heard of it.'

Nothing happened, but my source assured me I'd got it right.

Then, lo and behold, on Thursday, 10 November – three weeks almost to the day of my exclusive – what *Sun* readers already knew was officially announced. Hanagan had lost his job. It was almost an exclusive from beyond the grave.

Over many years David Yates – 'Newsboy' of arch rivals the *Daily Mirror* – had not exactly been a pal. I enjoyed our red-top rivalry. But on the very day the Hanagan story was confirmed, Yates appeared on Racing UK reviewing all the newspaper headlines. 'Let's be fair,' said Yates: 'Claude Duval wrote this exclusive story nearly a month ago and, as usual in these cases, it was firmly denied by those closest to the truth.'

Hanagan had ridden seven Group 1 winners for his Arab retainer since replacing Richard Hills in the famous blue-and-white silks in 2012. Taghrooda gave him his first English Classic in the 2014 Oaks, and the same season he won the King George VI and Queen Elizabeth Stakes on the filly at Ascot, as well as Sandown's Coral-Eclipse on Mukhadram. He also won three Group 1 sprint successes in 2015, on Muhaarar: the July Cup, Prix Maurice de Gheest and the Qipco Champions Sprint.

But 2016 was not a great year for Hamdan Al Maktoum and his trainers, and by now Hanagan, champion jockey in 2010 and 2011, had just 51 wins from his 299 rides for his Arab owner. His seasonal total of just over 70 winners was his lowest since 2003.

I believe his downfall could have been his ride on Muntahaa in the St Leger. After only a furlong and a half Muntahaa, trained by John Gosden and a much-fancied 4-1 shot, was pulling like a train and out in front. No horse could have been expected to keep up that position, and in the end he faded into fourth behind the 22-1 Harbour Law, whose trainer Laura Mongan became the first woman to saddle a St Leger winner in its 240-year history.

In the November, Angus Gold revealed that Jim Crowley, the newly crowned Flat champion jockey, would replace Hanagan, who, unsurprisingly, quit Newmarket and rerouted to Yorkshire to rejoin the Malton trainer Richard Fahey, with whom he had previously had such a successful partnership as the darling boys of punters on the northern circuit. I sincerely hope the likeable Hanagan bounces back to the top.

At a pre-season cricket match at Canterbury in March 2017, who should be watching Kent than David Yates? I thanked him sincerely for his unexpected gesture in highlighting on TV the background to the Hana-gone fiasco.

'I revealed that Joseph O'Brien was giving up riding because of endless weight problems, and was going to train,' he told me. 'All hell broke loose, and they threatened to sue. Of course, later all my predictions were confirmed. The very best exclusive stories are always denied…'

26

Blind Faith

ONE MAJOR REGRET WHEN I RETIRED was that I was not able to cover Andrew Thornton reaching 1,000 winners in his career. For at least two years I'd been reporting that the lanky jump jockey from County Durham was about to join the Grand Club. But the final few winners did seem to come in a slow trickle, and I'd waited long enough.

Sure enough, weeks after I quit *The Sun*, Thornton booted home a double at Wincanton on Boxing Day, 2016, on the Seamus Mullins-trained pair Somchine and Kentford Myth, to finally reach his goal. When he came back to the winner's enclosure after the second win, he attempted a Frankie Dettori-style flying dismount, but twisted his ankle and had to give up his remaining rides for the day!

But Thornton had already come back from a succession of bone-crunching injuries that would have crucified lesser jockeys. As a lifelong Newcastle United football fan he knows all about life's ups and downs.

One of his nicknames was 'John Wayne', because of his long-legged cowboy riding style, and like John Wayne he has shown true grit to become the 24th jump jockey to ride 1,000 career winners. Ironically, twelve of them were Irish-born. When I rang Thornton to congratulate him on his achievement he said, 'I want to pass Peter Niven's record of 1,004 winners. I'd like nothing better than to beat that miserable Scotsman's record – although I actually quite like him!'

John Francome always rated Thornton, calling him 'a real old-fashioned horseman'. Everybody remembers Thornton's win on Cool Dawn in the 1998 Cheltenham Gold Cup, a 25-1 shock, but the most emotional success was on Miko De Beauchene in the 2007 Coral Welsh Grand National. Sally Alner had just taken over her husband Robert's licence after he was paralysed in his horror car crash.

Bought as 'a safe ride for a lady', Cool Dawn was picked up by Robert Alner for less than £10,000 as a point-to-point ride for the owner and businesswoman Dido Harding, who would later emerge as the chief executive of TalkTalk. In the Gold Cup, Thornton gave him an inspired ride, and made virtually every yard of the running from the front to hold off Strong Promise by one and a quarter lengths. 'I reckon Strong Promise went half a length up on me from the last fence,' recalled Thornton, 'but Cool Dawn simply would not give in. I've got to pinch myself that this has happened,' he went on. 'Dido rode Cool Dawn at Wincanton the previous November, but the partnership did not click. That's when Robert Alner suggested that maybe a professional rider would have more success. Me, the great professional? I can't believe it!'

Thornton was always very coy with me about his age. 'Just say I'm 35 plus VAT,' he'd joke. He rode his first winner on Wrekin Hill at Sedgefield in 1991 for WA Stephenson. When he started he was originally nicknamed Eddie the Eagle, because of his big thick glasses. Then he became Blindman, then Lensio because of his contact lenses. 'Actually, with contact lenses I think I have better vision than most jockeys,' Thornton told me. 'Far more jockeys wear contact lenses than you would imagine – young Tom Scudamore swears by them. I only once forgot to turn up with my lenses. I didn't say anything, but I did manage to win the Anthony Mildmay/Peter Cazalet Chase at Sandown on Lancastrian Jet. Afterwards I told Henry Daly, and he suggested I should forget my contact lenses more often.

'They found out I needed to wear glasses back when I was a child, and I mistook a sheep for a cow. I went to the rugby-playing school Barnard Castle, which produced many England internationals, including Rob Andrew, Matthew Tait and the brothers Rory and Tony Underwood. I played fly-half. Even now when I ride in the north some of WA Stephenson's old staff call me Eddie the Eagle. But I always wanted to be a jockey despite all my eyesight problems. I don't mind my nicknames like Lensio. Whenever I cut up other jockeys in races and the lads complain I always shout, "What do you expect? You know I can't see." I always try and go down the inner because at least there's a white rail!'

In 2003 Thornton produced the best ride of the season. On King-scliff in a three-mile chase at Ascot his reins snapped at the third fence, but he guided the horse round with superb skills to win by eighteen lengths. Carl Llewellyn was watching the race on TV in the jockeys' weighing-room. 'Doesn't the blind bugger realise that his reins have broken?' he exclaimed. 'He's never looked so stylish!'

'I started out with Stephenson,' explains Thornton. 'He told me one day, "You've got long legs – use them." When the great trainer died I came south. It was a big mistake. I pulled my leathers up but I kept falling off. By Christmas one year I had ridden just four winners. I recall one day at Market Rasen when I had five rides and fell off four of them.

'In recent years Seamus Mullins and Caroline Bailey have been my most supportive trainers. I'll go anywhere to ride winners – Sedgefield one day and Plumpton the next. I reckon I spend more miles on the motorways from my home near Thirsk than any other jockey. I involve myself as much as I can with owners. I've always thought that if an owner is paying you £100 or more for each ride the least you can do is have a drink with them afterwards and explain how it has all gone. I know that it upsets other riders, but it's just my philosophy.

'The worst thing about being a jump jockey, apart from falling off, is putting up overweight. And being so tall' – Thornton is a 5-foot-11-inch beanpole – 'means I have had to starve myself literally for years. I should naturally be over 12 stone, but have dieted down to as low as 10st 4lb. Dieting and sweating is the hideous side of a jockey's life – but it has to be done. Dieting is all between your ears – it's all in the mind.

'I once did a five-mile run at Haydock before racing. In the car on the way to the races I also had the heater turned full on. I lost over seven pounds that morning – I was like an oven-ready turkey – but I had completely overdone it, and I was as weak as a kitten. The secret is to lose weight without getting drained.'

At the end of 1999, with Timmy Murphy injured, Paul Nicholls called Thornton up to ride See More Business in the King George at Kempton. 'That season I seemed to have become the super sub. I think I was about seventh in line, and it came as a complete shock. I had to lose a lot of weight very quickly. It was exactly 19 years after I won on See More Business when I reached my 1,000th winner.'

In December 2014 *The Sun* ran a column about top sportsmen and how they survived the Christmas festivities. 'We are having 14 family members to lunch,' Thornton revealed, 'including our son Harry, who will be enjoying his first Christmas.

'I shall have one meal of roast turkey, which is white meat, and I will treat myself to one roast potato, as I know I will have to be riding at Kempton Park on Boxing Day. I will have to sweat down to ride in any handicaps. That means that when I get to Kempton I will put on a tracksuit, plus a sweat suit, two pairs of socks, a hat and gloves, and run round the track. I usually run off six pounds this way.'

Thornton has often been hired by BBC Radio 5 Live at the major meetings, and a media career looms on the horizon; with his vast experience he was also an ideal candidate to be the Professional Jockeys

Association's Safety Officer. 'We should not have to defend the Grand National,' he says emphatically, 'because there is nothing to defend. With the changes to the fences, jockeys can get away with a lot more than they used to. I was thrilled when Auroras Encore won the 2013 Grand National at 66-1, as it showed that any horse can still scale the heights at Aintree.'

Thornton may have had 89 rides before he had his first fall, but says plainly that 'all jump jockeys suffer terrible injuries. We are in the only profession where sometimes as many as two ambulances follow our every move. Tony McCoy has the best saying: "If you don't want to get hurt, don't get on a horse." But as I neared my 1,000th winner I would bump into AP and he would always tell me, "Don't give up. You'll regret it when you do."' The likeable Lensio has walked tall for years and is a credit to his profession. He has proved that blind faith can move mountains.

27

The Last Day of All

AFTER 47 YEARS AS *THE SUN*'S racing correspondent, my final day was truly emotional.

Over the years I'd met so many lovable, generous racing people, and watched so many brave-hearted horses. I'd always enjoyed racing's self-made success stories – Barry Hills, Nigel Twiston-Davies, David Elsworth, Mark Johnston, Jack Berry and Paul Nicholls are great examples. I'd always found it hard to admire the silver spoon brigade. Like Martin Pipe, one of my heroes, I'd come into racing without any background in the sport.

I'd loved the racing world for being full of amusing stories and repartee, and one of my favourites remains Radio 5 Live's Rob Nothman's: 'There have been three great love stories in the history of the world: Antony and Cleopatra, Romeo and Juliet... and Derek Thompson and Derek Thompson.'

I learned a lesson very early on not to get too big-headed. After one glowing review in the Sporting Life of an article of mine I bumped into local Lower Beeding trainer-vet John Hicks at Plumpton. He said: 'If I knew as little about racing as you, I'd be riding a push bike.'

A chance meeting on a Paris train for the Arc de Triomphe started a brilliant friendship with fun-loving owner Andy Stewart and his charming wife Judy. They included me in their parties at Cheltenham and Aintree and I shared in their pride of owning the great stayer Big Buck's. Even greater was the joy when their eldest son Paul, who was told that he would never walk again after a horror snow-boarding accident in France in December, 2008, managed a fairly normal life with two sticks.

'I tried to show the same courage as Big Buck's showed in all his races" he said. I admired the fierce enthusiasm of champion trainer Paul Nicholls. But I had one major fall-out with another top jumps trainer Nick Henderson, which surprised me as I supported him when he was given a record £40,000 BHA fine in 2009 when a horse owned by the Queen had been given a banned drug.

But Simon Philip, one of the part-owners of Henderson's hugely exciting chaser Might Bite, remains a close friend. In 2017 he was voted chairman of Kent County Cricket Club and we spend many happy hours together.

He laughs: "I went to Lambourn's open day in 2017. Massive crowds turned up at Nicky's stables and I obviously went to see my horse. As I nearer his box an anxious father with three youngsters said "Come away and don't get too near this one." Then I spotted the sign Might Bite!'

I'd met so many rogues and villains in racing, too. The swashbuckling Scottish stockbroker and old Harrovian Tony Collins was definitely not one of them, despite being fined £1,000 and banned by the Jockey Club for ten years in 1974 for trying to defraud the bookies in the infamous Gay Future betting coup at Cartmel, where he, the trainer and some shady Irishmen had placed doubles and trebles on three horses when Gay Future was only ever going to be the sole runner, and the bets became heavily-disguised singles. Gay Future duly won by 15 lengths, but the bookies tumbled the scam. Collins had few regrets, however, and I've always remembered his wise words: 'In life,' he told me, 'you can never put the toothpaste back in the tube.'

In my reporting era, Lester Piggott and Tony McCoy had been the outstanding jockeys. Back in 1972 I'd written a book about Lester, who throughout his career had starved himself to 30 pounds below his natural weight, and interviewed his trainer father Keith. 'We Piggotts have always thought a lot about money,' he told me. 'If we had a good bet, we always expected to win. In my riding days if I was beaten on a horse my father had backed he didn't talk to me for a fortnight.'

In 1998 I'd done a book with Tony McCoy, and I'd ghosted his column in *The Sun* for many years, but he'd been merely the conditional jockeys' champion in 1994 when we first signed him up. He then proceeded to be the champion jockey for 20 years. I recall his first trainer Billy Rock telling me how Nicky Henderson had come over to see some horses and spotted teenage AP riding them and asked, 'Who is that kid trying to impersonate Lester Piggott?' McCoy rewrote jumping's history books, but to the end of a glittering career in the saddle he remained as modest as the day I first met him.

Set Tony McCoy's impeccable professionalism and sobriety against the scene that had greeted me in the bar of the Adelphi Hotel in Liverpool back in 1975, in the early hours of Grand National day.

'Is he all right?' Someone was pointing out a little figure on the floor in the corner, clearly tired and emotional, curled round the base of the hat-stand, fast asleep and hugging it for comfort.

'Oh, that's Tommy Carberry', I had to tell him. 'He's on the second-favourite L'Escargot in the National later today…'

And L'Escargot, of course, won.

How racing had changed over the years since I'd started on *The Sun*! When I'd started, exclusive stories on the racing pages (apart from

Sir Peter O'Sullevan's) were almost nil. As a Man of Kent I rued the days when both my local racecourses, Wye and Folkestone, were closed. The Jockey Club's iron-fisted rule was largely transformed by the inception of the British Horseracing Authority. Marketing moguls started messing about with the racing calendar, and tradition was often destroyed by the relentless march of so-called progress.

Now at last, Champions Day at Ascot, Saturday, 15 October 2016, was a fitting finale.

Kelvin MacKenzie sent me a text that read, 'Congratulations on still being full of running when the finishing post arrived. You were brilliant for *The Sun*. They were lucky to have had you.' A terrible Ascot memory suddenly came back to me.

Many years earlier I'd written in *The Sun* that a disqualified Royal Ascot winner was *certain* to be reinstated on appeal. If I was proved wrong, I boasted, I would streak round Portman Square outside the Jockey Club's headquarters.

I was proved wrong.

A day later I was sitting at the Oval watching the Test match when my mobile rang.

'What's all this about streaking round Portman Square?' boomed Kelvin MacKenzie.

'I only meant it as a joke,' I protested pathetically.

'We have the highest professional standards on *The Sun*!' he shouted. 'Get round there and get your kit off!'

And so I did, much to the amusement of all the office workers leaning out of the windows for my revelation of the naked truth.

On my last day at Ascot for *The Sun* I wasn't going to make the same mistake.

'Duval's Diary was an institution,' wrote Ladbrokes' CEO Jim Mullen in a charming letter. '*The Sun* without the Punter's Pal will be unrecognisable.'

In the *Daily Telegraph*, under the shoutline, 'Duval ensured my debut was never forgotten', Marcus Armytage wrote,

The biggest surprise of the autumn has been the retirement of Claude Duval. He is one of the great professionals, and our first encounter as journalistic colleagues taught me a salutary lesson.

At Goodwood in the early 1990s I was at a dreary three-day meeting. Nothing much was happening until Walter Swinburn won a race and came back and complained that his horse had jumped a road track after the winning-line and that it was dangerous. Claude and all the others made a big deal out of it, and next day it led most of the racing pages.

I pooh-poohed the story, and pointed out that Swinburn had spent half his life in the hunting fields, and suggested that a two-year-old jumping a track was hardly a daring exploit, and 'a mountain had been made out of a molehill.'

The next day I arrived, rather pleased with myself, but Duval spotted me and said, 'Oi, Molehill. You will soon learn what makes a good story on a quiet racing day.' Luckily, the nickname did not stick, and we have been the best of friends ever since.

'You were the greatest racing journalist Fleet Street has ever known, and certainly ever will,' my last racing editor Dave Cook wrote to me. 'It's been like working with my hero.' I am still blushing.

I also received a call from the retired stipendiary steward and fellow cricket lover Major Jeremy Ker. He had obviously forgiven me for the rumpus I caused one day when he was officiating at Epsom. In one finish there was the most clear-cut case of interference by a winner I had ever seen. But there was no inquiry. When I asked Ker why no action had been taken he joked, 'I think the stewards were all too busy watching the Test match.' Reporting his remark in *The Sun*, I stressed he had made it as a joke. I was astounded, therefore, when the galloping Major was summoned to Portman Square and given a dressing-down by the Jockey Club's hierarchy.

The Sun itself certainly let me go out with a bang: a two-page spread and a picture of me with Frankie Dettori. 'This is it, folks!'

I wrote:

> *I am the only remaining staff member of the red-top tabloid from the first day it hit the streets – November 17, 1969 – later to become the country's best-selling newspaper.*
>
> *Yet on the day when* The Sun *was launched by Rupert Murdoch,* Daily Mirror *grandees threw a dinner party in their High Holborn boardroom with dead sunflowers running the length of the table.*
>
> *But within years we blossomed, galloped past the* Mirror *and have been leading the field ever since…*

Although, like many, I had always questioned the wisdom of having the end-of-season jamboree in the middle of October, when there was always going to be the threat of seasonal rain and the inevitable heavy going, the highly paid marketing moguls who'd dreamt up the idea to switch the traditional big races from Newmarket to Ascot after centuries of history were never going to concede defeat. I was in no mood to go out on a low.

Inevitably Frankie Dettori, who had clearly read *The Sun*'s big send-off to me, greeted me with the inevitable Italian hug and planted two kisses on my cheeks.

I love this excitable little jockey. He is a very human being, and I have seen both sides of his character. A typical Latin, he is either on cloud nine or plunged into the depths of despair. I first interviewed him in Newmarket in the early eighties when he was an unknown stable boy with Luca Cumani who could hardly speak English, his accent half-Italian and half-Arsenal-fans' language.

I've had dozens of kisses from Dettori over the years, but have never been quite as embarrassed as Sir Michael Stoute after the 2008 St Leger. The Doncaster Classic was beginning to become an almost unmentionable hoodoo for this very intense trainer, but Dettori put that right on the 8-1 Conduit and completely ambushed Stoute in the winner's enclosure.

I didn't get a kiss from Sir Mark Prescott, Newmarket's longest-serving trainer, but we established that we had both done the same 47 years, as he had started out as a trainer in 1969.

I was enjoying a convivial lunch that final day in Coral's private box high up in the magnificent Ascot grandstand when the jockey Jamie Spencer, already in his riding silks, was introduced to 'go through the card' with his tips for all the guests. Having given his selections, Spencer glanced across at me at the back of the box and said, 'I'd just like to wish Claude Duval a long and happy retirement.'

Delighted but utterly surprised by Spencer's kindness, my mind drifted back to an afternoon at Lingfield in January 1999, when I requested the chance to speak to him outside the weighing-room. At a mere 18 years old he was already a riding sensation in his native Ireland, and had won the Irish 1,000 Guineas the previous spring on Tarascon.

Prior to that first meeting, Spencer had won for the master gambler-trainer Barney Curley on Magic Combination in a conditional jockeys' hurdle race at Kempton, heavily backed down to 11-2 (no prizes for guessing who had the on-course bet of £5,000 to £1,000), and it had caught my attention that afterwards Curley had described him as 'the best I've seen since Martin Molony', the Irish champion jump jockey of the 1940s and 1950s.

The baby-faced Spencer duly appeared from the weighing-room, and I introduced myself. I was quickly struck how closely he resembled the 13-year-old Lester Piggott when he rode his first winner at Haydock in 1948.

'Mr Curley is not here today,' he said, 'but his last orders were not to speak to *anybody*.'

Fortunately, mobile phones had been invented by then, and I was able to speak to Barney, who allowed his shy young protégé to give me an interview.

'I don't see why I can't continue to ride over hurdles and on the Flat,' Spencer told me. 'TP Burns rode over both codes for Vincent

O'Brien for 20 years. But Mr Curley will not let me ride over fences.' Spencer came across as a very mature jockey for his slender years.

I was still firing in the questions when his mobile rang, and I heard Barney say, 'I want you back here – there's work to be done.' Then Curley asked to speak to me. 'Jamie doesn't need any publicity,' he told me forcefully. 'A blind man can see he has great potential.'

Spencer is the Dick Turpin of jockeys – a real hold-up horseman, who loves coming with a penetrating late run from off the pace. He admits he copied the style of the ace American jockey Angel Cordero. He likes to get horses to settle, get them into a rhythm, and then cruise past tired horses – seldom wastes ground by going on the wide outside.

Racing's forums are always buzzing when Spencer overplays the waiting tactics, or goes for the late run only to be blocked by a wall of horses. When it comes off, he's a genius; not so otherwise. I was cruel enough in *The Sun* one day, after an especially painful defeat, to dub him 'Frank Spencer' after the accident-prone TV character played by Michael Crawford. The next time he saw me as he came out of the weighing-room he swished his whip uncomfortably close to my private parts. That last day in Coral's box it seemed I'd been forgiven.

Finally that day, Steve Jones, 'Templegate' of *The Sun*, helped me with my very last report and, reluctant to retire and still full of running, I left the busy Ascot press room and never looked back.

On the Sunday after my retirement, At The Races' Robert Cooper interviewed me over the telephone, and a guest in the studio that day was Julian Muscat, who had joined *The Times* in the 1980s, and went on to the *Racing Post*. When he first entered the press room I dubbed him 'Philby' after the well-known double agent, as he was working for both Rupert Murdoch and Robert Maxwell at the same time. It has been his nickname ever since. Of his *Times* days he recalled, 'I first met Claude on the platform at King's Cross as we were walking towards the train to York races. Suddenly he stopped where the train carriages divided between the First and Second class sections. He said, "Mr Muscat, this is where we part. I am travelling in here with your readers, and I suspect that you are travelling further down the train with mine…"'

This is how I finished my final column in *The Sun* on Champions Day:

Sir Peter O'Sullevan always was my idol. He completed 35 years as racing correspondent on the Daily Express, *so I guess I just outstayed him. In every single conversation I had with Peter over nearly five decades he always left me with the two words: 'Be lucky'.*

I can't beat that.

Acknowledgements

LOOKING BACK ON MY CAREER IN racing has made me realise how incredibly lucky I have been. Anecdotes about the great and the good in the Sport of Kings have come flooding back. I doubt whether any other sport has produced such amusing characters.

I must say a sincere thanks to *Racing Post* Books' hierarchy of Brough Scott, Julian Brown and Alan Byrne for giving me the green light to tell my story. My skilled editor Graham Coster has also been exceedingly helpful, although on many occasions from his Thames-side office I looked lovingly across at the nearby Prospect of Whitby, one of my favourite London pubs, and could easily have 'run out'.

When *The Sun* sub-editors incurred my wrath I always recalled the words of Luke in the Bible: 'Father, forgive them, for they know not what they do.' But on countless occasions they rescued me from total embarrassment.

My press room colleagues Cornelius Lysaght, Jim 'Croc' McGrath, Marcus Armytage and Alastair Down have been very helpful and supportive. I owe enormous thanks to John McCririck for so often highlighting my exclusive stories on TV and the *Yorkshire Post*'s Tom Richmond who has been a tremendous ally. Sally Masson, Ryan Price's one-time secretary, recalled so many of the hilarious exploits of the Controversial Captain.

At Price's funeral his coffin was carried out to Frank Sinatra's 'My Way'. I've had plenty of laughs and the odd cry. I hope you've enjoyed this account of one lucky scribe.

Claude Duval

July 2017
Rolvenden Layne
Kent

Index